These Truths We Hold

JUDAISM IN AN AGE OF TRUTH

These Truths We Hold

JUDAISM IN AN AGE OF TRUTHINESS

Wendy Zierler and Joshua Garroway, editors

HEBREW UNION COLLEGE PRESS

HEBREW UNION COLLEGE PRESS

© 2022 Hebrew Union College Press

Cover Design by Paul Neff Design LLC

Set in Arno Pro by Raphaël Freeman MISTD, Renana Typesetting

Library of Congress Cataloging-in-Publication Data

Names: Zierler, Wendy, editor. | Garroway, Joshua D., editor.

Title: These truths we hold: Judasim in an age of truthiness / Joshua Garroway and Wendy Zierler, editors.

Description: Cincinnati: Hebrew Union College Press, [2022] | Includes index. | Summary: "The authors of this collection, comprising leading scholars, journalists, entertainers, and religious leaders, were asked to examine the idea of truth from a variety of Jewish textual and disciplinary perspectives-biblical, rabbinic, liturgical, scientific, and artistic. The volume's intention is to hold out the hope that deep, thoughtful teaching from some of the world's leading Jewish voices might lead not to deeper understanding not just of Jewish texts, but of the nature and accessibility of truth itself" – Provided by publisher.

Identifiers: LCCN 2022007501 (print) | LCCN 2022007502 (ebook) | ISBN 9780878201983 (paperback) | ISBN 9780878202287 (adobe pdf)

Subjects: LCSH: Truth – Religious aspects – Judaism. | Truthfulness and falsehood. | Truth – Biblical teaching. | Jewish ethics. | Truth in literature.

Classification: LCC BJ1286.T7 T44 2022 (print) | LCC BJ1286.T7 (ebook) | DDC 177/.3 – dc23/eng/20220302

LC record available at https://lccn.loc.gov/2022007501

LC ebook record available at https://lccn.loc.gov/2022007502

Dedicated to the memory of Aaron Panken, z"l

ૐ

אתה תחזה מכל־העם
אנשי־חיל יראי אלהים, אנשי אמת שנאי בצע

And you shall select from the nation,
valiant God-fearers, people of truth who hate dishonesty.

— EXODUS 18:21

Contents

Preface

"These Truths We Hold," the 2018 Symposium on Truth that gave rise to this volume, was first envisioned in 2016 by my predecessor, former HUC-JIR President, Rabbi Aaron Panken (z"l), two years prior to his tragic death in May of 2018. It was the result of an effort by President Panken to elevate HUC-JIR's role in developing ideas that would shape our world. The presentations at that Symposium and the essays that emerged were part of his more perspicacious vision of the Reform Movement's role in addressing the broader truth crisis that had fully arisen within Western democracies.

In the years since President Panken initiated this project, the truth crisis has grown, becoming a threat to the foundation of our democratic civil society, dependent as it is on citizen deliberation, public education, and confidence that we can agree at least upon a set of facts, if not the best solutions, when debating public policy and law.

As I write this in February of 2022, the issue of truth has become an issue of life and death. Even in the third year of a global pandemic many still question the proven safety and effectiveness of vaccines. And more than one year after a presidential election showed no evidence of fraud, it continues to be contested by those in the highest echelons of power who cynically argue that it was "stolen."

What can Judaism teach us about this crisis? How has this crisis affected Judaism? The essays in this volume explore these questions by providing interpretive, analytical, and historical answers by some of the world's leading scholars of religion and science.

One way to understand today's crisis of truth is to see it as a battle between faith and reason. Those who reject the effectiveness of vaccines or the validity of the 2020 presidential election sometimes claim that both lack evidence. In fact, the evidence for both is clear and compelling. Thus, rejecting either claim requires an assertion of faith. The truth crisis of democratic society might thus be seen as a question of whether our faith (in party, ideology, or tribal association) should trump what reason and science indicate to be true.

It is thus worth explaining why a religious approach to these questions might be helpful.

The tension between faith and reason has been a common theme of Jewish debate for a long time. Though some of the more fundamentalist Jewish communities today prioritize faith over reason, modern Judaism has more often viewed the two in dialogue. Our greatest scholars and teachers have often sought to revise and accommodate our faith to what reason and science discovered. Even prior to the Enlightenment, Maimonides was an exemplar of this approach. Spinoza, later, pushed it to its limits (or in the views of some of his contemporaries, well beyond them).

Hebrew Union College – Jewish Institute of Religion is not just an institution of Jewish higher education that seeks to advance the highest caliber academic scholarship; it is the center for professional leadership development of Reform Judaism. Reform Judaism recognizes both faith and science as paths to Truth. However, celebrating reason as that which distinguishes humans as created *b'tzelem Elohim*, made in the image of God, we generally view faith as being limited by reason. We thus must give up ideas based on faith, when they conflict with what reason and science reveal about our world. Religious life gives meaning to what we come to know through science. Religious ideas provide a framework for engaging eternal questions on a speculative basis that extends beyond what can be known through the methods of science alone.

Because Reform Judaism, and other liberal approaches to religious life, demand that our faith be bounded by reason, it elevates the process of discovery. Our beliefs are tied inextricably to the process of revision in the light of evidence. As Reform Jews, we are committed to a process of reasoned, systematic exploration of the world, embracing experimentation and evidence to learn what is true. Revisability in the face of new information becomes a religious commitment.

Seen in this light, the crisis of truth in the United States today may be thought of as a battle about whether we make truth or discover it. The argument that "if you believe it, it is true for you!" reflects a narcissistic approach to the world, as if each of us is a god capable of making the world in our image. Humility before God might inspire instead the idea that perhaps, just perhaps, we are not actually able to make or change reality simply through the beliefs we hold. Acceptance of a religious view that acknowledges the limitations of our knowledge should lead to a position of curiosity, humility, and openness, as we strive to learn what really is true, no matter what we may believe.

Hebrew Union College – Jewish Institute of Religion was founded in 1875 to raise up rabbis for a new American Judaism based on the principle of a faith bounded and limited by reason. We now operate educational programs in Cincinnati, Los Angeles, New York, and Jerusalem, raising up hundreds of students each year to be rabbis, cantors, non-profit professionals, teachers, and scholars. We maintain unparalleled research collections in Cincinnati that are used by thousands of international scholars to discover truth about the history and ideas of Jewish civilization and the American Jewish experience. Throughout that history we have insisted on incorporating the most contemporary knowledge of the social and physical sciences into the education of our students. We have demanded that our faculty's scholarship be held to the highest standards of academic evaluation.

In 2017, under President Panken's leadership, the HUC-JIR board reaffirmed our commitment to truth-seeking in its mission statement, identifying one of our institution's three core activities to be, "Advancing the critical study of Judaism and Jewish culture in accordance with the highest standards of modern academic scholarship."

We are not gods. We do not make the world through our beliefs. We seek instead to understand the world that God created through the process of discovery, standing ready to revise our understanding in the face of new evidence.

There is after all no amount of "believing" that will change the events of May 5, 2018 and bring back Aaron Panken, our beloved former President. But perhaps your engagement with the thoughtful essays in this volume will help you discover a bit more about the commitments of the person, the parent, the sibling, the spouse, the teacher and the rabbi that this world, in truth, lost much too soon.

Andrew Rehfeld

President, Hebrew Union College-Jewish Institute of Religion

Introduction

JOSHUA GARROWAY AND WENDY ZIERLER

"What is truth? Said jesting Pilate, and would not stay for an answer."[1]

"I was a boy who told lies. This came from reading."[2]

Two stories separated by nineteen centuries: one from the Gospel of John in the Christian scriptures; another by the Russian-Jewish writer, Isaac Babel (1894–1940). Two stories not likely to be juxtaposed except in a volume edited by scholars with expertise in vastly different fields. And yet, two stories that combine to invite reflection on the subject treated in the present volume, namely, the truth.

The first story features the famous question, *Quid est veritas?* posed to Jesus of Nazareth by the Roman governor of Judea, Pontius Pilate. Brought before Pilate to answer for the allegation that he proclaimed himself the king of the Jews, the playfully evasive Jesus eventually declares his real purpose: "For this I was born, and for this I came into the world, to testify to the truth. Everyone who belongs to the truth listens to my voice." Then comes Pilate's notoriously curt response: "What is truth?"[3]

---

1. Francis Bacon, *The Essays, or Councils, Civil and Moral, of Sir Francis Bacon, Lord Verulam, Viscount St. Alban. With a Table of the Colours of Good and Evil. And a Discourse on the Wisdom of the Ancients* (London, 1701), 1.
2. Isaac Babel, *The Complete Works of Isaac Babel* (New York, NY: W.W. Norton & Company, 2005), 635.
3. John 18:37–38 (NRSV).

As Francis Bacon later quipped, Pilate does not stay for an answer. He returns abruptly to the Jewish officials with his offer to release either Jesus or Barabbas. His question – three words in both Latin and English (as well as in the original Greek) – just hangs there, bald and dangling, awaiting a reply. No shortage of philosophers and theologians have taken a stab at it. Most have answered descriptively, arguing for this or that understanding of the truth. Others, however, such as the ancient sophists or contemporary postmodernists, seem rather to share the cynicism of jesting Pilate: truth is an illusion, a perspective, or merely a word.

Perhaps the simplest answer one might offer Pilate is that truth is the opposite of falsehood or deception, but even this modest proposal is belied by the insights of one of Isaac Babel's most memorable stories. "In the Basement" is about a young boy who invents outlandish tales about his family in order to impress Borgman, an affluent, intellectually gifted peer. The relationship between truth and storytelling is one of the central issues of this coming-of-age story. None of what Babel's narrator tells Borgman about his own family and background existed in reality. What did exist, however, "was far more extraordinary than anything I had invented, but at the age of twelve I had no idea how to grapple with the truth of my world."[4]

Writers and literature professors love "In the Basement" because, in addition to being a literary masterpiece, it shows how the art of lying – in other words, fiction – can serve to uncover deep human truths. Babel (1894–1940), who fell victim to Stalin's Great Purge and for decades was "erased" from Soviet memory, produced fiction that is taut, complex, and ambiguous, yielding rich meanings and interpretations that grow and develop over time with different readers. The idea that stories, though fictitious, convey complex truths and give rise to multiple interpretations is central to our understanding not just of great literature but also of Jewish tradition.

Generative as this blurred distinction between truth and fiction may be, however, it comes at a cost. Sometimes we wish to assert an incontrovertible truth. Certainly, we Jews sometimes do. But often there is another side, a countervailing truth that cannot be reconciled with

---

4. Babel, *The Complete Works*, 638.

our own. A case in point: a trip to Babel's childhood Odessa neighbor-hood of Moldavanka, where many of his stories were set, reveals that Babel has been rehabilitated and acknowledged by a sidewalk star in a Ukraine's version of the Hollywood Walk of Fame. At the same time, one readily witnesses the ubiquitous Ukrainian celebration of Bogdan Khmelnytzky, the Cossack leader who presided over the uprising against Poland in 1648, during which thousands of Jews were massacred. He is so revered that he appears on the 5 hryvnia bill. The same man whom Jews consider an arch villain is held up by Ukrainians as a national hero! Adding to this confusion in early 2022 is the Russian invasion of Ukraine, which has seen the state-sponsored Russian media deliberately misrepresent facts on the ground. And the fact that Ukranian president, Volodymyr Zelenskyy, is a Jew! Can truth really be so utterly subjective and contingent?

Or consider the passion narratives in the Christian scriptures. What Christians might call "gospel truth," an accurate accout of the misguided Jews who dragooned Pilate into carrying out their murderous plot, Jews might see as ancient "fake news," a fictitious account drawn up by a Christian apologist to curry favor with Rome by pinning the blame for an allegedly innocent man's execution on the fractious Jews. And these different truth claims have mattered very much. Untold generations of Jews have suffered at Christian hands on account of the passion narra-tives and the deicide charge – indeed, they contributed to the hatred of Jews that motivated the Cossacks under Khmelnytzky!

Recent developments in American culture have made it even harder to tolerate falsehood as a possible vehicle for expressing truth. Simply put, brazen lying and deception have become routine in public life. Nowadays it is challenging to read the line, "I was a boy who told lies. This came from reading," with the same delight and abandon in a society where public officials – indeed, the highest of public officials – look straight into a camera and lie, and lie, and lie over and again; where social media abound with fake descriptions of events designed intentionally to deceive; where professional media aim more to craft narratiaves to entertain their self-selecting partisan audiences than to "get down to the facts," as they used to say. And all this in a country whose founding docu-ment begins with the words: "We hold these truths to be self-evident."

With all these considerations, and with a deep desire to delve into the wisdom that Jewish tradition might offer on the subject of truth, we and our colleagues at the Hebrew Union College-Jewish Institute of Religion embarked on HUC-JIR's Symposium 2, entitled "These Truths We Hold: Judaism in an Age of Truthiness," a two-day conference, which took place at Steven Wise Temple in Los Angeles in November, 2018. The title made reference to the Declaration of Independence as well as to a familiar expression in American popular culture made famous by comedian Stephen Colbert. Way back in 2005, Colbert – a liberal fictitiously masquerading as a conservative in order reveal deeper truths, ironically enough – famously offered up the term "truthiness" to satirically expose attempts, especially by politicians, to pass off assertions as true despite their patent falseness. "Who is Britannica to tell me the Panama Canal was finished in 1914?" the conservative persona declared. "If I want to say it happened in 1941, that's my right!" At the time, Colbert was targeting unsubstantiated claims about the war in Iraq, but the "truthiness" term spoke to a broader anxiety among American viewers about the status of truth in contemporary society. It speaks even louder today. What was emerging as a problem in 2005 has in recent years become a full-blown epistemological crisis.

Our invited speakers, comprising leading scholars, journalists, entertainers, and religious leaders, were asked to examine the idea of truth from a variety of Jewish textual and disciplinary perspectives – biblical, rabbinic, liturgical, scientific, and artistic. If Babel's child narrator warned of the lies that can result from reading, we held out the hope that deep, thoughtful teaching from some of the world's leading Jewish voices might lead not to lies but to deeper understanding. We took hold of that premise and set out with our assembled attendees to learn what we could.

To be sure, our desire to uncover the nature of truth in Jewish terms is not unprecedented. In publishing this book, we join the company of many august scholars. To name just a few notable predecessors in this endeavor, Abraham Joshua Heschel made the subject of truth and its relation to such values as love and the good the subject of his comparative study of the religious thought of Israel Ba'al Shem Tov, Menahem

Mendel of Kotzk, and Soren Kierkegaard.[5] Louis Jacobs dedicated a number of essays to the subject of truth in classical and medieval Jewish thought, often emphasizing, as Marc Brettler and Christine Hayes[6] argue in their contributions to this book, that "[t]he main thrust in the appeals for Jews to be truthful is in the direction of moral truth and integrity."[7] David Weiss Halivni, Moshe Halbertal, and others grappled with what appears to a be two-tiered approach to truth in Jewish classical sources: a notion of heavenly truth, on the one hand, and a practical, worldly sense of truth based on majority rule.[8] More recently, Chaya Halberstam published a book-length study exploring "two different modes juridical rhetoric: the Hebrew Bible, which deploys an authoritative discourse of knowledge, certainty, and divine truth; and tannaitic literature, which assumes a stance of perpetual uncertainty despite the biblical tradition, and demands the authoritative construction of legal truth."[9] This book joins those important, discipline- or period-specific voices and, as it were, brings them into conversation with one another, assembling work by scholars across the disciplines of Jewish Studies, readers of ancient, medieval, and modern texts alike, in the hope of creating a broad, honest,

---

5. Abraham Joshua Heschel, *A Passion for Truth* (New York, NY: Farrar, Strauss and Giroux, 1973).

6. In addition to her contribution here, see Christine Hayes, *What's Divine About Divine Law?: Early Perspectives* (Princeton, NJ: Princeton University Press, 2015).

7. Louis Jacobs, "Truth," in *The Jewish Religion: A Companion* (Oxford: Oxford University Press, 1995), 568. See also Louis Jacobs, "Truth," in *Jewish Values* (Eugene, OR: Wipf and Stock, 2008), 145–54.

8. See David Weiss Halivni, *Peshat and Derash: Plain and Applied Meaning in Rabbinic Exegesis* (New York, NY: Oxford University Press, 1991) 101–5; Moshe Halbertal, "Authority, Controversy and Tradition," in *The People and the Book* (Cambridge, MA: Harvard University Press, 1997), 45–89. See also Daniel R. Schwartz, "Law and Truth: On Qumran-Sadducean and Rabbinic Views of Law," in *The Dead Sea Scrolls: Forty Years of Research*, ed. Devorah Dimant and Uriel Rappaport (Leiden: Brill, 1992), 229–40, and Jeffrey Rubenstein's critique of Schwartz's approach in Jeffrey Rubenstein, "Nominalism and Realism in Qumranic and Rabbinic Law: A Reassessment," *Dead Sea Discoveries* 6.2 (1999): 157–83.

9. Chaya Halberstam, *Law and Truth in Biblical and Rabbinic Literature* (Bloomington: Indiana University Press, 2010), 3.

multi-valent, and relevant contemporary discussion of Jewish notions of truth.

Despite the array of disciplines and perspectives represented here, one theme in particular surfaces again and again. While Jews and Judaisms across time routinely affirm the existence of absolute truth and its importance, as well as the virtue of truth-telling, they acknowledge at the same time that the fraught, fleshly reality of human existence renders impossible a perfect recognition of the truth, or an unadulterated commitment to it. Sometimes the limits of the human ken prevent us from ascertaining the truth as it really is. Sometimes ethical considerations, like the need to promote compassion, peace, and humility, supersede total steadfastness to the truth. Sometimes liturgical considerations, like the need to create communities of meaning, do the same. Likewise, there is the need to maintain social order, establish systems of justice, and cultivate relationships with non-Jews, all of which, at times, require one to compromise the truth. It was Clarence Darrow who said, "Chase after the truth like all hell and you'll free yourself, even though you never touch its coat tails." It seems Jewish tradition would agree: the truth is real, and warrants our admiration and aspiration, even as we recognize that absolute adherence is ultimately beyond our grasp.

Following the organization of the symposium, the chapters in this book are divided into textual or disciplinary sections. The first section, entitled *"Torat Emet"* – or, "the Torah of Truth," an expression familiar to many Jews from the Torah-reading service in synagogues – examines what Judaism has traditionally identified as the foundation of all truth, the revelation of God to Israel recorded in the Torah. As each of the contributions demonstrates, a Jewish answer to the question "Is the Torah true?" is invariably both yes and no.

Marc Zvi Brettler opens the discussion with the trenchant, if provocative, observation that the authors of the Hebrew Bible, or at least two of them, might well be considered liars. He asks whether the phrase of Jeremiah 8:8, "the false pen of the scribes has made it into a lie," might be used justifiably to describe the authors of Deuteronomy and Chronicles. Overwhelming evidence indicates that these works engage in the sort of deceptive reportage that would hardly pass muster in contemporary historical writing. They manipulate or even fabricate sources and recast events in ways that cohere with their political or theological interests. The author of Deuteronomy even goes so far as to claim Mosaic authorship in the process! These observations force readers to decide whether Deuteronomy and Chronicles are, as some scholars have asserted, outright forgeries that deserve the negative valence accorded forgeries in the present day, or, as other scholars claim, creative and positive revisions that reformulate sources so as to articulate better what was originally meant.

Whereas Brettler deals with the so-called written Torah, Christine Hayes addresses the Oral Torah and its ancient advocates, the rabbis. Hayes contends that the impact of Hellenism, introduced to Jewish communities in Egypt, the land of Israel, and elsewhere following the conquests of Alexander the Great in the late fourth century BCE, had a substantial impact on Jewish thinking about the truth. The notion of a single, objective truth accessible by reason, as propounded by Philo, the Stoics, and other philosophers, led many Jews to claim that the Torah, although not philosophical in its appearance, was nonetheless an expression of rational, universal truth. The rabbis, Hayes argues, went in a different direction. Sometimes they challenged the idea of an absolute truth by proposing the existence of multiple truths. At other times, they acknowledged the existence of an objective truth but determined that the right course of action, as determined by the Torah, is not in accord with the truth. The Torah, in other words, which is distinct from the truth, occasionally commands behavior at odds with the truth! When determining the calendar, for example, Rabban Gamliel is reported in the Mishnah to have demanded adherence to the decisions of the rabbinic court even when they are patently at odds with astronomical reality. Elsewhere the rabbis encourage judges to resist enforcing strict, or true, justice on account of the need for mercy, compassion, or peace. Pursuing the truth is a value for the rabbis, but not an absolute one.

The next two essays concern peculiarly modern problems. It goes without saying that the Enlightenment and its reverberations have introduced Jews to questions that their ancient and medieval forbears could never have imagined. Since the nineteenth century, for example, the Torah has been treated as a historical document rather than a divine revelation in academic settings, with the result that most university-trained rabbis and Jewish scholars now view the Torah as a composite work of human hands. If that is so, must the Torah lose its stature as a repository of truly divine revelation?

Benjamin D. Sommer says no. Rather than disputing the findings of biblical criticism, Sommer reinterprets them. The Torah represents different authors expressing different views at different times – that is indisputable – but the motley product that resulted is precisely what one might expect in the wake of a divine revelation. Drawing on what he calls "a participatory theology of revelation," Sommer contends that Torah is not a stenographic recording of the revelation at Sinai, but a patchwork, an anthology reflecting various perceptions, memories, and interpretations of revelation. Because God reveals truth in ways that people can neither understand perfectly nor express precisely, the collaged character of the Torah is exactly what we might expect from ancient Israelites attempting to convey their experience of the numinous within the limits of human mind and language. The Torah is true, in this sense, even as it features contradictions and variations in perspective.

Rachel Adler builds on this notion of participatory revelation with its collage of truths and supplies an additional metaphor, namely of the Torah as our *chavruta* partner. Adler arrives at this metaphor after a series of observations about the role of interpretation, relationship, and of changing values and ethics in our understanding of truth. "The *viability* of revelation," she writes, "depends on dialogue, on *maḥloket*, on old words and obligations re-encountered in new contexts. This dual Torah is not an authority that dictates from beyond time. If Torah is our *chavruta*, then, just as we must be accountable to our *chavruta*, our *chavruta* must be accountable to us." We participate with the Torah, as it were, in hashing out its new meanings, and in its continual re-writing, engaging with it, in relationship and dialogue, in the same way that we engage with a study partner in a *beit midrash*.

The next section, *Tefilat Emet*, moves us from the study hall to the synagogue, and explores the problem of Jewish truth-telling specifically in liturgical contexts, a concern that has become especially acute in modern times as many Jews question whether they believe what is said in traditional prayers to be true, and whether it is permissible or desirable to change prayers to match changing convictions. As Dalia

Marx observes, we moderns are hardly the first to ask such questions. She examines a rich passage from the Babylonian Talmud (Yoma 69b) in which illustrious sages disagree: one group claiming that statements uttered in prayer must be true, and therefore the words of a prayer may be revised to accord with the truth; another that the prayer's words may not be revised, even if they seem to be untrue. Marx then goes on to consider several examples in which statements in the traditional liturgy appear false, contradictory, or deceptive, and the different approaches taken by Orthodox and Reform Jews to resolve these problems.

Whereas Marx examines liturgy from the standpoint of a so-called correspondence theory of truth, in which a statement is judged to be true if it corresponds to reality, Lawrence A. Hoffman suggests that an alternative solution to understanding liturgy might be achieved if we approach the notion of truth differently. Correspondence theory might work well in a discipline like science, Hoffman says, because science aims to describe accurately objects in the physical world. Prayer, on the other hand, expresses emotions, commitments, and aspirations, and the world it seeks to describe is more so the metaphysical world of God, Creation, Israel, and the like. Drawing on insights from the philosopher Ludwig Wittgenstein, Hoffman argues that the truth value of religious utterances should be assessed against the constellation of images, ideas, and experiences that a religious community uses to make sense of the human condition. As such, liturgical statements that seem untrue or even nonsensical from a scientific point of view might seem patently true for a Jew.

Moving beyond liturgical settings, the next section examines the ethics of truth-telling in general. If *Sefat Emet*, or truthful language, is a Jewish virtue, is it ever acceptable for a Jew to lie? David Ellenson considers the question as it arises in the responsa of Rabbi Haim David Halevi, the late Chief Sephardic Rabbi of Tel Aviv-Yafo. First, Ellenson shows that Halevi was willing to take a hard stand against lying and deception. In a responsum dealing with students who cheated on exams, Halevi invokes Psalm 119:29–30 ("the way of falsehood remove from me...") among other passages to indict the sin of both the cheaters and the peers who allowed them to copy from their papers. Halevi nonetheless believed that deception was at times acceptable, even desirable. As

Ellenson demonstrates, Halevi recognized that an absolutist approach to truth-telling proves incompatible with our imperfect world. Truth-telling is a virtue, but so is peace, for example, and in extreme cases the quest for peace might supersede the expectation of honesty. Thus, the sons of Jacob lied to their brother, Joseph, and even God reported Sarah's words deceptively to Abraham (Gen 18:13) to forestall a domestic dispute.

The next two sections extend the conversation beyond the bounds of Judaism. Since antiquity, but especially in modern times, two intellectual disciplines have aspired to discern the truth about the world as it really is: philosophy and science. The pair of essays in *Emet Umada'* ("Truth and Knowledge") explores the extent to which truths proclaimed in Judaism can be reconciled with foundational tenets of Enlightenment philosophy, on one hand, and the contemporary natural sciences on the other. Leora Batnitzky considers the emergence in the nineteenth century of "Jewish philosophy," an enterprise that she views as a response to the new political reality in which Jews could so easily choose to abandon Judaism. What special truth did Judaism offer to justify the continued adherence of the recently emancipated European Jew? The first thinker to take up this uniquely modern dilemma was Moses Mendelssohn, who famously proposed that Judaism constitutes a revealed legislation for a particular people, and that since it has no dogmas it can neither confirm nor contradict any universal truth claims uncovered through philosophy. While the successors of the so-called Socrates of Berlin widely criticized his project, Batnitzky shows that, nonetheless, the three most dominant trends in modern Jewish philosophy – the rational model (exemplified by Hermann Cohen), the historicist model (associated with Franz Rosenzweig), and the political model (represented by Leo Strauss) – are indebted to insights expressed originally by Mendelssohn.

Whereas philosophy is still widely considered the bailiwick of intellectual elites in the ivory tower, modernity has witnessed the emergence of science as a routine subject in popular discourse. Especially in recent years, as climate change, coronavirus, gender identity, and other issues have made their way to center stage, the media abound with tweets and articles about scientific claims. The very word "science" has become a rhetorical stand-in for truth: "I follow the science," for example, is often a standard declaration when proclaiming the correctness of one's perspective. Here, Geoffrey A. Mitelman challenges what he sees as the overly facile popular linkage of science with truth. In fact, he argues, scientists themselves tend to be humbler about the fruits of their labor. Yes, scientists devote themselves to methodological rigor in the hope of distinguishing correct from incorrect descriptions of the world and how it works, but their findings, on their own reckoning, are invariably tentative and provisional. Scientific truths are not exact, universal, and eternal, but the best available solutions to a problem at the given moment. Truth is not certainty. As such, Mitelman proposes, scientific truth resembles Jewish truth, a point he makes in connection with the rabbis' insistence on preserving minority opinions. Just as the rabbis anticipated that their own verdicts might one day be overturned by a court with greater wisdom, so scientists record their procedures and findings with the expectation that subsequent exploration will revise, refine, or perhaps even refute what they understand to be true at present.

In addition to the encounter with philosophy and science, one of the hallmarks of the modern Jewish experience has been the pervasive contact with non-Jewish people and ideas, especially in the diaspora. While the consequences of this encounter have at times been grim, it has also brought about the rich interaction of well-intentioned people of different faiths sharing the truths of their traditions. Mark Diamond writes of his struggles and achievements in such a multicultural setting. A rabbi who teaches Judaism and religious studies at a Jesuit university, Diamond contends that interreligious dialogue succeeds best when interlocutors are able to overcome the inclination to view the conversation as a competition, my view of the truth versus yours, in which only one view can emerge as the victor. Dialogue succeeds rather when participants endeavor to correct misconceptions they may have about the religion of another, to refine their own beliefs, and to appreciate better the theological and practical consequences of their own exclusivist or inclusivist claims about the truth.

Whereas Diamond focuses on his personal experience as a leader in interreligious dialogue, Michael Marmur examines the problem of truth in pluralistic settings from a theoretical perspective. He considers three different, but related, metaphors that have been deployed to account for disagreement about what is true among reasonable and well-intentioned people: (1) the "language as lens" theory, which holds that truth, however universal and absolute it might be, is expressed differently by different languages; (2) specular theories, which hold that truth, again possibly universal, is nonetheless seen differently by different eyes; and (3) horizontal versus vertical pluralism. Horizontal pluralism holds that people utilizing different modes of description – a poet as opposed to a scientist, for example – might offer different, but equally valid, descriptions of an event. Vertical pluralism goes further, suggesting that different, but equally valid, descriptions of an event might be offered even by people in the same mode. Marmur takes the last insight in an exciting new direction by proposing a "diagonal pluralism" that aspires to recognize truth from multiple points of view within Judaism (vertical) and multiple points of view generally (horizontal).

And what good is a Jewish book about truth without a treatment of the truth-telling power of comedy? The connection between humor and truth-telling is one the Symposium took seriously, going so far as to tap the comedic stylings of Stephen Colbert for its title. Indeed, Colbert mused recently about the connection between truth and laughter in an interview on National Public Radio. Observing that overt government deception can produce crippling anxiety in its constituents, Colbert finds an antidote in humor: "When you laugh, you can't be afraid at the same time. So if you can laugh, you can think."[10] In other words, the disarming power of laughter allows viewers, for the moment at least, to overcome their fear and find the truth amidst the dishonesty.

The essay on laughter in the present volume deals not with American political satire, but with a work of Israeli television. In "Truth and Satire in the Bible, Yesterday and Today: Reflections on *Hayehudim Ba'im* (*The Jews are Coming*)," Wendy Zierler (with contributions by Asaf Beiser and Natalie Marcus) considers the truth-telling capacities of satire in relation the award-winning Israeli comedy/satire show, *Hayehudim Ba'im*, a show that mines the entire textual and cultural history of the

---

10. https://www.npr.org/2021/04/27/991149701/stephen-colbert-on-missing-his-audience-and-making-comedy-a-family-business.

Jewish people since biblical times for laughs as well as hard-hitting truths about issues of religious and contemporary political significance. The various skits surveyed and analyzed demonstrate the role of comedy and satire in exposing vice as well as virtue, and in fostering intellectual as well as moral excellence. Finally, Wendy Zierler's concluding essay considers the relationship between truth and death in a selection of modern Jewish literary sources. Ultimately, she finds, death or the threat thereof does not so much simplify the Jewish quest for truth as lend it a sense of moral and historical urgency. Even so, in almost every case, the quest for absolute truth is countered in these texts, as in biblical and rabbinic sources, by other virtues: pluralism, ethical consideration, and changing social norms.

A couple of provisos before turning to the essays. First, any volume that endeavors to treat a subject so vast and variegated as Jewish tradition is bound to have gaps. So, too, here. The make-up of our Symposium, limitations on space, the expertise of available scholars, and other factors have meant that some aspects of Judaism are left unexplored. Medieval Jewish thinkers are largely absent, for example, as are sources from the Second Temple period. The contributions nonetheless span a wide range of eras and perspectives, and there is tremendous breadth within many of the essays themselves, such that Jewish tradition can be said to have been treated fairly, if not comprehensively.

Second, the observation made here in the introduction and in many of the contributions, namely that Jewish sources demonstrate tolerance, flexibility, and openness to change with respect to truth and its inter-pretation, does not mean that truth should be seen as an instrumental construct, invoked merely for expedience rather than principle. This exact point comes to the fore at the end of Franz Kafka's famous novel, *The Trial*, when the Priest offers his recitation and commentary on the parable, "Before the Law." Joseph K. rejects the Priest's riddling interpre-tation of the parable, saying that in order to accept it, one would need to need to accept that "everything said by the doorkeeper [who guards the Law and prevents the man from the country from entering until finally he dies] is true... "No," said the priest, "you don't need to accept every-thing as true. You only have to accept it as necessary." "Depressing view," said K. "The lie made into the rule of the world."[11] K.'s rejection of the Priest's commentary thus becomes a rejection of the rule of lying, itself an important truth, and an assertion of principle against the backdrop of a world filled with inscrutable laws and inaccessible judges. With COVID fear and confusion, widespread distrust of government institutions, and (justified) paranoia surrounding the workings of police and our justice system, our own world has taken on a nightmarish, absurd, Kafkaesque aspect: K.'s singular refusal to accept the rule of lying, however, is one of the few unriddled, unambiguous messages of the novel – a resonant message, indeed, for our current moment.

---

11. Franz Kafka, *The Trial*, trans. Edwin and Willa Muir, (New York, NY: Schocken, 1992), 119.

Section 1

Torat Emet:
The Torah of Truth

"The False Pen of the Scribes Has Made It into a Lie" (Jeremiah 8:8): The Truthiness of Scripture*

Marc Zvi Brettler

For many of us, it is hard to gauge the truthfulness – or even truthiness – of current events. The case for events which occurred long ago, preserved in highly curated texts such as the Hebrew Bible, is certainly much more complex.[1] How well does the Bible capture or map the real past?[2] Modern scholarship suggests that often biblical texts, even those written not long after the events that they narrate, are more "truthy" than truthful.[3]

* I would like to thank Professors Jonathan Klawans, Bernard Levinson, and Hindy Najman for their helpful comments and conversations on this topic, and Jonathan Homrighausen and Matthew Arakaky for their helpful assistance. The translations from the Bible used below are NJPS, sometimes modified slightly.

1. For the Bible as a "curated" text, see, e.g., Eva Mroczek, *The Literary Imagination in Jewish Antiquity* (New York, NY: Oxford University Press, 2016), 136. Similarly, William G. Dever describes the Bible as a "curated artifact" in Dever, *Recent Archaeological Discoveries and Biblical Research* (Seattle: University of Washington Press, 1990), 11.

2. For my understanding of historical writing as a "map," based on John Lewis Gaddis, see Marc Brettler, "The Hebrew Bible and History," in *The Cambridge Companion to the Hebrew Bible/Old Testament*, ed. Stephen B. Chapman and Marvin Sweeney (Cambridge: Cambridge University Press, 2014), 108–25.

3. The literature on this topic is immense; see Lester L. Grabbe, *Ancient Israel: What Do We Know and How Do We Know It?*, rev. ed. (London: T&T Clark, 2017); and the recent collection, *The Hebrew Bible and History*, ed. Lester L. Grabbe

But this will not be my focus here, not least because the relation of the Bible to historical events is contested in almost every case. I will instead explore the complexities of truthfulness in Scripture by looking at a more objective issue, namely, the ways in which the authors of Deuteronomy and Chronicles rework their respective source texts, examining whether they do so in a manner we might deem "truthful."

Both Deuteronomy and Chronicles use earlier sources but transform them remarkably. Deuteronomy (more properly, the D source within Deuteronomy) retells many of the laws and narratives of Exodus–Numbers, especially those of the E source,[4] while most of Chronicles is a retelling of the earlier Samuel–Kings. Deuteronomy is the better-known example of textual transformation, and is especially problematic because it explicitly attributes its words to Moses – its first-person discourse is typical of pseudepigraphic writing.[5] Even though Chronicles is not especially well known outside of biblical studies, it is as much a part of the Bible as Deuteronomy, and is, in fact, especially important within Judaism since it illustrates many points of transition between biblical texts from the classical period and the rabbinic literature that followed. Both books engage and revise their sources in a variety of noteworthy ways and thus offer important, early evidence on the issues we are exploring in this volume. In evaluating the content of Chronicles and Deuteronomy, should we conclude, to borrow a phrase from Jeremiah 8:8, that "the false pen of the scribes has made it into a lie"?[6]

(London: T&T Clark, 2018). For some, the gap between the "real" history of Israel and its history as told in the Bible is so great that each should be treated separately; see, e.g., Mario Liverani, *Israel's History and the History of Israel* (London: Equinox, 2003).

4. It is not important for the arguments advanced below if this is exclusively so, or if D interprets some J material as well; in any case it is often difficult to disentangle J from E after Exodus 3, and it would be wise not to use circular reasoning to isolate passages that belong to E on the basis of their reflection in D.

5. Eibert Tigchelaar, "Forms of Pseudepigraphy in the Dead Sea Scrolls," in *Pseudepigraphie und Verfasserfiktion in frühchristlichen Briefen*, ed. Jörg Frey. WUNT 246 (Tübingen: Mohr Siebeck, 2009), 99–100.

6. In most cases, translations follow NJPS, often revised slightly; here I use NRSV.

I. CHRONICLES AND ITS SOURCES

Most biblical scholars believe that Chronicles, written in the fourth pre-Christian century,[7] used Samuel and Kings, more or less in the form now known to us, as its main source.[8] This relationship was already identified by W.M.L. de Wette, one of the founders of modern biblical scholarship, at the beginning of the nineteenth century (1805), and then adopted and bolstered by Wellhausen in his masterful synthesis, *Prolegomena to the History of Israel*, at the end of that century.[9] This is the most likely explanation for the similarities between Samuel–Kings and Chronicles – about fifty percent of the latter overlaps with the former. Although some scholars have doubted this model, assuming instead that Chronicles and Samuel–Kings both derive from a now-lost source, most agree that the model of dependency of Chronicles on some version of Samuel–Kings (which may not be identical to those

---

7. See, e.g., the commentaries of Sara Japhet, *I & II Chronicles*, OTL (London: SCM, 1993), 23–28; Gary N. Knoppers, *I Chronicles 1–9*. AB (New York, NY: Doubleday, 2004), 16; Ralph W. Klein, *I Chronicles*. Hermeneia (Minneapolis, MN: Fortress, 2006), 13–16. In terms of the broader arguments I adduce below, I wonder if it is a coincidence that, according to Grafton, the fourth century was "the first real heyday of the forger." Anthony Grafton, *Forgers and Critics: Creativity and Duplicity in Western Scholarship* (Princeton, NJ: Princeton University Press, 1990), 10.

8. Most scholars agree that the text of Kings used by the Chronicler is closer to the current Hebrew text of Kings than his text of Samuel is to the current Hebrew text of Samuel, but this issue does not affect the cases below. On this topic, see, e.g., Isaac Kalimi, *The Reshaping of Ancient Israelite History in Chronicles* (Winona Lake, IN: Eisenbrauns, 2005), 89–90; Knoppers, *I Chronicles 1–9*, 69–71. For a useful brief bibliography on Chronicles and discussion of the Chronicler as an interpreter of earlier texts, see Bernard M. Levinson, *Legal Revision and Religious Renewal in Ancient Israel* (Cambridge: Cambridge University Press, 2008), 176–81. For those interested in seeing firsthand how the Chronicler revised earlier sources, see the collection of synoptic parallels in *Chronicles and its Synoptic Parallels in Samuel, Kings, and Related Biblical Texts*, ed. John C. Endres, William R. Millar, and John Barclay Burns (Collegeville, MN: Michael Glazier, 1998); or Abba Bendavid, *The Twice-Told Tale: Parallels in the Bible* (Jerusalem: Carta, 2017).

9. Julius Wellhausen, *Prolegomena to the History of Israel* (1885; repr., Atlanta, GA: Scholars Press, 1994), 171–72.

books as they are now preserved in MT) best explains how Chronicles was produced.[10]

Stated differently, "Chronicles is the only comprehensive book of the Bible whose sources are, for the most part, available to us."[11] This makes it invaluable as we examine truthfulness (and truthiness): we can see how Chronicles revises its sources, rewriting historical accounts penned several centuries earlier. In examining how the Chronicler uses and revises his sources it is important not to straightjacket his methods, remembering instead that "Chronicles dealt in *many* different ways with the literature held to be authoritative by its implied author and its intended and primary readerships."[12] In the following, I offer several representative examples that allow some reflection on the "truthiness" of the Chronicler's complex reworking of his earlier sources.[13]

Hiram/Huram and the Temple

1 Kings 9:12–13, after describing Solomon's construction projects, reads:

12 ויצא חירם מצר לראות את־הערים אשר נתן־לו שלמה ולא ישרו בעיניו: 13 ויאמר מה הערים האלה אשר־נתתה לי אחי ויקרא להם ארץ כבול עד היום הזה

But when Hiram came from Tyre to inspect the towns that Solomon had given him, he was not pleased with them. "My brother," he said, "what sort of towns are these you have given me?" So they were named the land of Cabul, as is still the case.

---

10. The common-source theory, as it is called, is associated especially with A. Graeme Auld; see *Kings Without Privilege: David and Moses in the Story of the Bible's Kings* (Edinburgh: T&T Clark, 1994); and most recently *Life in Kings: Reshaping the Royal Story in the Hebrew Bible* (Atlanta, GA: SBL Publications, 2017). This view has been criticized, e.g., by Knoppers, *1 Chronicles 1–9*, 66–68.

11. Kalimi, *The Reshaping of Ancient Israelite History in Chronicles*, 1.

12. Ehud Ben Zvi, "One Size Does Not Fit All: Observations on the Different Ways the Chronicler Dealt with the Authoritative Literature of Its Time," in *What Was Authoritative for Chronicles?*, ed. Ehud Ben Zvi and Diana Edelman (Winona Lake, IN: Eisenbrauns, 2011), 34.

13. Most of these examples are taken from, and discussed in greater detail in, Marc Zvi Brettler, *The Creation of History in Ancient Israel* (London: Routledge, 1995), 20–47, though the discussion below updates the bibliography of these items.

These verses likely reflect payment by Solomon to the Phoenician King Hiram for goods and services related to Solomon's building projects. They depict Solomon negatively, but this is not very surprising in the Book of Kings: its portrayal of this king is quite uneven, and, in the final chapters of its Solomonic narrative, tends to be ambivalent or outright negative.[14] As it needs to justify the establishment of the competing Northern Kingdom, it emphasizes Solomon's problematic behavior, including "Solomon spurn[ing] the land of Israel granted by YHWH by giving it back to the Canaanites."[15]

The Chronicler,[16] however, has a much more positive view of Solomon, in part because he could largely ignore the Northern Kingdom, which had disappeared by the time of his writing. He thus had no need to use the reign of Solomon to justify the Northern Kingdom's existence.[17] Furthermore, as several scholars have noted, the Chronicler appears invested in promoting an idealized vision of the king, with some even describing the Chronicler's Solomon as "indeed flawless."[18] It is thus not surprising that Chronicles, in revising its source, has omitted these verses concerning payment with land for services rendered. But the Chronicler, quite remarkably, goes much further, writing instead (2 Chr 8:2), והערים אשר נתן חורם לשלמה בנה שלמה אתם ויושב שם את־בני ישראל – "Solomon

---

14. Marc Zvi Brettler, "The Structure of 1 Kings 1–11," *Journal for the Study of the Old Testament* 49 (1991): 87–97; Jerome T. Walsh, "The Characterization of Solomon in First Kings 1–5," *Catholic Biblical Quarterly* 57, no. 3 (1995): 471–93; Isaac Kalimi, *Writing and Rewriting the Story of Solomon in Ancient Israel* (Cambridge: Cambridge University Press, 2018).

15. Marvin A. Sweeney, *I & II Kings*. OTL (Louisville, KY: Westminster John Knox, 2007), 144.

16. I am using this term for the author of the Book of Chronicles (and not for the author of Chronicles + Ezra-Nehemiah, as some other scholars do).

17. This is the majority view of Solomon in Chronicles; see, e.g., Roddy L. Braun, "Solomonic Apologetics in Chronicles," *JBL* 100 (1973): 503–16; Sara Japhet, *The Ideology of the Book of Chronicles and Its Place in Biblical Thought*, trans. Anna Barber (Frankfurt: Peter Lang, 1989), 478–80. I do not find the critique of this view in Yong Ho Jeon, *Impeccable Solomon? A Study of Solomon's Faults in Chronicles* (Eugene, OR: Wipf & Stock, 2013), to be compelling.

18. Japhet, *I & II Chronicles*, 48; for an expanded discussion of this, see Braun, "Solomonic Apologetics in Chronicles."

also rebuilt the cities that Huram [Chronicles's rendition of the name Hiram] had given to him, and settled Israelites in them." The Chronicler actually reverses who gives the cities to whom – in Wellhausen's words, the narrative "is changed into the opposite."[19] This was done, as a recent commentary on Chronicles has noted, for a variety of overlapping reasons: "The Chronicler introduced this change because he did not want to imply that Solomon was short of resources, that he would willingly give away part of the land of Israel in a business transaction, or that Huram would dislike anything that Solomon had given him."[20] Sara Japhet, using a term of the historian of early Judaism E.J. Bickerman, explains this change in terms of "historical probability"[21] – that is, the author wrote the account that fit best with what he believed *had to be true*. The Chronicler has here, in Japhet's words, "corrected" his source to harmonize it with his notion of what *might* or *should* have happened in the past. This certainly is one way of writing, or rewriting, history.

Walking before Me or Following the Torah?

The following example, which involves the change of a single word, may seem minor compared to the previous one. But the change of even a single word may be very significant. In Solomon's prayer in 1 Kings 8:25, Solomon quotes the promise made to his father David: "And now, O Lord God of Israel, keep the further promise that You made to Your servant, my father David: 'Your line on the throne of Israel shall never end, if only your descendants will look to their way and walk before Me (ללכת לפני) as you have walked before Me.'" In other words, covenant obedience will be rewarded with an eternal line of Davidic kings. The author of 1 Kings 8 phrased this obedience as "walk[ing] before Me" (ללכת לפני), using the broad terms typical of ancient Near Eastern treaties; the Torah did not exist in this author's period and thus could not be used to express covenant obedience. However, the Torah,

---

19. Wellhausen, *Prolegomenon*, 187.
20. Ralph W. Klein, 2 *Chronicles*. Hermeneia (Minneapolis, MN: Fortress, 2012), 119.
21. For more on this principle, Brettler, *The Creation of History in Ancient Israel*, 25–26.

largely in the same form as we now know it, was complete by the time the Chronicler wrote. Because he viewed observing the Torah as the central expression of covenant obedience from the time of Moses, it must have been observed already by the righteous Kings David and Solomon.[22] 2 Chronicles 6:16 thus changes 1 Kings 8's "to walk before Me" (ללכת לפני) to read "to walk [following] my Torah" (ללכת בתורתי). Physically, this is a small change, involving just one word in a verse; however, conceptually, it is a large change: here, the Chronicler retrojects the Torah and Torah-observance into the period of David and Solomon, reflecting the new centrality of this document in postexilic Judaism.

How Long is Sukkot?

The influence of the entire Torah on Chronicles may also be seen in some very specific changes it makes to its source material. According to 1 Kings 8:2, Solomon dedicates the Temple during "the festival," namely *sukkot*. In Deuteronomy 16:13 and 15 this is stated to be a seven-day festival:

חג הסכת תעשה לך שבעת ימים

You shall hold the Feast of Booths for seven days. (Deut 16:13)

שבעת ימים תחג ליהוה אלהיך

You shall hold a festival for the Lord your God seven days. (Deut 16:15)

1 Kings 8:65, which reflects the terminology and ideology of the Deuteronomist, records Solomon commemorating the festival for שבעת ימים, "seven days,"[23] as expected. The next verse states clearly that ביום השמיני שלח את־העם – "on the eighth day he let the people go."

Various Priestly sources (Lev 23:36, 39; Num 29:35–38), by contrast, follow the seven-day sukkot festival with an eighth-day "sacred occasion" (מקרא־קדש), "complete rest" (שבתון), or "solemn gathering" (עצרת). This is not recognized in 1 Kings 8, which predated the completed

---

22. See, e.g., Zipora Talshir, "Several Canon-Related Concepts Originating in Chronicles," *ZAW* 113 (2001): 386–90.

23. The Hebrew text of 1 Kings 8:65, which records two seven-day festivals, is widely regarded as corrupt; see *BHS*, and among the commentators, e.g., Mordechai Cogan, *1 Kings.* AB (New Haven, CT: Yale University Press), 290.

Torah and was not influenced by Priestly writings. However, since the
Chronicler knew the entire Torah, for him, the idea that Solomon would
not know of, and observe, this eighth day of the festival was unthinkable.
For this reason, in 2 Chr 7:8–10, he rewrites the earlier passage:

8 ויעש שלמה את־החג בעת ההיא שבעת ימים וכל־ישראל עמו קהל גדול
מאד מלבוא חמת עד־נחל מצרים: 9 ויעשו ביום השמיני עצרת... 10 וביום
עשרים ושלשה לחדש השביעי שלח את־העם לאהליהם שמחים וטובי לב
על־הטובה אשר עשה יהוה לדויד ולשלמה ולישראל עמו:

⁸ At that time Solomon kept the Feast for seven days – all Israel
with him – a great assemblage from Lebo-hamath to the Wadi
of Egypt. ⁹ On the eighth day they held a solemn gathering....
¹⁰ On the twenty-third day of the seventh month he dismissed
the people to their homes, rejoicing and in good spirits over the
goodness that the Lord had shown to David and Solomon and
His people Israel. (2 Chr 7:8–10)

The Chronicler had no evidence other than his own logic that Solomon observed this eighth day of the festival – and he wrote this into
his text despite the fact that his source said "on the eighth day he let the
people go." He deduced this by supposing that since Solomon was a
righteous king who observed the Torah, he must have observed the law
as reflected in the Torah. This was his basis for revising, or "correcting,"
his source material. Would we deem this truthful?

The Chronicler and the Priestly Source

While the previous revision was accomplished through a brief addition,
in many other places the Chronicler adds more extensive material –
which could not have possibly been in Kings – to show that David and
Solomon observed various regulations found in the Priestly literature,
or regulations that were normative in his own period that he was sure
dated from hoary antiquity. One short example of this type of addition
is his expansion of 1 Kings 9:25:

והעלה שלמה שלש פעמים בשנה עלות ושלמים על־המזבח אשר בנה
ליהוה והקטיר אתו אשר לפני יהוה ושלם את־הבית:

Solomon used to offer burnt offerings and sacrifices of well-being three times a year on the altar that he had built for the Lord, and he used to offer incense on the one that was before the Lord. And he kept the House in repair.

Much more extensively, 2 Chronicles 8:12–16 reads:

אז העלה שלמה עלות ליהוה על מזבח יהוה אשר בנה לפני האולם: 12
ובדבר יום ביום להעלות כמצות משה לשבתות ולחדשים ולמועדות 13
שלוש פעמים בשנה בחג המצות ובחג השבעות ובחג הסכות: 14 ויעמד
כמשפט דויד־אביו את־מחלקות הכהנים על־עבדתם והלוים על־משמ־
רותם להלל ולשרת נגד הכהנים לדבר־יום ביומו והשוערים במחלקותם
לשער ושער כי כן מצות דויד איש־האלהים: 15 ולא סרו מצות המלך
על־הכהנים והלוים לכל־דבר ולאצרות: 16 ותכן כל מלאכת שלמה עד
היום מוסד בית יהוה ועד כלתו שלם בית יהוה:

[12] At that time, Solomon offered burnt offerings on the altar that he had built in front of the porch. [13] What was due for each day he sacrificed according to the commandment of Moses for the sabbaths, the new moons, and the thrice-yearly festivals – the Feast of Unleavened Bread, the Feast of Weeks, and the Feast of Booths. [14] Following the prescription of his father David, he set up the divisions of the priests for their duties, and the Levites for their watches, to praise and to serve alongside the priests, according to each day's requirement, and the gatekeepers in their watches, gate by gate, for such was the commandment of David, the man of God. [15] They did not depart from the commandment of the king relating to the priests and the Levites in all these matters and also relating to the treasuries. [16] And all of Solomon's work was well executed from the day the House of the Lord was founded. And he kept the House in repair.

The beginning and final words of this Chronicles unit reflect Kings. But in between them the Chronicler retrojects his later, much more complex cultic system into the laws of Deuteronomy that underlie Kings. In the older system, the main way of worshipping YHWH was through three annual pilgrimage festivals (Deut 16:1–17; cf. Exod 23:14–19). The Chronicler's system, derived from the Priestly literature, insists upon sacrifices every day and special sacrifices for the Sabbath and the New Moon (see esp. Lev 23). Likewise, the Priestly writer clearly distinguished priests from Levites (see, e.g., Exod 38:21), as does the Chronicler, while Deuteronomy typically speaks of the "levitical priests" (הכהנים הלוים) as a single group (see, e.g., Deut 17:9). As in the previous case, new, additional material regarding religious observance has been retrojected into the past because the Chronicler, it would seem, believed that Solomon, as a righteous king, *must have* observed these traditions.

Did David Sin and Was He Punished?

The Chronicler not only rewrites history by changing words or verses, or by adding new material: he also makes substantial deletions. As I explain to my students, he bought white-out by the truckload! This is especially evident in the Chronicler's description of the reigns of David and Solomon, both of whom he idealized.[24] (In contrast, the authors of Samuel and Kings used their reigns to show that all people, even kings, sin [see 1 Kgs 8:46], and that even kings are subordinate to the Deuteronomic law.) For example, David's affair with Bathsheba and its aftermath – the killing of Uriah and the rebuke of Nathan (2 Sam 11:2–12:25) – are all omitted by the Chronicler, who only copies over the framework of this story (1 Chr 20:1–3, paralleling 2 Sam 11:1, 12:26, 30–31), erasing most of two chapters. He also skips over the story's aftermath, beginning with the rebellion of Absalom and extending through the rebellion of Sheba son of Bichri – eight full chapters (2 Sam 13–20)! He even erases the competition over the throne in David's old age (1 Kgs 1), countering it with a single sentence (1 Chr 29:24) "all – וכל־השרים והגברים וגם כל־בני המלך דויד נתנו יד תחת שלמה המלך: the officials and the warriors, and the sons of King David as well, gave their hand in support of King Solomon." The language of Chronicles here clearly reflects knowledge of the earlier source and polemicizes against it.[25] These erasures are not minor: they are part of a radical change of the images of David and Solomon carried out in Chronicles.

---

24. Braun, "Solomonic Apologetics in Chronicles;" Japhet, *The Ideology of the Book of Chronicles*, 468–69, 478–80.
25. Japhet, *I & II Chronicles*, 514.

They also pose a challenge for anyone upholding the truthfulness of the Tanakh: the Chronicler himself seems to think that the author of 2 Samuel–1 Kings was untruthful because his source depicted a power struggle in David's old age. For the Chronicler, this *had* to be wrong, for this showed disrespect toward David and Solomon. Thus he "corrected" the earlier account.

King Manasseh

In some cases, the Chronicler both adds and deletes material. The quintessential example of this concerns the reign of the seventh-century King Manasseh, who is credited in both Kings and Chronicles with a fifty-five-year-long reign. In Kings, he is depicted as the worst Judean king of all, committing all sort of sacrilegious acts and filling Jerusalem with the blood of the innocent. Furthermore, Manasseh is blamed for the exile of 586 several times in the later sections of Kings (2 Kgs 23:26, 24:3), as well as in a long passage in 2 Kings 21:10–16 – a passage written after Manasseh's death, indeed after the destruction and exile of 586.[26] This lengthy passage is totally absent from Chronicles, which instead adds seven verses (2 Chr 33:11–17) in which an (unnamed) Assyrian king captures Manasseh and leads him in chains to Babylon, where he repents and then returns to Jerusalem to purify the Temple of the non-Yahwistic cultic items he had introduced there. This tradition is especially problematic since Babylon was never the capital of Assyria, but the capital of Babylonia, to which some Judeans were exiled later, in the early sixth century. But it fits the Chronicler's significant interest in the efficacy of repentance.[27]

Scholars have long debated whether this added passage in Chronicles has any historical veracity, with Wellhausen suggesting that the Chronicler's depiction of Manasseh "is entirely on the same plane with

---

26. Mordechai Cogan and Hayim Tadmor, *II Kings: A New Translation*. AB (Garden City, NY: Doubleday, 1988), 271.

27. Japhet, *The Ideology of the Book of Chronicles*, 176–91; Gary N. Knoppers, "Saint or Sinner? Manasseh in Chronicles," in *Rewriting Biblical History: Essays on Chronicles and Ben Sira in Honor of Pancratius C. Beentjes*, ed. Jeremy Corley and Harm van Grol (Berlin: de Gruyter, 2011), 211–29.

Nebuchadnezzar's temporary grass-eating."[28]Although some scholars continue searching for a basis of some kind, either in historical reality or in the Chronicler's likely sources, to explain this change,[29] it is likely that most if not all of the new account in Chronicles was composed by the author himself in order to justify the lengthy reign of this king.

Does Chronicles Fabricate Sources?

In order to substantiate his claims to authority regarding the (new and largely fabricated) material in his account, the Chronicler added many citations to fictitious ancient sources; for example: ויתר דברי אביה ודרכיו ודבריו כתובים במדרש הנביא עדו – "The other events of Abijah's reign, his conduct and his acts, are recorded in the story of the prophet Iddo" (2 Chr 13:22).[30] These sources, however, especially those attributed to prophets, are largely invented.[31] A particularly clear case of such a fabrication is the letter (מכתב) sent by Elijah to King Jehoram according to 2 Chronicles 21:12. This letter is problematic in many respects: according to the biblical chronology, Elijah was likely dead when Jehoram ascended to the throne;[32] according to Kings, Elijah communicated in speech rather than sending letters; and, finally, the letter's wording resembles the Chronicler's own use of language, not Elijah's.[33] Stated simply: the Chronicler fabricated this letter, exemplifying the "claim[s] to have consulted far-off documents" which typify forgeries.[34] This, in turn, naturally raises the question of how much else he fabricated.

---

28. Wellhausen, *Prolegomena*, 207.

29. See, e.g., Japhet, *I & II Chronicles*, 1002–4; Klein, *2 Chronicles*, 474–77; and the especially nuanced depiction in Ehud Ben Zvi, "Reading Chronicles and Reshaping the Memory of Manasseh," in *Chronicling the Chronicler: The Book of Chronicles and Early Second Temple Historiography*, ed. Paul s. Evans and Tyler F. Williams (Winona Lake, IN: Eisenbrauns, 2013), 121–40.

30. Steven J. Schweitzer, "Judging a Book by Its Citations: Sources and Authority in Chronicles," in Ben Zvi and Edelman, *What Was Authoritative for Chronicles?* (Winona Lake, IN: Eisenbrauns, 2011), 37–65.

31. See, e.g., David A. Glatt-Gilad, "Regnal Formulae as a Historiographic Device in the Book of Chronicles," *Revue Biblique* 108 (2001): 200–1.

32. Japhet, *I & II Chronicles*, 812.

33. Klein, *2 Chronicles*, 306–7.

34. Grafton, *Forgers and Critics*, 9; see also 16, on the use of quotation to bolster the authority of a forgery.

How, then, should we understand the Chronicler, this author of one of the biblical books? On what basis did he make his changes? Although some scholars think that he had additional sources unknown to us that informed his revisions, most feel that the majority of his omissions, additions, and alterations were rooted in his own ideology and the application of what Bickerman termed "historical probability."[35] Based on his ideology, he was convinced he knew better than his sources what must have *really* happened, and he composed Chronicles by modifying those earlier sources to fit his belief system. This may be seen as analogous to the free composition of speeches in classical historiography, well known from the study of Acts and Thucydides.[36]

The ultimate result of the Chronicler's (re)writing is the presence of both Samuel–Kings and Chronicles in the canon. This presents a problem for anyone upholding the truthfulness (not truthiness!) of the Tanakh: the authors of two of its books would hold each other to be untruthful. From the Chronicler's perspective, the authors of Samuel–Kings interjected too much unreliable and disrespectful tabloid-level gossip into their narratives of the kings of Israel and Judah; the Chronicler was trying to remove what he saw as the "fake news" in his source. Conversely, had the authors of Samuel–Kings lived to read what the Chronicler made of their work, they might have accused him of censorship and radical historical revisionism.

---

35. On ideological reasons behind forgeries, see Bart D. Ehrman, *Forgery and Counterforgery: The Use of Literary Deceit in Early Christian Polemics* (Oxford: Oxford University Press, 2013), esp. 98–99 concerning "Political and Religious Authorization," and 119–20 on forgeries "To Establish the Validity of One's Views."
36. Marion L. Soardes, *The Speeches in Acts: Their Content, Context, and Concerns* (Louisville, KY: Westminster John Knox, 1994); Richard I. Pervo, *Acts*. Hermeneia (Minneapolis, MN: Augsburg Fortress, 2009), 14. On made-up speeches in classical historiography, most closely identified with Thucydides, see most recently Antonis Tsakmakis, "Speeches," in *The Oxford Handbook of Thucydides*, ed. Ryan K. Balot, et al. (New York, NY: Oxford University Press, 2017), 267–81, esp. 271: "Speeches in classical historiography are not the authentic orations that were delivered by historical actors. They rather serve a historian's historiographical and philosophical aims." Also see Neville Morley, *Thucydides and the Idea of History* (London: I.B. Tauris, 2014), 115–37 for a helpful survey of the speeches and their function.

II. DEUTERONOMY AND ITS SOURCES

Deuteronomy, like Chronicles, reworks earlier source materials.[37] The case of Deuteronomy, however, is potentially even more damning than that of Chronicles, for the following three reasons. First, Deuteronomy not only reworks narrative sources, but legal sources as well – God's commands. Second, Deuteronomy notes לא תספו על־הדבר אשר אנכי מצוה אתכם ולא תגרעו ממנו – "You must neither add anything to what I command you nor take away anything from it" (Deut 4:2; see the slightly different form in 13:1: את כל־הדבר אשר אנכי מצוה אתכם אתו תשמרו לעשות לא־תסף עליו ולא תגרע ממנו, "Be careful to observe only that which I enjoin upon you: neither add to it nor take away from it.")[38] – and yet, it both adds to and deletes from its sources. Third, while the Chronicler fakes sources, the Deuteronomist fakes ancient authorship – he claims Mosaic authorship for the entire book, making it an early Hebrew pseudepigraphon (or forgery).[39] This dissimilation may be even more egregious than it first appears, depending on how we should understand Deuteronomy's self-presentation in its introduction, specifically if it is claiming to re-present an earlier revelation to Moses.[40] However, even

---

37. On legal reworking, see the works of Bernard M. Levinson, esp. *Deuteronomy and the Hermeneutics of Legal Innovation* (New York, NY: Oxford University Press, 1997); and more briefly on narrative reworking, Brettler, *The Creation of History in Ancient Israel*, 62–78.

38. Bernard M. Levinson has written extensively on this verse and its implications; see Jeffrey Stackert and Bernard M. Levinson, "Between the Covenant Code and Esarhaddon's Succession Treaty: Deuteronomy 13 and the Composition of Deuteronomy," *Journal of Ancient Judaism* 3 (2012): 127n6. This verse also serves as the point of departure for Levinson, *Legal Revision and Religious Renewal*; see esp. 12.

39. This is a central and oft-quoted point of Morton Smith, "Pseudepigraphy in the Israelite Tradition," in *Entretiens sur l'antiquité classique 18 Pseudepigrapha* I, ed. K. von Fritz (Geneva, 1971), 191–215 [197–98]. Some now see Smith's desire to call the book a pseudepigraphon rather than a forgery as an improper attempt to whitewash its reputation; see, e.g., Jonathan Klawans, "Deceptive Intentions: Forgeries, Falsehoods and the Study of Ancient Judaism," *JQR* 108 (2018): 489–501. Also, of course, by the standards of modern biblical scholarship (and of Klawans), all the passages that record Mosaic discourse are pseudepigraphic or forgeries.

40. Levinson, *Deuteronomy and the Hermeneutics*, 151, expresses the typical view

so, it revises that revelation so extensively that the original author(s) would not have been able to recognize it.

Intergenerational Punishment in the Decalogue and Elsewhere

In Exodus 20:5–6, the Decalogue describes the punishment for worshipping other deities:[41]

לא־תשתחוה להם ולא תעבדם כי אנכי יהוה אלהיך אל קנא פקד עון 5 אבת על־בנים על־שלשים ועל־רבעים לשנאי: 6 ועשה חסד לאלפים לאהבי ולשמרי מצותי:

[5] You shall not bow down to them or serve them. For I the Lord your God am an impassioned God, visiting the guilt of the parents upon the children, upon the third and upon the fourth generations of those who reject Me, [6] but showing kindness to the thousandth generation of those who love Me and keep My commandments.

Although the Decalogue in Deuteronomy contains many differences from that in Exodus,[42] these verses are reproduced in nearly identical form in Deuteronomy 5:9–10:

לא־תשתחוה להם ולא תעבדם כי אנכי יהוה אלהיך אל קנא פקד עון 9 אבות על־בנים ועל־שלשים ועל־רבעים לשנאי: 10 ועשה חסד לאלפים לאהבי ולשמרי מצותו [מצותי]

[9] You shall not bow down to them or serve them. For I the Lord your God am an impassioned God, visiting the guilt of the

---

that Deuteronomy presents itself as a retelling of earlier material, though this is disputed by Itamar Kislev, "Understanding Deuteronomy on Its Own Terms," TheTorah.com, July 21, 2015, https://thetorah.com/understanding-deuteronomy-on-its-own-terms/; Kislev, "Numbers 36:13: The Transition between Numbers and Deuteronomy and the Redaction of the Pentateuch," in *From Author to Copyist: Essays on the Composition, Redaction, and Transmission of the Hebrew Bible in Honor of Zipi Talshir*, ed. Cana Werman (Winona Lake, IN: Eisenbrauns), 120–21.

41. This entire section is based on Levinson, *Legal Revision and Religious Renewal*, 57–88.

42. For a chart of the major differences between the Decalogue in Exodus and Deuteronomy, including some variations found in the ancient versions, see Moshe Weinfeld, *Deuteronomy 1–11*. AB (New York, NY: Doubleday, 1991), 279–80.

parents upon the children, upon the third and upon the fourth generations of those who reject Me, [10] but showing kindness to the thousandth generation of those who love Me and keep My commandments.

Both versions agree that such egregious religious behavior may be punished by God intergenerationally, עַל־שִׁלֵשִׁים וְעַל־רִבֵּעִים, "upon the third and upon the fourth generations." Both also note, to paraphrase these verses, that God is two hundred and fifty times more generous, as Exodus 20:6 states, וְעָשָׂה חֶסֶד לַאֲלָפִים, "showing kindness to the thousandth generation."

But a serious debate developed within ancient Israel about whether intergenerational punishment was fair – after all, it involved vicarious punishment of the innocent. Indeed, a number of biblical texts explicitly polemicize against the practice.[43] Strikingly, one such text is none other than Deuteronomy 7:9–10, a mere two chapters after the Decalogue:

9 וְיָדַעְתָּ כִּי־יְהוָה אֱלֹהֶיךָ הוּא הָאֱלֹהִים הָאֵל הַנֶּאֱמָן שֹׁמֵר הַבְּרִית וְהַחֶסֶד לְאֹהֲבָיו וּלְשֹׁמְרֵי מִצְוֹתוֹ [מִצְוֹתָיו] לְאֶלֶף דּוֹר: 10 וּמְשַׁלֵּם לְשֹׂנְאָיו אֶל־פָּנָיו לְהַאֲבִידוֹ לֹא יְאַחֵר לְשֹׂנְאוֹ אֶל־פָּנָיו יְשַׁלֶּם־לוֹ:

9 Know, therefore, that only the Lord your God is God, the stead-fast God who keeps His covenant faithfully to the thousandth generation of those who love Him and keep His commandments, [10] but who instantly requites with destruction those who reject Him – never slow with those who reject Him, but requiting them instantly.

As Levinson has shown, the parallels in vocabulary between 7:9–10 and the Decalogue are very strong; it is virtually certain that this passage refers to the Decalogue, and has reworked and transformed it.[44] And what a remarkable transformation this is: instead of intergenerational punishment, God "instantly ... requites" those who sin. This notion is stated three times in different ways in 7:10: (1) וּמְשַׁלֵּם לְשֹׂנְאָיו אֶל־פָּנָיו

43. This is outlined very clearly in Levinson, *Legal Revision and Religious Renewal*, 57–88.

44. Levinson, *Legal Revision and Religious Renewal*, 72–81.

להאבידו, "but who instantly requites with destruction those who reject Him"; (2) לא יאחר לשנאו, "never slow with those who reject Him"; (3) אל־פניו ישלם־לו, "but requiting them instantly." Such repetition characterizes polemical texts, and when polemicizing against the Decalogue, of all texts, emphatic use of such tactics is certainly necessary.

To intensify the problem: Deuteronomy 7:9–10 is presented, like the Decalogue, as divine speech – although, unlike the Decalogue, it is revealed to Moses alone and not directly to all Israel. The long unit containing these verses is introduced[45] in 6:1 as follows:

וזאת המצוה החקים והמשפטים אשר צוה יהוה אלהיכם ללמד אתכם
לעשות בארץ אשר אתם עברים שמה לרשתה:

And this is the Instruction – the laws and the rules – that the Lord your God has commanded [me] to impart to you, to be observed in the land that you are about to cross into and occupy. (Deut 6:1)

A Deuteronomic author has placed words in God's mouth that contravene the Decalogue – presumably, because he did not believe that the theology of the Decalogue was correct. But it is one thing to disagree with a theological position; it is quite another to put the contrary position in God's mouth to Moses! And this is not even the only place where a Deuteronomist overturns the legislation of the Decalogue on this matter; the central Deuteronomic law collection (24:16) also reads: לא־יומתו אבות על־בנים ובנים לא־יומתו על־אבות איש בחטאו יומתו – "Parents shall not be put to death for children, nor children be put to death for parents: a person shall be put to death only for his own crime." This disagreement with the Decalogue on two different occasions is especially striking.

Creating the Judicial System
Exodus 18:13–26 and Deuteronomy 1:12–18 both present accounts of the creation of the judicial system; these accounts, however, differ in at

---

45. This issue may be a bit more complicated due to the history of the composition of Deuteronomy, and the possibility that 6:1–3 concludes chap. 5, rather than, or in addition to, introducing what follows; see Weinfeld, *Deuteronomy 1–11*, 327.

least three ways.[46] First, in Exodus, Moses's father-in-law is responsible for initiating the judicial system:

13 ויהי ממחרת וישב משה לשפט את־העם ויעמד העם על־משה מן־הבקר
עד־הערב: 14 וירא חתן משה את כל־אשר־הוא עשה לעם ויאמר מה־הדבר
הזה אשר אתה עשה לעם מדוע אתה יושב לבדך וכל־העם נצב עליך
מן־בקר עד־ערב: 15 ויאמר משה לחתנו כי־יבא אלי העם לדרש אלהים:
16 כי־יהיה להם דבר בא אלי ושפטתי בין איש ובין רעהו והודעתי את־חקי
האלהים ואת־תורתיו:

Next day, Moses sat as magistrate among the people, while the people stood about Moses from morning until evening. [14] But when Moses's father-in-law saw how much he had to do for the people, he said, "What is this thing that you are doing to the people? Why do you act alone, while all the people stand about you from morning until evening?" [15] Moses replied to his father-in-law, "It is because the people come to me to inquire of God. [16] When they have a dispute, it comes before me, and I decide between one person and another, and I make known the laws and teachings of God." (Exod 18:13–16)

In Deuteronomy, however, the initiative is taken by a seemingly rather burnt-out Moses:

12 איכה אשא לבדי טרחכם ומשאכם וריבכם: 13 הבו לכם אנשים חכמים
ונבנים וידעים לשבטיכם ואשימם בראשיכם:

[12] How can I bear unaided the trouble of you, and the burden, and the bickering! [13] Pick from each of your tribes men who are wise, discerning, and experienced, and I will appoint them as your heads. (Deut 1:12–13)

The second difference between the accounts is illustrated in Deuteronomy 1:14, in which the nation approves of establishing the judicial system, saying that טוב־הדבר, "the idea is good." No such approval is to be found in the parallel section of Exodus. In fact, in Exodus, the same phrase is used, but in a negative statement: Moses's father-in-law tells

---

46. This section is based on Brettler, *The Creation of History in Ancient Israel*, 65–70; see there for additional details and documentation.

Moses, לֹא־טוֹב הַדָּבָר – "this is not a good matter" (18:17). These are the only two times in the Torah where the phrase טוֹב הַדָּבָר (the idea/matter is good) is used together with the verb עשה, (to do), presenting yet another lexical parallel which suggests that Deuteronomy is reworking Exodus. Third, the nature of the judges to be appointed in both texts differs sharply: in Exodus 18:21 they are אַנְשֵׁי־חַיִל יִרְאֵי אֱלֹהִים אַנְשֵׁי אֱמֶת שֹׂנְאֵי בָצַע, "capable men who fear God, trustworthy men who spurn ill-gotten gain"; while in Deuteronomy 1:15, they are אֶת־רָאשֵׁי שִׁבְטֵיכֶם אֲנָשִׁים חֲכָמִים וִידֻעִים, "tribal leaders, wise and experienced men." Exodus emphasizes religious virtue; Deuteronomy insists on secular acumen.

Despite these differences, shared vocabulary suggests that this passage in Deuteronomy is a conscious reworking of Exodus. For example, in addition to the lexical parallel noted above, these are the only two texts in the entire Bible to use the phrase שָׂרֵי אֲלָפִים וְשָׂרֵי מֵאוֹת וְשָׂרֵי חֲמִשִּׁים וְשָׂרֵי עֲשָׂרֹת, "chiefs of thousands, hundreds, fifties, and tens" (Exod 18:21, 25; Deut 1:15), and the language of Deuteronomy 1:17, וְהַדָּבָר אֲשֶׁר יִקְשֶׁה מִכֶּם תַּקְרִבוּן אֵלַי, "And any matter that is too difficult for you, you shall bring to me" is based on Exodus 18:22, אֶת־הַדָּבָר הַקָּשֶׁה יְבִיאוּן אֶל־מֹשֶׁה, "the difficult matters they would bring to Moses."[47] In short, these passages are close enough to suggest that the Deuteronomist reworks Exodus, but different enough to reveal intentional changes hinting at a broader authorial agenda, likely explained, in part, by the influence of the wisdom tradition on Deuteronomy.[48]

After the Revelation of the Decalogue

The Deuteronomist also revises Exodus's account of the Israelites' reaction to God's revelation at Sinai. At first glance, Exodus and Deuteronomy describe Israel's reaction to the revelation in similar terms: after "seeing" (Exod 20:18: וַיַּרְא הָעָם, "the people saw"; Deut 5:25 רְאֵינוּ, הֶרְאָנוּ, "has shown us," "we have seen"), they raise concerns that they will die

---

47. On ascertaining that two texts are related, and knowing which is earlier, see now *Subtle Citation, Allusion, and Translation in the Hebrew Bible*, ed. Ziony Zevit (Sheffield: Equinox, 2017).

48. Moshe Weinfeld, *Deuteronomy and the Deuteronomic School* (Oxford: Clarendon, 1972), 233, 244–45. Bernard M. Levinson, *"The Right Chorale": Studies in Biblical Law and Interpretation*. FZAT 54 (Tübingen: Mohr Siebeck, 2008), 62–68.

(Exod 20:19, פֶּן־נָמוּת, "lest we die"; Deut 5:25 לָמָּה נָמוּת, "let us not die"). In both cases, in response to the people's reaction, Moses alone approaches God (Exod 20:21; Deut 5:30–31). Moses's role as an intermediary is established in both accounts, though more clearly and extensively in Deuteronomy.[49] Once again, the similarities are significant enough to suggest that Deuteronomy knows Exodus. However, a comparison of Exodus and Deuteronomy shows that the latter has reworked and expanded the account of the former quite significantly:

EXOD 20:18–21 MT / 20:15–18 NJPS	DEUT 5:23–33 MT / 5:20–30 NJPS
20 וכל־העם ראים את־הקולת ואת־הלפידם ואת קול השפר ואת־ההר עשן וירא העם וינעו ויעמדו מרחק: 19 ויאמרו אל־משה דבר־אתה עמנו ונשמעה ואל־ידבר עמנו אלהים פן־נמות: 20 ויאמר משה אל־העם אל־תיראו כי לבעבור נסות אתכם בא האלהים ובעבור תהיה יראתו על־פניכם לבלתי תחטאו: 21 ויעמד העם מרחק ומשה נגש אל־הערפל אשר־שם האלהים:	23 ויהי כשמעכם את־הקול מתוך החשך וההר בער באש ותקרבון אלי כל־ראשי שבטיכם וזקניכם: 24 ותאמרו הן הראנו יהוה אלהינו את־כבדו ואת־גדלו ואת־קלו שמענו מתוך האש היום הזה ראינו כי־ידבר אלהים את־האדם וחי: 25 ועתה למה נמות כי תאכלנו האש הגדלה הזאת אם־יספים אנחנו לשמע את־קול יהוה אלהינו עוד ומתנו:26 כי מי כל־בשר אשר שמע קול אלהים חיים מדבר מתוך־האש כמנו ויחי: 27 קרב אתה ושמע את כל־אשר יאמר יהוה אלהינו ואת תדבר אלינו את כל־אשר ידבר יהוה אלהינו אליך ושמענו ועשינו: 28 וישמע יהוה את־קול דבריכם בדברכם אלי ויאמר יהוה אלי שמעתי את־קול דברי העם הזה אשר דברו אליך היטיבו כל־אשר דברו: 29 מי־יתן והיה לבבם זה להם ליראה אתי ולשמר את־כל־מצותי כל־הימים

---

49. Richard D. Nelson, *Deuteronomy*. OTL (Louisville, KY: Westminster John Knox, 2002), 77.

למען ייטב להם ולבניהם לעלם:
30 לך אמר להם שובו לכם לאהליכם:
31 ואתה פה עמד עמדי ואדברה אליך
את כל־המצוה והחקים והמשפטים
אשר תלמדם ועשו בארץ אשר אנכי
נתן להם לרשתה: 32 ושמרתם לעשות
כאשר צוה יהוה אלהיכם אתכם לא
תסרו ימין ושמאל: 33 בכל־הדרך אשר
צוה יהוה אלהיכם אתכם תלכו למען
תחיון וטוב לכם והארכתם ימים בארץ
אשר תירשון:

EXOD 20:15 All the people
witnessed the thunder and
lightning, the blare of the horn
and the mountain smoking; and
when the people saw it, they
fell back and stood at a distance.
16 "You speak to us," they said to
Moses, "and we will obey; but let
not God speak to us, lest we die."
17 Moses answered the people,
"Be not afraid; for God has come
only in order to test you, and in
order that the fear of Him may
be ever with you, so that you do
not go astray." 18 So the people
remained at a distance, while
Moses approached the thick
cloud where God was.

DEUT 5:20 When you heard the
voice out of the darkness, while
the mountain was ablaze with
fire, you came up to me, all your
tribal heads and elders, 21 and
said, "The Lord our God has just
shown us His majestic Presence,
and we have heard His voice out
of the fire; we have seen this day
that man may live though God
has spoken to him. 22 Let us not
die, then, for this fearsome fire
will consume us; if we hear the
voice of the Lord our God any
longer, we shall die. 23 For what
mortal ever heard the voice of
the living God speak out of the
fire, as we did, and lived? 24 You
go closer and hear all that the
Lord our God says, and then you
tell us everything that the Lord
our God tells you, and we will
willingly do it." 25 The Lord heard
may go

a that you made to me, and the
Lord said to me, "I have heard
the plea that this people made
to you; they did well to speak
thus. [26] May they always be of
such mind, to revere Me and
follow all My commandments,
that it may go well with them
and with their children forever! [27]
Go, say to them, 'Return to your
tents.' [28] But you remain here
with Me, and I will give you the
whole Instruction – the laws and
the rules – that you shall impart
to them, for them to observe in
the land that I am giving them
to possess." [29] Be careful, then,
to do as the Lord your God has
commanded you. Do not turn
aside to the right or to the left:
[30] follow only the path that the
Lord your God has enjoined
upon you, so that you may thrive
and that it may go well with you,
and that you may long endure in
the land you are to possess.

What gives the Deuteronomist the right to expand upon his source
text so extensively in this matter? And he does not engage only in
expansion, filling in details – though that is evident as well.[50]

Deuteronomy recasts its source. While Exodus 20 expresses the people's abject fear of revelation, and they are implicitly condemned for that
fear – in fact, verse 20 mentions "fear" twice, once as a noun and once

---

50. Pseudepigrapha typically fill in details of their sources, as noted by Ehrman,
Forgery and Counterforgery, 104–5.

as a verb (ירָאתו ,אל־תירָאו; "do not be afraid," "the fear of him") – this root is used only once in the eleven parallel verses from Deuteronomy 5, and there in the sense of "revere" (5:29: ליראה אתי, "to revere me"). Furthermore, in contrast to its source, God's attitude toward the people's reaction in Deuteronomy 5:28 is explicitly decidedly positive: היטיבו כל־אשר דברו:, "they did well to speak thus"!

The Hebrew Slave Revisited

The Deuteronomic law collection is introduced in verse 12:1, as follows:

אלה החקים והמשפטים אשר תשמרון לעשות בארץ אשר נתן יהוה אלהי
אבתיך לך לרשתה כל־הימים אשר־אתם חיים על־האדמה:

These are the laws and rules that you must carefully observe in the land that the Lord, God of your fathers, is giving you to possess, as long as you live on earth.

As has long been noted, and has been decisively shown by Levinson, many of the laws which follow this verse in Deuteronomy revise those of the Covenant Collection in Exodus.[51] A noteworthy example of this dynamic is found in the two books' respective slave laws. Given the many close similarities in phraseology and structure between the slave law presented in Exodus 21 and the slave law given in Deuteronomy 15, scholars have long recognized that the latter revises the former in accordance with different views on cultic practice and on the role of women slaves:[52]

EXOD 21:2–11	DEUT 15:12–18
² כי תקנה עבד עברי שש שנים יעבד ובשבעת יצא לחפשי חנם: ³ אם־בגפו יבא בגפו יצא אם־בעל אשה הוא	¹²כי־ימכר לך אחיך העברי או העבריה ועבדך שש שנים ובשנה השביעת תשלחנו חפשי מעמך:

---

51. Levinson, *Deuteronomy and the Hermeneutics of Legal Innovation*. Specifically on the slave law, see Levinson, "The Manumission of Hermeneutics…". SVT 109, 293–304.

52. See, e.g., already in 1895, S.R. Driver, *Deuteronomy*. ICC (Edinburgh: T&T Clark, 1895): "The present law is based upon the corresponding one in JE (Ex. 21:2–6)." More recently, see Nelson, *Deuteronomy*, 197: "This law represents a radical rewriting of the manumission law in the Covenant Code (Exod 21:2–6)."

ויצאה אשתו עמו: ⁴ אם־אדניו יתן־לו
אשה וילדה־לו בנים או בנות האשה
וילדיה תהיה לאדניה והוא יצא
בגפו: ⁵ ואם־אמר יאמר העבד אהבתי
את־אדני את־אשתי ואת־בני לא אצא
חפשי: ⁶ והגישו אדניו אל־האלהים
והגישו אל־הדלת או אל־המזוזה ורצע
אדניו את־אזנו במרצע ועבדו לעלם:
ס ⁷ וכי־ימכר איש את־בתו לאמה לא
תצא כצאת העבדים: ⁸ אם־רעה בעיני
אדניה אשר־לא [לו] יעדה והפדה לעם
נכרי לא־ימשל למכרה בבגדו־בה:
⁹ ואם־לבנו ייעדנה כמשפט הבנות
יעשה־לה: ¹⁰ אם־אחרת יקח־לו שארה
כסותה וענתה לא יגרע: ¹¹ ואם־שלש־
אלה לא יעשה לה ויצאה חנם אין כסף:

¹³ וכי־תשלחנו חפשי מעמך לא
תשלחנו ריקם: ¹⁴ העניק תעניק לו
מצאנך ומגרנך ומיקבך אשר ברכך
יהוה אלהיך תתן־לו: ¹⁵ וזכרת כי
עבד היית בארץ מצרים ויפדך יהוה
אלהיך על־כן אנכי מצוך את־הדבר
הזה היום: ¹⁶ והיה כי־יאמר אליך לא
אצא מעמך כי אהבך ואת־ביתך כי־
טוב לו עמך: ¹⁷ ולקחת את־המרצע
ונתתה באזנו ובדלת והיה לך עבד
עולם ואף לאמתך תעשה־כן: ¹⁸ לא־
יקשה בעינך בשלחך אתו חפשי
מעמך כי משנה שכר שכיר עבדך שש
שנים וברכך יהוה אלהיך בכל אשר
תעשה:

EXOD 21:2–11

² When you acquire a Hebrew
slave, he shall serve six years; in
the seventh year he shall go free,
without payment. ³ If he came
single, he shall leave single; if he
had a wife, his wife shall leave
with him. ⁴ If his master gave him
a wife, and she has borne him
children, the wife and her children shall belong to the master,
and he shall leave alone.

But if the slave declares, "I love
my master, and my wife and
children: I do not wish to go
free," ⁶ his master shall take him
before God. He shall be brought
to the door or the doorpost, and

DEUT 15:12–18

¹² If a fellow Hebrew, man or
woman, is sold to you, he shall
serve you six years, and in the
seventh year you shall set him
free. ¹³ When you set him free, do
not let him go empty-handed:
¹⁴ Furnish him out of the flock,
threshing floor, and vat, with
which the Lord your God has
blessed you. ¹⁵ Bear in mind that
you were slaves in the land of
Egypt and the Lord your God
redeemed you; therefore I enjoin
this commandment upon you
today. ¹⁶ But should he say to you,
"I do not want to leave you" – for
he loves you and your household
and is happy with you – ¹⁷ you

his master shall pierce his ear with an awl; and he shall then remain his slave for life. [7] When a man sells his daughter as a slave, she shall not be freed as male slaves are.

[8] If she proves to be displeasing to her master, who designated her for himself, he must let her be redeemed; he shall not have the right to sell her to outsiders, since he broke faith with her. [9] And if he designated her for his son, he shall deal with her as is the practice with free maidens. [10] If he marries another, he must not withhold from this one her food, her clothing, or her conjugal rights. [11] If he fails her in these three ways, she shall go free, without payment.

shall take an awl and put it through his ear into the door, and he shall become your slave in perpetuity. Do the same with your female slave. [18] When you do set him free, do not feel aggrieved; for in the six years he has given you double the service of a hired man. Moreover, the Lord your God will bless you in all you do.

The revision by the Deuteronomist is extensive – however, the content of the law, at least as it concerns male slaves, remains essentially the same. I only comment on four changes. For male slaves, the ear-piercing ritual is moved from taking place אֶל־הָאֱלֹהִים, "before God" (Exod 21:6) – i.e., at a local temple – and instead is to be carried out at the slave-owners' דֶּלֶת, "door" (Deut 15:17). This is in keeping with Deuteronomy's rejection of local temples, which resulted in certain desacralizing tendencies.[53] Secondly, the Deuteronomist has added a provision in verses 13–14 declaring that slaves are to be "furnish[ed]" with various items, presumably to reduce the likelihood that freed slaves would become immediately impoverished and return quickly to slavery.

---

53. See, e.g., Jeffrey H. Tigay, *Deuteronomy*. NJPS Torah Commentary (Philadelphia, PA: Jewish Publication Society, 1996), 150; Nelson, *Deuteronomy*, 199.

This concern is entirely absent in Exodus.[54] These two changes modify the law, but do not change it in a fundamental way.

However, the two changes concerning female slaves arguably do fundamentally alter the law, and may be seen as a reflection of the improved attitude toward women present in Deuteronomy as a whole.[55] The law in Exodus 21 contains two sections: verses 2–6 concern male slaves, while 7–10 concern women sold into slavery by their fathers. Deuteronomy 15 lacks a special section on women slaves, and, furthermore, adds the words או העבריה, "or [Hebrew] woman" (v. 12) at the law's beginning, and, toward the end, the phrase ואף לאמתך תעשה־כן:, "Do the same for your female slave" (v. 17). These alterations communicate that, in Deuteronomy (unlike in Exodus), male and female slaves are to be treated in the same way.[56]

Finally, Deuteronomy lacks any equivalent to Exodus 21:4, which suggests that a slave-master can give his slave a wife to sire children and retain the wife and children as slaves after the male slave is freed. This omission likely reflects the abolishment of this possibility by the Deuteronomic author.[57] Thus, in light of these considerations, it is clear that the role of women slaves is reformulated quite significantly in Deuteronomy's revision of Exodus.

---

54. This addition may also be an expression of Deuteronomy's "humanism," which elsewhere characterizes its slave law; see Weinfeld, *Deuteronomy and the Deuteronomic School*, 282–83.

55. Eckart Otto, "False Weights in the Scales of Biblical Justice? Different Views of Women from Patriarchal Hierarchy to Religious Equality in the Book of Deuteronomy," in *Gender and Law in the Hebrew Bible and the Ancient Near East*, ed. Victor H. Matthews, Bernard M. Levinson, and Tikva Frymer-Kensky. JSOT Supp. 262 (Sheffield: Sheffield Academic Press, 1998), 128–46; for a contrary view, see Carolyn Pressler, *The View of Women Found in the Deuteronomic Family Laws*. BZAW 216 (Berlin: de Gruyter, 1993), 95–112.

56. See already Driver, *Deuteronomy*, 182–83; note especially Otto, "False Weights in the Scales of Biblical Justice?," 142; and the broader discussion in Carolyn Pressler, "Wives and Daughters, Bond and Free: Views of Women in the Slave Laws of Exodus 21:2–11," *Gender and Law in the Hebrew Bible and the Ancient Near East*, ed. Matthews, Levinson, and Frymer-Kensky, 147–72.

57. Nelson, *Deuteronomy*, 197–98.

Is Deuteronomy Truthful?

As noted in the introduction to this section, Deuteronomy is a classic pseudepigraphon – it puts into Moses's mouth the Deuteronomist's own legal and narrative rewritings of earlier material. This is, in some ways, even more theologically problematic than Chronicles, which merely rewrites an earlier account of history: Deuteronomy also rewrites law, and even ascribes this rewriting to Moses to bolster its authority.[58] Should we be horrified? Can Deuteronomy be legitimately deemed "truthful"?

III. TRUTHINESS, FORGERIES, AND INTERPRETATION

Comparing Deuteronomy and Chronicles with their source texts shows how both books rewrite earlier canonical sources – a fact which bears directly on the truth of the Bible, however one defines "truth."[59] It may be hard to stand back and view this issue dispassionately, but we must try, since "disinterested scholars are better at detecting forgeries than are scholars that have a vested interest in the content."[60] To phrase the issue bluntly: should Deuteronomy and Chronicles be considered forgeries? Should they be considered truthful? I will not present an answer to these questions; however, I will supply two frameworks through which to better ponder them – one developed by Jonathan Klawans, the other by Hindy Najman.

Forgery, or Merely Changing Notions of Authorship?

In this essay, I have presented both the Deuteronomist and the Chronicler as authors of *pseudepigrapha* – texts presented as of greater antiquity or

---

58. The main function of pseudepigraphic attribution is to give a new work authority; see, e.g., Ehrman, *Forgery and Counterforgery*, and *Fakes, Forgeries, and Fictions: Writing Ancient and Modern Christian Apocrypha: Proceedings from the 2015 York Christian Apocrypha Symposium*, ed. Tony Burke (Eugene, OR: Cascade, 2017).

59. For a variety of perspectives on this, including different understandings of how to construe "truth," see TheTorah.com symposium, "Meditations on Torat Emet" at https://thetorah.com/torat-emet/

60. Christopher A. Rollston, "Forging History: From Antiquity to the Modern Period," in *Archaeologies of Text: Archaeology, Technology, and Ethics*, ed. Matthew T. Rutz and Morag M. Kersel (Oxford: Oxbow Books, 2014), 176.

more venerable authorship than they actually are. Jonathan Klawans, in his recent article "Deceptive Intentions: Forgeries, Falsehoods and the Study of Ancient Judaism,"[61] provocatively suggests that there is no distinction between *pseudepigraphy* (a relatively neutral scholarly term) and *forgery* (a *very* loaded term). Klawans argues passionately that attempts to whitewash ancient pseudepigrapha, or to differentiate between pseudepigrapha and lies, must be resisted. He "can no longer countenance a categorical distinction between pseudepigraphy and forgery – for this too can be construed as defending lies."[62] Though his article primarily concerns post-biblical literature, it offers an important framework for exploring the question of the truthfulness of Chronicles, and especially of Deuteronomy, considering its false attribution to Moses. Klawans borrows arguments and terminology from discussions of forgery among scholars of the New Testament and early Christianity, especially a lengthy 2013 book by Bart Ehrman, *Forgery and Counterforgery*,[63] and the papers gathered in Tony Burke's 2017 collection, *Fakes, Forgeries, and Fictions*.[64] Ehrman, it should also be noted, utilizes Anthony Grafton's classic work, *Forgers and Critics*, which is directly relevant for studying ancient Jewish texts. In his analysis, Klawans acknowledges the contemporary relevance of this problem, observing, "We scholars stand at a crossroad, conjoining intersecting realms of lies. Political mendacity seems ubiquitous."[65]

The criteria of Klawans and Ehrman are helpful in evaluating whether the authors of Deuteronomy and Chronicles are liars. The Deuteronomist puts words into Moses's mouth without any record of Moses having spoken them, and the Chronicler reworks his sources, often drastically, on the basis of little more than "historical probability," that is, what he thought, based on his ideology, must or should have happened. Klawans's methodology and observations might even suggest that Deuter-

---

61. *JQR* 108 (2018): 489–501, and see now Jonathan Klawans, *Heresy, Forgery, Novelty: Condemning, Denying, and Asserting Innovation in Ancient Judaism* (New York, NY: Oxford, 2019), esp. 1–8; I am especially taken with the term he has created, based on the work of Harold Bloom and others: "the anxieties of innovation."
62. Klawans, "Deceptive Intentions," 489.
63. Ehrman is especially critical of what he calls in his conclusion "Lies and Deceptions in the Cause of Truth"; Ehrman, *Forgery and Counterforgery*, 529–48.
64. Burke, *Fakes, Forgeries, and Fictions*.
65. Klawans, "Deceptive Intentions," 489.

onomy's use of the formula about neither adding nor subtracting from the law is an example of the type of cover-up that typifies such lies – what he calls "pseudepigraphic deceit."[66] This deceit is also exemplified by the Chronicler's fabrication of sources to bolster his recreated history.[67] The Chronicler's opening of his works with genealogies could also be seen as an attempt to create an aura of verisimilitude. Similarly, although none of the authors of the collection *Fakes, Forgeries, and Fictions* discuss the Hebrew Bible – the book's focus is on the forged Gospel of the Wife of Jesus – the criteria[68] they present suggest that we should deem Deuteronomy and Chronicles forgeries, since each one is "a text written to deceive its intended readers as to its true origins."[69]

Hindy Najman, by contrast, laments that "some biblicists have come perilously close to accusing the ancient authors of forgery or fraudulence,"[70] imposing modern ideas of authorship and authority that may not apply to these ancient texts. Her use of the adverb "perilously" clearly illustrates her position, and, indeed, over the course of two books, *Seconding Sinai* and *Past Renewals*,[71] she develops her notion that "just as there was no distinction between citing and interpreting, so too there

---

66. Grafton, *Forgers and Critics*, 493–96. See also the observation in Levinson, *Deuteronomy and the Hermeneutics*, 152, that the phrase in Deuteronomy 5:22, ולא יסף, "those and no more," is "disingenuous."

67. See above, p. 14.

68. The significant exception is Pierluigi Piovanelli, "What Has Pseudepigrapha to Do with Forgery? Reflections on the Cases of the Acts of Paul, the Apocalypse of Paul, and the Zohar," in Burke, *Fakes, Forgeries, and Fictions*, 50–60; see esp. his quotation of Gershom Scholem: "Pseudepigraphy is far removed from forgery" (59).

69. Tony Burke, "Introduction," in Burke, *Fakes, Forgeries, and Fictions*, 1n1. Contrast the more restrictive (and to my mind, unnecessarily restrictive) definition of Bart D. Ehrman, who reserves the term forgery "for literary deceits that involve false authorial claims"; this would exclude the anonymous Book of Chronicles, which according to his terminology, would instead be a "fabrication." Ehrman, "Apocryphal Forgeries: The Logic of Literary Deceit," in Burke, *Fakes, Forgeries, and Fictions*, 36.

70. Hindy Najman, *Past Renewals: Interpretive Authority, Renewed Revelation and the Quest for Perfection in Jewish Antiquity*. SJSJ 53 (Leiden: Brill, 2010), viii.

71. Hindy Najman, *Seconding Sinai: The Development of Mosaic Discourse in Second Temple Judaism*, SJSJ 77 (Leiden: Brill, 2003); Najman, *Past Renewals*.

was no clear distinction between interpreting and interpolating."[72] She further clarifies her stance in "The Vitality of Scripture Within and Beyond the 'Canon,'"[73] where she argues that we need to consider the possibility of transformations of prophecy, for "there was no straightforward cessation of divine encounter."[74] She uses Nietzsche's notion of "Homeric" as extending beyond what Homer wrote, conjoined with Walter Benjamin's idea that texts have lives – that they are *vital*, and should not be diminished by focusing on the original text in its original form. She, in decidedly positive terms, calls this vitality "generative."[75] A recent article written together with Irene Peirano reframes "'pseudepigraphy' as an act of interpretation, or as a generative mechanism that enables growth of a tradition," and claims that such texts are not "intruders or interlopers into the canon but...creative responses to their respective traditions."[76] Her ideas are echoed by Pierluigi Piovanelli, who, in his analysis of Christian apocrypha, suggested that such texts should not be called forgeries because they are "constantly reactualizing and re-legitimizing such a tradition as time goes by."[77]

Najman's understanding is diametrically opposed to that of Klawans, Ehrman, and Grafton.[78] For Najman, texts are organic, and people mediate or facilitate their growth and transformation. This is a natural process, related to the life – the *vita*, the vitality – of texts, especially in the premodern world. Thus, someone who reworks a text is treating it with respect and is working in continuity with its originator(s), rather than deceiving later readers.

---

72. Najman, *Past Renewals*, 84.

73. Hindy Najman, "The Vitality of Scripture Within and Beyond the 'Canon,'" *JSJ* 43 (2012): 497–518.

74. Najman, "The Vitality of Scripture," 507.

75. Najman, "The Vitality of Scripture," 512–18.

76. Hindy Najman and Irene Peirano, "Pseudepigraphy as an Interpretative Construct," in *The Old Testament Pseudepigrapha: Fifty Years of the Pseudepigrapha Section at the SBL*, ed. Matthias Henze and Liv Ingeborg Lied (Atlanta, GA: SBL Publications, 2019), 351.

77. Cited from Tony Burke, "Introduction," 14.

78. As I read him, Bernard Levinson stands somewhere between these two poles.

Is There a Clear Truth about Truthiness?

Who is right: Klawans or Najman? How should we evaluate the authors of Deuteronomy and Chronicles? Do we give them the benefit of the doubt and assume that they were rewriting earlier traditions and laws according to what they believed was the true spirit of the earlier formulations? Or are they fundamentally deceptive, rewriting the past to serve their ideological interests? Of course, the same question may be asked (and also not so clearly answered) regarding the rabbis who "rewrote" biblical law by interpreting it in a fashion that clearly differed from its original meaning. So, were the rabbis deceitful when they used the narrow law: לא־תבשל גדי בחלב אמו, "You shall not boil a kid in its mother's milk," to claim that you cannot cook any meat and milk together (m. Hullin 1:8 and b. Hullin 115b)?[79] Or were they giving new life to the text by expanding it, and no deceit is involved?

Asked in relation to the opening quotation from Jeremiah, should we understand either the Deuteronomist or the Chronicler as scribes writing with false pens? Moreover, if "forgery is a sort of crime,"[80] should we view these authors as criminals?

A definitive answer to this question would involve understanding the intentions of these two authors, which seems very difficult, if not impossible:[81] as I asked above, did they rewrite their sources because of a belief that they were conveying the core meaning of the text, honing and improving the original, or were they rewriting because they had a different idea of what the source should have said? Perhaps related to

---

79. David C. Kraemer, *Jewish Eating and Identity Through the Ages* (London: Routledge, 2007), 39–54.

80. Grafton, *Forgers and Critics*, 37.

81. The issue of the possibility and utility of determining any literary work's intention is very vexed; for a recent survey, see Noël Carrol, "Interpretation," in *The Routledge Companion to Philosophy of Literature*, ed. Noël Carrol and John Gibson (New York, NY: Routledge, 2016), 305–12; and, more simply explained, see *Literary Theory and Criticism: An Oxford Guide*, ed. Patricia Waugh (Oxford: Oxford University Press, 2006), esp. 178–79, "Intention is 'neither available nor desirable,'" and 184, "Intentions are not private and inaccessible." If, as Ehrman holds, intention is key to determining forgery, then we are stymied in our efforts to judge if these works are forgeries. See Ehrman, *Forgery and Counterforgery*, 30: "The intention to deceive is part and parcel of what it meant to produce a forgery."

this question is another issue confronted by biblical scholars – were these later authors hoping to replace their earlier sources, or did they assume that the earlier sources would remain in circulation, and that their newer texts would exist side-by-side with them, perhaps as original and interpretation?

It thus remains uncertain whether these biblical texts can help us find definitive answers to contemporary issues of "truthiness." Nevertheless, examining these two cases – the Deuteronomist and the Chronicler – and viewing them through the respective lenses of Najman and Klawans, can teach us a great deal about assessing what is or is not to be deemed "truthful." Finally, looking at the complexities of truth and deceit through the Bible is particularly valuable, since it can provide us with a model of ancient forgeries that deserves further study[82] – and, perhaps, even veneration. This thought leads directly into the observations of the following paper by Christine Hayes, which highlights that truth is not the only value, and that the most original version of a text is not always best or most true.

---

82. On the importance of studying ancient forgeries, see esp. Stanley G. Porter, "Lessons from the Papyri: What Apocryphal Gospel Fragments Reveal about the Textual Development of Early Christianity," in Burke, *Fakes, Forgeries, and Fictions*, 65–69.

Truth, Goodness, and the Rabbis

CHRISTINE HAYES

In an age when many public officials and national leaders find it as easy to lie as to breathe, truth takes on the aura of an unconditional good. In Jewish tradition, however, the only unconditional good is the divine being. Certainly, truth is highly valued and lying is a sin, but is it correct to say that truth is an *unconditional* good in the Jewish moral economy?

The answer is complex because "truth" is a culturally conditioned concept. The Hebrew term אמת (*emet*) is related (etymologically and semantically) to the word אמונה (*emunah*), which means "faithfulness," and refers to something that, or someone who, is firm and reliable, can be trusted, and does not deceive. *Anshe emet* ("people of truth") are people who can be trusted not to take bribes and distort justice (Exod 18:21) and those who practice *hesed ve'emet* honor agreements and act dependably and kindly (Josh 2:14). God's *hesed ve'emet* (i.e., faithfulness) is everlasting (Ps 117:2) and His words, commandments, and Torah are *emet*, meaning that they are trustworthy (2 Sam 7:28), or simply good and just (Mal 2:6; Neh 9:13). But about 2,300 years ago, as new understandings of truth emerged, some ancient Jews begin to think of the Torah as conveying a single, unchanging, divine "Truth." Other ancient Jews resisted this new way of thinking. Understanding what was at stake in the truth wars of Jewish antiquity may shed light on the truth wars of our own time.

Following the successful eastward campaign of Alexander the Great in the late fourth century BCE, ancient Jews were increasingly exposed to the riches of Hellenistic culture. Literate and learned Jews gained familiarity with the basic contours of Greek philosophical teachings and inevitably brought these teachings into conversation with their own biblical heritage. The results of their intellectual labors are preserved in important works from the centuries before and after the turn of the millennium (i.e., the pre-rabbinic and rabbinic periods). Many of these writings work to characterize the relationship between Torah and the new understanding of truth absorbed from the Greek philosophical tradition.

As Richard Hidary explains in a recent volume,[1] ancient Greek epistemology offered two basic views of truth. The first of these two understandings is reflected foremost in the teachings of Plato. As Hidary explains, "Plato taught that truth is singular, objective, and unchanging" (24) – "Truth" with a capital T. It can be accessed through reason, since reason is also objective and – because it is immaterial and therefore not subject to the cycle of generation and decay – unchanging. Two apples plus two more apples equal four apples in the third century or the twentieth century, in Alaska or in Fiji. In fact, if the whole material cosmos were to vanish so that there were no apples and no people to count them, two plus two would still equal four because reason (*logos*) is immaterial (transcending space and time) and the Truth it reveals is thus static and immutable. For Plato, it is only through philosophy (the activity of reasoning toward wisdom) that we "rise above the world of illusions and [mutable, material] bodies in order that our souls may understand the ideal forms, the realm of unchanging truth" (Hidary, 25).

The Stoics were heirs to this view of Truth but took the idea of the *logos* in a new direction. *Logos* permeates, animates, and governs nature, which is identified with God (for the Stoic, God is nature and nature is God). Indeed, in Stoic thought, the *logos* (reason) that permeates divine nature and makes knowledge of Truth possible, is itself divine.[2] Reason, Truth, and the divine become inextricably linked in Stoic thought.

But not all Greek thinkers agreed with Plato on the idea of a single Truth or with the Stoics on the idea of a divine *logos*. As Hidary explains,

---

1. Richard Hidary, *Rabbis and Classical Rhetoric: Sophistic Education and Oratory in the Talmud and Midrash* (New York, NY: Cambridge University Press, 2018).
2. Unlike Plato, the Stoics held that the *logos* is material.

a second view of truth was held by the sophists, who believed truth to be relative and thus rejected the notion of truth as static, singular, and eternal. Nihilists, for their part, denied the existence of truth altogether.

While we cannot always trace the path of transmission, we do know that ancient Jews encountered these Greek ideas in the Hellenistic period, beginning in the third century BCE, because, around this time, they began to write about reason and truth and the divine in new ways. Where did ancient Jews stand on this debate between the *positive* absolutism of philosophers who enshrine a single, static, rationally-accessed divine Truth AND the *relativism* of the sophists or the *nihilism* of those who claim no truth? More important, how did they conceive of the Torah's relationship to "Truth" as it came to be understood in the Hellenistic period?

In Rabbinic Hebrew, as in Biblical Hebrew, there is no word equivalent to the Greek *aletheia*, which connotes the notion of a universal, transcendent, absolute Truth. Nevertheless, some ancient Jews scrambled on board the philosophers' Truth train. If Truth is divine, and if Israel's Torah was indeed given by a divine being, then the Torah must be divine Truth which, following the Greek definition, means that the Torah is utterly rational and immutable. Its laws and teachings must be universal and singular in meaning, contain no contradictions, and reflect objective and static verities of the divine realm that transcend the ever-shifting circumstances of material existence.

The problem, however, was that the written Torah did not appear to possess these qualities. Nor did it *look* very much like a work of philosophy that uses reason to demonstrate a universal and immutable Truth which transcends the material realm. On the contrary, the Torah is full of myths and stories with fantastical elements – narratives which convey neither universality nor rationality – and contains a set of written laws that govern even the most mundane aspects of material life! To make matters worse, the biblical God states explicitly that the laws given to Israel are designed to *separate* Israel from the rest of humanity, which would indicate that the Torah is particular, unlike Truth, which is universal. Nor are the Torah's laws entirely rational. Certainly, some laws, such as those prohibiting murder and robbery, might be arrived at through a process of reasoning; others, however, such as the purity laws and the dietary laws, would not be arrived at by natural reason![3] Indeed, it is precisely their arbitrary imposition by the divine will that makes them a serviceable means of separating Israel from other nations, because other nations would not discover them through reason. Finally, the Torah's laws – even in biblical times – are not static and eternally fixed but are susceptible to revision over time as new needs arise.[4]

The fact that the Torah of Israel did not appear to teach a universal, rationally accessed, immutable Truth of the kind that dominated the Greek conceptual universe made certain Hellenistic-era Jews anxious: was the Torah merely human, then, and not divine? To forestall such a conclusion some wrote apologetic works insisting that the Torah, the divine law of Israel, was indeed utterly rational and unchanging, as any work of divine Truth (in the Greek sense) should be. Thus, in the Letter of Aristeas (written in Greek in second–first century BCE Alexandria), a Jewish protagonist defends the dietary laws as rational truth: "The legislation was not laid down at random or by some caprice of the mind, but with a view to *Truth* (*aletheia*) and as a token of *right reason* (*orthos logos*)…" (161). One must understand the dietary laws allegorically as a system of symbols, the author argues; only then does one see the deep philosophical and ethical truths that they convey. Similarly, in the Stoic-influenced Book of 4 Maccabees (first century CE), a Jewish protagonist defends the dietary laws against the attacks of a mocking Greek tyrant saying: "You scoff at our philosophy (*philosophia*), as though our living by it were not sensible [*eulogistia*, rational]…[but] believing that the law is divine, we know that the creator of the world shows us sympathy by imposing a law that is in accordance with nature" (5:22, 25).

The greatest exemplar of this apologetic approach was Philo, a

---

3. The rabbis themselves make this point explicitly in Sifra Aḥare Mot Perek 13. For a full discussion see Hayes, *What's Divine about Divine Law: Early Perspectives* (Princeton, NJ: Princeton University Press, 2015), 248–53.

4. A classic example is God's decision to change the laws of inheritance in Num 27:1–11 after hearing the plea of the daughters of Zelophehad. Some laws are discarded or modified when the Israelites enter the land (see for example, the altar law in Deut 13), and Deut 17 provides for the promulgation of new rulings as new or difficult cases arise. In addition, ancient readers were not blind to the fact that Deuteronomy repeats laws from Exodus with modifications.

first-century Alexandrian Jew who, in his writings, defended the Torah's verisimilitude, its correspondence to universal rational and philosophical Truth, its lack of contradiction, and its immunity to historical development. Writing in Greek, Philo declares, "in every respect the Holy Writings are true" (*QA on Gen* 1:12) and "in agreement with the principles of eternal nature" (*Life of Moses* 2:52). Moreover: "In the poetic work of God you will not find anything mythical or fictional but the canons of truth all inscribed" (*AC, Det.* 125).[5]

But not everyone jumped on the philosophers' Truth train. The rabbis of the classical talmudic period (second–seventh centuries CE) resisted the rationalist philosophers' devotion to a single static Truth and rejected the identification of the Torah with this understanding of Truth. They did so in at least two different ways. The first way has been the focus of much scholarly attention in recent decades. Instead of claiming one unchanging Truth in matters of divine law, the rabbis often assert the existence of *multiple* truths, as many scholars have demonstrated.[6] The second way in which the rabbis resisted the philosophers' devotion to a single unchanging Truth has received much less attention. This second, and more radical, mode of resistance will be explored in detail here.[7]

On many occasions, the rabbis do indeed recognize that there is a single objective truth, but after some consideration decide that *they do not have to follow its dictates*. Not only is truth distinct from Torah – truth does not always determine the path of Torah. This means that, when interpreting the Torah and applying its laws to real-world situations, the rabbis are, at times, willing to overrule truth. They do so explicitly and transparently – openly acknowledging the truth, but then setting it aside in their declaration of the halakhah in order to achieve some other good.

---

5. For more on Philo's reconciliation of Torah and Stoic thought see Maren Niehof, *Jewish Exegesis and Homeric Scholarship in Alexandria* (Cambridge: Cambridge University Press, 2011) and Hindy Najman, "A Written Copy of the Law of Nature: An Unthinkable Paradox?" in *Studia Philonica Annual* 15 (2003): 51–56.
6. See Hidary, *Rabbis and Classical Rhetoric*, 26–28, 277–87, and Hidary, *Dispute for the Sake of Heaven: Legal Pluralism in the Talmud* (Atlanta, GA: SBL Publications, 2010) and literature cited there.
7. The discussion that follows draws extensively from chapter 5 ("The 'Truth' about Torah") of my *What's Divine about Divine Law*.

They do so because, as important as truth is, it is not God; truth does not exhaust the category of the divine. There is more to the divine, more to God, more to Torah, than a static, rational, immutable "Truth."

The evidence for this claim can be organized according to three forms of truth: formal, empirical, and judicial. Formal or logical truths are analytically or definitionally true as in the case of simple arithmetic claims ($2 + 2 = 4$) or syllogisms (for example: if bachelors are, by definition, unmarried and if Socrates is unmarried, then the statement that "Socrates is a bachelor" is logically true). Empirical truth describes any claim that conforms to empirical evidence of objective reality (for example: "it is nighttime" is empirically true if one confirms by observation that the time is 11 p.m.). Finally, judicial truth describes a just determination, i.e., a determination that, following a consideration of the facts and the law, properly acquits the innocent and condemns the guilty. Below, we examine rabbinic sources in which the divine Torah may be seen to deviate from all three forms of truth: formal, empirical, and judicial.

We consider first the Torah's deviation from logical truth. On hundreds of occasions the rabbis take the time to point out that divine law doesn't necessarily accord with formal, logical truth. In such cases, the rabbis create a syllogism and then declare that Scripture contradicts the formal truth produced by the syllogism.

Mishnah Menaḥot 8:5

אף המנחות היו בדין שיטענו שמן זית זך מה אם המנורה שאינה לאכילה
טעונה שמן זית זך המנחות שהן לאכילה אינו דין שיטענו שמן זית זך
תלמוד לומר (שמות כז) זך כתית למאור ולא זך כתית למנחות

Meal offerings might logically be thought to require the purest olive oil, for if the menorah, which is *not* intended for consumption, requires the purest olive oil then the meal offerings, which *are* intended for consumption, is it not logical (בדין, *badin*) that they should require the purest olive oil? [And yet], Scripture says (Exod 27:20) "Pure olive oil beaten for the light" and not "pure olive oil for meal offerings!"

This passage claims that, although logic would dictate one outcome, Scripture dictates another (a recurrent argumentative pattern in rabbinic

Scriptural exegesis). Note, however, that the syllogism is entirely manu-
factured by the rabbinic reader. It is not *logically, definitionally* necessary
that the oil used for a meal offering be of the purest quality, since the
purity of the oil may be significant for reasons unrelated to whether or
not it is consumed. Moreover, the assertion that Scripture disallows
the purest oil for the cereal offering is equally forced. Exodus 27:20
merely states that the purest oil should be used for the *menorah*. It
does not mention the cereal offering at all. Nevertheless, our rabbinic
author makes the following unwarranted (but typical) inference: when
Exodus 27:20 states that the purest oil must be used for the menorah,
this means such oil is to be used *precisely and only* for the menorah and
for nothing else! Thus, Scripture teaches that the purest oil is not to
be used for cereal offerings, which contradicts the earlier conclusion
reached through (faulty) logic that it should. What are we to do in such
a case of contradiction between Scripture and formal logic? We follow
Scripture's ruling, *against the dictates of formal logic.*

What is remarkable about this passage and the hundreds of passages
like it is the fact that the rabbis go out of their way to manufacture a
contradiction between formal, logical truth and Scripture (logically, the
law should be X but Scripture teaches not-X) in order to declare that
Scripture deviates from formal truth. Philo, who dedicated himself to
the demonstration of the inherent rationality and truth of the Torah,
would have been scandalized!

Not only can Torah deviate from logical truth, the rabbis also tell us
that Torah does not always align with physical reality or natural facts
as ascertained by empirical observation. In Stoic thought, of course,
divine law is, by definition, in conformity with nature and physical
reality. And within sectarian Jewish circles, as evidenced by documents
from Qumran, an effort was made to align the calendar with the "true"
364-day calendar established by God (Community Rule 1:14–15) and
followed in heaven (Jubilees 2 and 6). But Mishnah Rosh HaShanah
2:9–12 contains what is perhaps the most well-known formulation of the
idea that the laws of the Torah can defy natural reality. In this passage,
R. Gamliel knowingly accepts false testimony about the phases of the
moon and, on its basis, sets the calendar, establishing the dates of Rosh
HaShanah and Yom Kippur. His colleagues object – how can he say that

this is the first of the lunar month, when this clearly is not astronomically true? He will lead people to observe Yom Kippur on the wrong day and to eat on the "true" Yom Kippur, a sin punishable by death at the hands of heaven! But R. Gamliel prevails – the rabbinic court has the right to set the calendar in defiance of astronomical reality. The Torah need not conform to the truths of nature. The Babylonian Talmud attributes a scripturally-based justification to R. Akiva:

Bavli Rosh HaShanah 25a

אמר לו: הרי הוא אומר דאתם, האתם, ואתם, שלש פעמים, אתם - אפילו
שוגגין, אתם - אפילו מזידין, אתם - אפילו מוטעין. בלשון הזה אמר לו:
עקיבא, נחמתני, נחמתני.

[R. Akiva] then said to [R. Joshua]: The text says, "you," "you," "you," three times (Lev 22:31, 23:2, 23:4) to indicate that "you" [may fix the festivals] even if you err inadvertently, "you," even if you err deliberately, 'you," even if you are misled. [R. Joshua] replied to him saying: Akiva, you have comforted me, you have comforted me...

Here, R. Akiva refers to the three verses in Leviticus in which God tells Israel "you are to do the commandments" or "you are to proclaim the festivals."[8] R. Akiva argues that this three-fold repetition gives rabbinic authorities the right to determine the calendar even if those declaring it are misled, or are inadvertently mistaken, or even deliberately in error – because divine law need not operate in accordance with empirical facts.

Similarly, the rabbinic interpretation of Torah tolerates counterfactual rulings and legal fictions if they help achieve humane and compassionate goals, as exemplified in the famous case of the woman who remarries after witnesses report incorrectly that her husband has died (m. Yevamot 10:1). When her husband returns, one authority allows the court to employ a legal fiction and declare that the returning husband simply

---

8. In each verse, the object of doing or proclaiming is *otam*, "them" (i.e., the commandments or the festivals), spelled defectively as אתם, which can be read as *atem* or "you." The threefold defective spelling of "them" to resemble "you" is understood by R. Akiva as conveying an additional meaning.

is not himself, in order to allow the woman's new marriage to continue without disruption (y. Yevamot 10:1). Fictive legal presumptions, such as the presumption that all women are in a state of ritual purity when their husbands return from a journey, are also tolerated (m. Niddah 1:1). Clearly, this will not always be factually true, but the facts alone are an insufficient basis for determining the law when a larger good – such as the promotion of marital intimacy and procreation – can be achieved.

Another noteworthy example of this contrary-to-fact orientation can be seen in the Tannaitic laws of bloodstains in Mishnah Niddah 8:2–3. The mishnah states that a woman may presume that a bloodstain of unknown origin is not menstrual blood if she is able to attribute it to some other source, even if remote, such as a louse killed by another person. Though the rabbis do limit the permissibility of this presumption, restricting it to small bloodstains – attributing a large bloodstain to such a tiny creature as a louse is deemed too great a legal fiction to be permitted – this example still strikingly communicates a general, and rather remarkable, rabbinic willingness to ignore the most reasonable factual explanation in a case of doubt. After all, one might expect that when interpreting and applying *divine* law, one should strive to stay as true to the facts as possible, and, in cases of doubt, err on the side of caution and rule according to the circumstances most likely to conform to empirical truth. But that is not the rabbis' position. Empirical truth is important, but it is not the sole determinant of the law.

Lest the radical nature of the rabbis' position be lost on us, the Babylonian Talmud pointedly draws our attention to it, directly following the laws presented in 8:2 with a story in which a woman brings a bloodstain to R. Akiva for a ruling. The status of the bloodstain as menstrual or non-menstrual in origin cannot be determined as a matter of *fact* and thus a legal presumption is required. R. Akiva adopts the presumption that the blood is non-menstrual based on a far-fetched attribution that strains credulity. R. Akiva's own disciples are astonished by his presumption and R. Akiva himself acknowledges their surprise.

The Torah's deviation from truth continues in judicial contexts, where several rabbinic texts depict an uncompromising adherence to truth – in this context, a single, inflexible standard of strict justice without moderation by other values – as less than ideal. Indeed, Tosefta Sanhedrin 1:3

contains a dispute over *bitsu'a* – a tactic of simply "dividing," or splitting the difference, in a dispute rather than rendering a formal judgment upholding the claim of one side against the other.[9] R. Elazar condemns *bitsu'a* and supports the uncompromising application of the law with the exhortation "Let justice (*ha-din*) cut through the mountain." By contrast, R. Joshua ben Qorḥa argues that a division that avoids declaring one person right and the other wrong is not only a religious duty; it is also the prime example of the biblical notion of a "judgment that combines both truth and peace" mentioned in Zechariah.[10] Indeed, a "judgment of truth" alone is deemed deficient – "where there is a judgment of truth there is no peace."[11]

According to some rabbinic sources, pious judges should contextualize the law and not judge according to the strict line of the law (*shurat hadin*); similarly, pious persons will not insist on the strict line of the law but will occasionally stay within the line of the law (*lifnim mishurat hadin*), foregoing their full rights under the law to achieve some greater good. The phrase *lifnim mi-shurat hadin* is based on a legal metaphor in which the formally true legal ruling is represented as a line. Those who sit on the line demand precise and formal justice (*din* or *shurat hadin*). Those who cross over the line (*'avar*) commit a transgression (*averah*), a negative deviation from the law. But those who stop short of the line of the law and stay *lifnim mishurat hadin* – renouncing the full rights and entitlements due to them by law while remaining within the area of permitted acts bounded by the line of the law – act piously and mercifully (examples are found in b. Berakhot 45b; b. Bava Metzi'a 24b, 30a–b; b. Bava Qamma 99b; b. Ketubbot 97a). Like the pious individual, the pious judge must apply the laws of the Torah with consideration for a range of values – not only truth but also values such as compassion, modesty, peace, humility, or charity.

God, too, judges best when He does not focus solely on the truth but stays within the line of the law (*lifnim mishurat hadin*). One tradition

---

9. For a full discussion of this passage, see Haim Shapira, "The Debate Over Compromise and the Goals of the Judicial Process" in *Dine Israel 26–17* (2010): 183–228.

10. Zechariah 8:16 reads: אֱמֶת וּמִשְׁפַּט שָׁלוֹם, שִׁפְטוּ בְּשַׁעֲרֵיכֶם, *Execute the judgment of truth and peace in your gates.*

11. Zechariah 8:16

in the Talmud (b. Avodah Zarah 4b), which states that it is best to come before God for judgment in the second part of the day, illustrates this notion: in the first part of the day God is studying Torah and will therefore apply the formally correct law, and no one wants to receive a judgment based on the abstract judicial truth; in the second part of the day, however, God engages in judgment which does not follow truth exclusively, but stops short of the formal "truth" or line of the law (i.e., when judging, God acts *lifnim mishurat hadin*). The rabbis portray the decision to forgo true justice as a conscious one on God's part. When the judgment is tending toward condemnation, God intentionally gets up from the seat of justice and sits in the seat of mercy (b. Avodah Zarah 3b). In Bavli Berakhot 7b, God prays that His attribute of mercy will overpower His attribute of justice, and in many rabbinic stories, God is depicted as urging various advocates in the heavenly court to employ whatever tactics are necessary (even dishonest ones!) to enable mercy to prevail over true justice.[12]

The destructive danger of an absolutist adherence to truth in matters of justice is dramatized in a midrash on the story of the Golden Calf (Exod. Rab. 43:4). When Israel sins by worshipping the calf, God realizes that He, according to the law that He Himself pronounced in Exodus 22:19 condemning idolaters to death, must now execute the Israelites. Although God wishes desperately to forgive Israel, how could this be achieved without giving the lie to the earlier vow to destroy idolaters? Isn't true justice eternal and unchanging? The midrash places in God's mouth the following cry of despair: "I cannot retract an oath which has proceeded from my mouth!" But Moses has the answer. Relying on Numbers 30:3, he instructs God to petition for release from a rash vow. God submits to the procedure, humbly admits that He regrets His rash vow, after which Moses – the presiding sage – declares that

---

12. For a full description of the defeat of truth in the rabbinic divine courtroom, see the excellent analysis in Richard Hidary, *Rabbis and Classical Rhetoric*, chapter 7. As Hidary notes, the divorce of truth from divine justice found in a number of aggadic sources stands in stark contrast to the conception of divine justice found in Plato's writings (25–26). Hidary describes the divine judgment imagined by Socrates in Plato's *Gorgias* as one in which nothing is hidden from the eye of the divine judge and the disembodied soul receives a judgment that is true.

the vow is released. This is an astonishing portrait of God trapped by His own "truth" and dependent upon the ingenious intervention of a human partner in order to escape the devastating consequences of the execution of true justice.

The destructive potential of truth holds equally in the human realm. It is said that Jerusalem was destroyed only because the people gave judgments according to strict or formal law (*din haTorah*), when under certain circumstances they should have stayed *lifnim mishurat hadin* – within the line of the law (b. Bava Metzi'a 30a–b). The failure to deviate from the strict line of the law in deference to a larger good can incur terrible consequences, since the *right* ruling is not always the (morally) *best* ruling.

When and how, precisely, is truth dangerous? After all, truthfulness is essential to the smooth conduct of human affairs, and the rabbis, no less than the biblical prophets, denounced lying and deception. But the rabbis understood that a commitment to "truth" is dangerous if misapplied or absolutized.

There are some domains to which the categories "true" and "false" do not apply. As Aristotle already noted, universal, exception-less "truth" may be attainable in arithmetic and logic but it is unattainable in the realm of practical and moral affairs. When deliberating over the morality of an action, we appeal not to concepts of truth and falsehood but, rather, to concepts of good and bad, which are not easily absolutized. However *good* a general rule or law might be in theory, and however *well* a previous moral decision may have served us in the past, it is entirely possible that it is not the best course of action in a similar new case. We must ask: do the demands of the hour indicate that a modification of the earlier rule or decision would be a *better* course of action? We do not have the luxury of simply whipping out some fixed rule on the assumption that it will secure the best moral outcome in every situation. Not only would this be lazy, but it could also cause great damage. The determination of what is best to do in any given situation requires a particularized judgment. Thus, moral reasoning does not prove that something is *immutably true*; it argues that something is *situationally good* – today, and maybe often, and maybe for a very long time, but not *absolutely* and *immutably* because the circumstances of life are ever-shifting. Wouldn't a truly *divine* law – one that can be relied upon now *and* in the future – need to be dynamic and responsive rather than absolute and eternally fixed (*pace* the Stoics)? Wouldn't it need to be open to critique and revision as new situations, new challenges, new information, and new moral insights arise?

The rabbis understood the danger that lies in the *misapplication* of immutable truth language to the dynamic realm of morality, especially given the human tendency to absolutize truth and to assume that nothing – not even God – has the power to displace this ideal "Truth." To the rabbis' way of thinking, declaring truth an *absolute* value – especially in the dynamic realm of moral inquiry – makes truth more sacred than God. And that is the cardinal sin of idolatry.

The refusal to absolutize any one value such as truth should not be confused with the rejection of values in general or with relativism. The rabbis' position is not a *value-less* position but a *value-rich* position. Rabbinic sources eulogize many virtues and values (especially truthfulness) and even hierarchize them on occasion, but they refuse to install any one value as permanently and absolutely supreme. They recognize that each moment of moral judgment requires the dynamic activation, weighing, and balancing of these values to determine the morally best course of action.

According to many midrashim, God too engages in this kind of moral calculus, adjusting the abstract Torah in consideration of actual human experience. In a recent study,[13] Dov Weiss examines more than a hundred midrashim in which God's actions, rulings, or laws are criticized by humans, leading to a modification of some kind. In one instance, Moses informs God that intergenerational punishment is perceived by humans as unfair, and God institutes a policy of individual punishment instead (Num. Rab. 19:33). In the same midrash, Moses tells God that it would be better to first sue for peace before engaging in a war and God consequently adopts this policy, replacing an earlier protocol which called for war without any consideration of first attempting to reach a peaceful resolution. Elsewhere, Moses objects to capital punishment as too severe a consequence for certain sins and God responds by instituting

---

13. Dov Weiss, *Pious Irreverence: Confronting God in Rabbinic Judaism* (Philadelphia: University of Pennsylvania Press, 2017).

lashes instead (Tanḥ. Num. 23). In these midrashim, humans act as local informants providing invaluable feedback for the further refinement of the Torah. They "test-drive" the Torah as it emerges from the pristine conditions of the divine factory and report back to God regarding the Torah's performance. Are its demands feasible? Tolerable? Do they achieve what they intend to achieve or generate perverse consequences? Even if a particular law is just, might there be a *better* way to accomplish that law's goal? In these midrashim, God relies on the concrete, embedded experience and moral insight of humans as He fine-tunes both the divine mores and the divine law.

The rabbis believed that this same deliberative approach was required of them as they interpreted the Torah and applied its teachings. For them, the Torah was not a mathematical or metaphysical treatise on abstract Truth; nor was it a fixed and unchanging law. They viewed the Torah as providing trustworthy training for the moral life. For the rabbis, the Torah's divinity did *not* reside in its immutability or its conformity to a single, universal Truth. Rather, they saw the Torah's divinity in its dynamic responsiveness to concrete human experience and adaptability – through moral reasoning and critical inquiry – to the challenge of living in a constantly changing world.

In *The Rhetoric of Innovation: Self-Conscious Legal Change in Rabbinic Literature*,[14] Aaron Panken highlights the rabbis' unabashed self-awareness when introducing legal changes. Legal changes introduced by the term *barishonah* ("formerly") occur when it is determined that a law is inadequate in light of changing social, agricultural, or economic conditions, changes in the behavior of the general populace, or changing views of fairness, among other possible contributing factors. In addition, *taqqanot*, of which there are more than 200, "represent innovations in law that layer entirely new practices, prayers or regulations never considered before onto the already accepted corpus of Jewish custom and law."[15] These modifications and innovations do not mean that the older law was not "true"; rather, when viewed in the light of new circum-

---

14. Aaron Panken, *The Rhetoric of Innovation: Self-Conscious Legal Change in Rabbinic Literature* (Lanham, MD: University Press of America, 2005).
15. Panken, xviii.

stances or evolving values, the older law was, *but no longer is,* as good as it could be, prompting the rabbis to introduce a "better" – morally better – ruling.

In short, for the rabbis, Torah rulings that may be just or correct in the abstract do not necessarily provide the best answer in concrete situations. Universal immutable truths may be possible in mathematics or in formal logic but they are not possible in the messy, complex business of moral living, which is the proper domain of Torah. Indeed, humans must perpetually serve as God's partners in the hard work of adapting the law to the circumstances of human life, so that it may better serve the good.

In the cases we have examined, there is a single truth that is, of course, valued and considered, but does not always prevail because "truth" is not God. Other rabbinic texts, however, speak of multiple truths. In these texts, which have drawn more scholarly attention than those that assume a single truth, values have an important role to play, as illustrated by b. Eruvin 13:1. Here the contradictory teachings of Beit Hillel and Beit Shammai are both declared to be the words of the living God (i.e., correct). And yet the rabbis avoid the paralysis of indeterminacy precisely by activating their values. Even though the rulings of Beit Hillel and Beit Shammai are both "true," the law follows Beit Hillel – not because their interpretation was somehow *more* true but because Beit Hillel were kindly, modest, conscientious in studying the rulings of their opponents, and humble in presenting their opponents' view first. Indeterminacy is overcome not by invoking a claim of absolute truth but by invoking a vision of the good.

Genesis states that after each act of creation, God looked at what had been created and saw not that it was true, but that it was good. The task of humankind is to maintain the goodness of God's creation to the best of our ability (a task at which we often do not succeed). This task requires a dynamic responsiveness to the ever-shifting circumstances of life in the material universe. The rabbis understood the Torah to be crucial for this task, not because it offers a single abstract and fixed truth but because it tells particular stories and offers particular legal cases that challenge us to think – to consider what justice and equity actually look like in specific instances without recourse to the idea that these can be conveyed by immutable rules. The Torah's very divinity lies in its capacity to respond dynamically to human life in all its of material and embodied complexity.

*   *   *

When the rabbis say that Torah is true, they do not mean (as the Hellenistic Jewish philosophers did), that it aligns with philosophical axioms and can be verified through logical argumentation. They do not mean (as the sectarians at Qumran did), that it aligns with natural facts ascertained through empirical observation or calculation. Nor do they mean that the Torah's judgments can be verified through reference to a fixed principle of true justice.

But it would be equally incorrect to imagine that the rabbis had no regard for formal, empirical, and judicial truth. Quite the contrary. The rabbis regularly avail themselves of formal logic in their deliberations; they excoriate those who lie, deceive, and mislead; and they condemn judges who pervert justice owing to bribes or bias. However, while truth is highly prized and given its due in all of these contexts, it is not absolutized or divinized as an unconditional good. Truth must serve God's good ends. That is why, on occasion, the truth is acknowledged and then set aside in the name of more pressing realities.

The rabbis remind us that the biblical and Jewish God is not the static and absolute unmoved mover of the philosophers, whose divinity entails transcendence and fixity, but a dynamic living presence whose divinity entails a responsive engagement with creation; that His Torah is not an eternal *logos* (as Philo maintained), but a set of moral teachings adaptable to facts on the ground; that to say God is true is not the same as saying that Truth is god; and that an overzealous devotion to an absolute and immutable "Truth" abstracted from the realities of particular moral situations, immune to critical inquiry, and lacking a shared commitment to a world-sustaining good, is nothing short of idolatry.

Can the Torah Still Be a Source of Truth?

Benjamin D. Sommer

When taking the Torah out of the ark during the morning service, many Jews recite the following passage from the Zohar:

אנא עבדא דקודשא בריך הוא, דסגידנא קמיה, ומקמי דיקר אורייתיה,
בכל עידן ועידן. לא על אינש רחיצנא, ולא על בר אלהין סמיכנא, אלא
באלהא דשמיא, דהוא אלהא קשוט, ואורייתיה קשוט, ונביאוהי קשוט,
ומסגי למעבד טבוון וקשוט.

I am the servant of the Holy Blessed One, and I bow before Him and before the glory of His Torah at all times. I rely not on a human, nor on an angel, but on the God of heaven who is the God of truth, whose Torah is truth, whose Prophets are truth, and who carries out myriad acts of goodness and truth.[1]

Can modern people really mean these words? Can we believe that the Torah and Prophets are truth? In the eyes of many people, my own academic field, biblical criticism, has severed the link between Torah and truth. Not only have critical scholars called into question the accuracy of many of the Torah's historical narratives; they have also demonstrated that it presents multiple and self-contradictory memories of historical events, multiple and self-contradictory perceptions of the nature of God, multiple and self-contradictory prescriptions of the law Israel should follow – at best, multiple and self-contradictory truths.[2] In light

---

1. Zohar Vayaqhel 2:206a. All translations in this essay are my own.
2. Many of my fellow biblical critics would phrase this sentence more skeptically; they would have written that the Bible presents multiple and self-contradictory

of modern biblical criticism, can the Torah still be a source of truth? If it can, what sort of truth does it contain or embody? What sort of truth does it endorse? The most basic meaning of the Hebrew word *torah* is "guidance" or "pointing."[3] Toward what sort of truth does the Torah point us, given its ambivalence and multivocality – that is, given the presence within the Torah of voices belonging to multiple ancient authors who often disagree with each other? In what follows, I will first describe the several distinct ways in which members of my guild (biblical critics) have undermined the role of the Bible as a source of truth. But then I will go on to argue that what I call "the participatory theology of revelation" provides a corrective to the view that אורייתא and קשוט, Torah and truth, have parted ways.[4] The participatory theology, which builds upon the work of thinkers such as Franz Rosenzweig, Abraham Joshua

---

constructions of historical events (rather than memories of them), multiple and self-contradictory *constructions* of the nature of God (rather than perceptions). Of course, both memory and perception involve construction, and the constructive nature of the memories and perceptions of biblical authors will play a crucial role in what follows. But I differ from many of my academic colleagues in this regard. As a person of faith, I regard the Bible as presenting memories and perceptions of real things, rather than purely fictional constructions.

3. The noun תורה comes from the root יר״ה, which has several meanings: point, shoot, throw, teach, provide an omen, provide a legal ruling. On the question of how these meanings relate to each other, see G. Liedke and C. Peterson, "Torah," in *Theological Lexicon of the Old Testament*, ed. E. Jenni and C. Westermann, trans. M.E. Biddle (Peabody, MA: Hendrickson Publishers, 1997), 1415; F. García-López, "Tôrāh," in *Theological Dictionary of the Old Testament*, ed. G.J. Botterweck, H. Ringgren, and H.-J. Fabry (Grand Rapids, MI: Eerdmans, 1977–2006), 611, 640; and Michael Fishbane, "*Tôrâ*," [Hebrew] in *Encyclopaedia Biblica* (Jerusalem: Bialik, 1955–88), 8:469–70. Particularly useful is the terse but rich treatment in F. Brown, S.R. Driver, and C. Briggs, *A Hebrew and English Lexicon of the Old Testament* (Oxford: Oxford University Press, 1907), 435f., which succeeds in showing that there is only a single root, יר״ה, in contrast to scholars cited above, who find two or three. The historical (and unanswerable) question of which meanings derived from which is, for our purposes, moot; what matters is that teaching, providing omens, and providing legal rulings all have in common a basic meaning of the root, which is to point, to shoot, to send in a particular direction.

4. I lay out this theory in greater detail in Benjamin Sommer, *Revelation and Authority: Sinai in Jewish Scripture and Tradition* (New Haven, CT: Yale University Press, 2015).

Heschel, and Louis Jacobs, allows contemporary religious Jews to see the very multivocality of scripture, and of Jewish tradition more broadly, as presenting a theory of truth. According to this theory, divine truths revealed from heaven are unavoidably subject to the imperfections inherent in human perception, which inevitably leads towards some degree of error or untruth. Recognizing this can enhance rather than destroy a religious worldview. While affirming the reality of divine revelation, this theology acknowledges the partial nature of human reception of revelation. It thus warns against the dogmatism, overconfidence, and self-righteousness that religions too often produce and that undermine the epistemological humility that ought to be the foundation of religious consciousness and behavior. The Torah's multivocality *cum* self-contradiction, by contrast, encourages such humility.

THE CHALLENGE FROM BIBLICAL CRITICISM

Most ancient and medieval interpreters, both Jewish and Christian, regarded the Bible as having come directly from heaven, and thus understood its content to be not only sacred but also completely reliable. The words of the Five Books of Moses, according to most classical Jewish thinkers, were composed not by Moses or by any other human being, but by God. The remaining books of the Bible were also understood to be of heavenly origin, in their content if not their precise phrasing.[5] This consensus began to break down in seventeenth-century Europe, when various freethinkers, such as the philosophers Thomas Hobbes and Baruch Spinoza (followed a century later by David Hume), began to question whether the Bible really stemmed from a heavenly source. In their wake, in the eighteenth century, several scholars – most of them Protestant, primarily in France and Germany – investigated the origins of these texts, and they doubted that they were literary unities, much less divinely written and perfect ones. The Book of Genesis, they

---

5. That this consensus was widespread does not mean that it met no challenges whatsoever. On ancient and medieval doubts concerning the self-consistency and accuracy of biblical texts, and rabbinic responses to these doubts, see Norman Solomon, *Torah from Heaven: The Reconstruction of Faith* (Oxford: Littman Library of Jewish Civilization, 2012), 113–32.

showed, contained what seemed to be material from multiple earlier works. Moreover, these sources, they found, contradicted one another on several narrative details. It appeared that the author (or, rather, editor) of Genesis had brought together these older documents without reconciling the contradictions among them. As this author/editor was relying on older documents that contradicted one another and could not be authoritatively reconciled, it seemed clear that this author/editor was not an omniscient, otherworldly being. These scholars presumed that the author/editor in question was Moses, but it was not long before it became clear that this method of analyzing the origins of Genesis also worked for Exodus, Leviticus, Numbers, and Deuteronomy, works which tell the story of Moses himself. Once it was clear that the whole Pentateuch was composite in origin, the notion that the author/editor of this work was Moses became untenable; after all, Moses would not have needed to rely on multiple and contradictory sources to narrate recent events in which he was the central character.

Nineteenth-century scholars of the origin of the Pentateuch attempted, with considerable success, to identify the sources from which the Pentateuch was put together. The theories that emerged continue to be refined to this day; but among all specialists in this field, from the mid-1800s through today, a consensus emerged that speaks of three or four main bodies of material, designated Priestly material, or P; Deuteronomic material, or, D; and non-P, non-D material. Some scholars (myself included) further divide this non-P, non-D material into two blocks that we call J and E, and some scholars also detect supplements added after all these sources were brought together. Many Jews and Christians felt that scholars of the Pentateuch's origins attacked the root of their respective religions by asserting that Genesis, Exodus, Leviticus, Numbers, and Deuteronomy were not books at all but a *melange* of originally separate, post-Mosaic, and to some degree contradictory texts. Similar theories were developed regarding other biblical books, showing, for example, that Isaiah could not have written all of the Book of Isaiah and that Jeremiah's original prophecies were supplemented by various texts that later scribes or editors attributed to him.[6] For Jews,

6. Overviews of these theories in modern biblical scholarship are legion. Espe-

however, it was especially the critical approach to the study of the Pentateuch that stung. The discovery that the laws found in Exodus through Deuteronomy were not Mosaic – or, to put it differently, that they are a mosaic but with a small m – has been greeted with dismay by many Jews over the past two centuries, as has the realization that the Pentateuch contains contradictions, and thus imperfection. The very core of Jewish scripture, תורת משה, was not written down by Moses, and, since its constituent parts contradicted one another, it could not have had one author, much less One Author.[7]

In addition, many Jews and Christians have regarded biblical criticism as unnerving because it casts doubt on the historical reliability of biblical texts. (This issue has been more pressing for Christians – especially modern Protestants – than for Jews.[8]) Now, on the one hand,

---

cially useful are articles on each book in standard dictionaries of the Bible, such as *The New Interpreter's Dictionary of the Bible*, ed. Katharine Doob Sakenfeld (Nashville, TN: Abingdon Press, 2006–9); *Anchor Bible Dictionary*, ed., David Noel Freedman, 6 vols. (New York, NY: Doubleday, 1992), and Eliezer Sukenik, et al., *Encyclopaedia Biblica*, 9 vols. [Hebrew] (Jerusalem: Mossad Bialik, 1950–88), as well as various introductions to the Bible, such as Jan Christian Gertz, et al., *T&T Clark Handbook of the The Old Testament*, trans. Linda M. Maloney (London: T&T Clark, 2012); Alexander Rofé, *Introduction to the Literature of the Hebrew Bible* (Jerusalem: Simor, 2009); Marc Zvi Brettler, *How to Read the Bible* (Philadelphia, PA: Jewish Publication Society, 2005), and John Collins, *Introduction to the Hebrew Bible* (Minneapolis, MN: Fortress Press, 2004).

7. On the ways theories concerning the Pentateuch's composition have challenged Jews since the nineteenth century, see Baruch Schwartz, "The Pentateuch as Scripture and the Challenge of Biblical Criticism: Responses Among Modern Jewish Thinkers and Scholars," in *Jewish Concepts of Scripture: A Comparative Introduction*, ed. Benjamin Sommer (New York, NY: New York University Press, 2012), 203–29, and Solomon, *Torah*, 158–271. Scholars can gain considerable theological, historical, and psychological insight into effects of biblical criticism on traditional Jews, along with an example of one type of response to it, from Chaim Potok's novel, *In the Beginning* (New York: Alfred A. Knopf, 1975).

8. Traditional Jewish readings of scripture focus more on the Pentateuch and law than Christian readings do, since the Jewish canon regards the Pentateuch (which contains the Bible's legal collections) as holier and more authoritative than the rest of the Tanakh. Christians do not introduce this division of prestige within their Old Testament. Thus, historical inaccuracies in Joshua, Judges, Samuel, Kings, Ezra-Nehemiah, and Chronicles loom less large in Jewish evaluations

the extent of this second challenge for believers who are not overly concerned with minutiae has been vastly exaggerated. Contrary to what one sometimes reads in the popular press or hears from less learned pulpits, there are no archaeological reasons to doubt the core elements of the Bible's presentation of Israel's history: namely, that the ancestors of the Israelites included a core group originally from Mesopotamia; that at least some Israelites were enslaved in Egypt and were rescued from bondage there under surprising circumstances;[9] that they experienced

---

of scripture than they do for Christians. Further, starting in the early twentieth century, fundamentalist Protestants in the United States and Britain, reacting to various developments in modern Christian theology, began to put extraordinary emphasis on what they viewed as the "literal" meaning of scriptural narratives in a way that Jewish (and Catholic) traditionalists did not, in part because Jews and Catholics since late antiquity and the early Middle Ages have recognized the greater religious value of several non-literal strategies for reading scripture. On the importance for Christian denominations of the threat stemming from historical inaccuracies in scripture, see John Collins, *The Bible After Babel: Historical Criticism in a Postmodern Age* (Grand Rapids, MI: Eerdmans, 2005), 6–7; on its particular consequence for Protestants, see Enns' treatment in Marc Zvi Brettler, Peter Enns, and Daniel J. Harrington, *The Bible and the Believer: How to Read the Bible Critically and Religiously* (New York, NY: Oxford University Press, 2012), 149–56. On the lesser import Jews tend to accord to historical and scientific challenges to biblical narratives, see Brettler in *Bible and Believer*, 51–53 and 164. Concern with scripture's historicity is a recent development; it is shared by fundamentalist Protestants and antireligious skeptics, who are equally influenced, in their thoroughly modern view of scripture, by historical critics. On the modern rather than traditional nature of fundamentalist views of scripture, see Wilfred Cantwell Smith, *What Is Scripture? A Comparative Approach* (Minneapolis, MN: Fortress Press, 1993), 364n54.

9. For a devastating critique of contemporary claims that the Bible's exodus narratives cannot be based on historical memories, see James Hoffmeier, *Israel in Egypt: The Evidence for the Authenticity of the Exodus Tradition* (New York, NY: Oxford University Press, 1997), and James Hoffmeier, *Ancient Israel in Sinai: The Evidence for the Authenticity of the Wilderness Tradition* (Oxford; New York: Oxford University Press, 2005). One need not agree with Hoffmeier's own positive conclusions (some of which, I believe, go beyond the available evidence) to recognize that Hoffmeier exposes the ignorance and faulty reasoning of those who deny a historical kernel to the exodus story. For a possible reference to Israelite enslavement within Egypt, see Gary Rendsburg, "The Date of the Exodus and the Conquest/Settlement: The Case for the 1100's," *Vetus Testamentum* 42 (1992):

a revelation that played a crucial role in the formation of their national, religious, and ethnic identity; that they settled down in the hill country of the land of Canaan at the beginning of the Iron Age, around 1300 or 1200 BCE; that they formed kingdoms there a few centuries later, around 1000 BCE; and that these kingdoms were eventually destroyed by Assyrian and Babylonian armies. To be clear, let me stress that archaeological and historical research do not prove that each and every one of these core elements definitely did happen. My point here is simply to note the specious nature of claims that any of these elements have been contradicted or even attenuated by what archaeologists have or have not found. Those who put forward claims of this sort are unaware of the evidence actually available; moreover, they are unschooled about the nature of the evidence – that is, about what such evidence can and cannot prove.

However, there are other ways in which the historical approach of biblical criticism has undermined the notion that the Bible is a perfect record of truth with regard to history. In particular, such scholarship has profoundly challenged notions of historical causality. Biblical scholars of the nineteenth century fashioned alternate ways of understanding the history of ancient Israel that contradicted what Christians aptly call the Bible's salvation history (*Heilsgeschichte*). Where the Bible identifies the will of a just, gracious, and omnipotent God as the causal agent behind the events of ancient Israelite history, modern historians of ancient Israel focus on the political, economic, and sociological agents that are

---

510–27, esp. 517–518. On the overwhelming likelihood that some Israelites were enslaved in Ramesside Egypt, see further Richard Elliott Friedman, *The Exodus: How It Happened and Why It Matters* (New York, NY: HarperOne, 2007), who restates and extends the theory of Theophile Meek, "Moses and the Levites," *The American Journal of Semitic Languages and Literatures* 56 (1939): 113–20. See also the essays in *Did I Not Bring Israel Out of Egypt?: Biblical, Archaeological, and Egyptological Perspectives on the Exodus Narratives*, ed. James Hoffmeier, Alan Millard, and Gary Rendsburg (Winona Lake, IN: Eisenbrauns, 2016). For further discussion and debate, see *Israel's Exodus in Transdisciplinary Perspective: Text, Archaeology, Culture, and Geoscience*, ed. Thomas Levy, Thomas Schnedier, and William H.C. Propp (Heidelberg and New York: Springer, 2015), and the conversation among Joshua Berman, Richard Hess, Ronald Hendel, and myself at https://mosaicmagazine.com/essay/history-ideas/2015/03/was-there-an-exodus/.

at work in the history of all nations. A great many biblical scholars, for example, interpret the laws and narratives in the Pentateuch's P source as motivated by the desire to glorify and enrich the Aaronide priestly caste responsible for P. They see the Book of Deuteronomy as ministering to the economic needs and social prestige of the Levitical caste from which Deuteronomy's authors are thought to have stemmed. According to an extreme but common version of this type of interpretation (which scholars of religious studies term *reductionism*), the Priestly texts and Deuteronomy are not really about religion or God at all; they merely encode social, political, and economic interests of specific groups of people. This encoding is all the more effective precisely because the audiences of these works *thought* they were about God; indeed, even their authors may have believed they were about God. But the modern reductionist scholar claims to see through the delusions which ensnared both the authors of the ancient texts and their premodern readers. (Examples of the reductionist approach to biblical texts, whose occasional validity as an explanatory model does little to diminish its pervasive shallowness, are so common in biblical studies that citing examples in a comprehensive fashion would require a separate volume.[10]) Similarly, by providing alternate interpretations of historical events narrated in the

---

10. To cite one well-known work: this phenomenon is found throughout Richard Elliott Friedman, *Who Wrote the Bible?* (San Francisco, CA: HarperCollins, 1987). Friedman speaks of each of the four Pentateuchal sources exclusively in terms of the political, social, and economic needs each allegedly serves, without ever exploring the possibility that these texts might have some connection to religious or humanistic ideas. That the differences among the four sources might relate to the varied ways they perceive God, the world, and humanity is barely hinted at, except in a vague comment in the conclusion on the theological heterogeneity that resulted from the redactor's work (234–41). On source criticism as a theologically meaningful pursuit, see Benjamin Sommer, "The Bible as Torah: How J, E, P, and D Can Teach Us about God," in *Imagining the Jewish God*, ed. Leonard Kaplan and Ken Koltun-Fromm (Lanham, MD: Lexington Books, 2016), 83–102. For an eloquent articulation of a similar perspective, see David Frankel, "Contemporary Jewish Theology in Light of Divergent Biblical Views on Revelation's Content," *Zeramim: An Online Journal of Applied Jewish Thought* 3/3 (2019): 6–7, 20–21. For a discussion of reductionism in biblical studies, see Benjamin Sommer, "Dating Pentateuchal Texts and the Perils of Pseudo-Historicism," in *The Pentateuch: International Perspectives on Current Research*, ed.

Bible, modern scholars relativize the Bible's own explanations: where the biblical books of Isaiah, Ezra, and Chronicles tell us, for example, that God brought the Persian emperor Cyrus to punish Babylon and restore Judean exiles to their land (see Ezra 1:1–11; 2 Chronicles 36:22–23; Isaiah 44:28–45:6), the modern historian of biblical Israel may speak of geographic, economic, or even environmental factors that led to the decline of Babylonian power and the rise of Persian hegemony over the Near East. Biblical criticism allows (or requires) historical and natural forces to displace divine causality.[11]

Attention to all these forces yielded a sense that the Bible is less than one thought: rather than transmitting heavenly wisdom, it reflects the political, social, economic, and psychological contingencies of this world. An anthology that contradicts itself, that serves the varied ideological needs of particular groups or individuals, and that puts forward

---

Thomas Dozeman, Konrad Schmid, and Baruch Schwartz (Tübingen.: Mohr Siebeck, 2011), 85–108, esp. 106–8.

11. In this regard, biblical criticism is simply one manifestation of broader historicist trends in modern Europe. On theological critiques of these trends, see David Myers, *Resisting History: Historicism and Its Discontents in German-Jewish Thought* (Princeton, NJ: Princeton University Press, 2003), *passim* and esp. 2; on their relationship to biblical theology specifically, see Daniel Harrington's discussion in Brettler, Enns, and Harrington, *Bible and Believer*, 94–95, as well as Keith Ward, *Religion and Revelation: A Theology of Revelation in the World's Religions* (Oxford: Clarendon, 1994), 232–35. Like Harrington and Ward, I reject the notion that historical study inevitably leads to reductionist and anti-transcendental results. For an example of anti-historicist thinking that nonetheless accords an important place for historiography, see Myers' discussion of Hermann Cohen's hope for a non-reductionist historical study at 40 and 50–51, and Sommer, "Dating," 104–7. Cohen's hope was realized in the work of Yehezkel Kaufmann; see Kaufmann's *Toledot Ha'emunah Hayisra'elit* [Hebrew] 4 vols. (Jerusalem and Tel Aviv: Bialik and Dvir, 1937–56), available in an English abridgement as *The Religion of Israel From Its Beginnings to the Babylonian Exile*, trans. and abridged by Moshe Greenberg (Chicago, IL: University of Chicago Press, 1960). On the exquisite synthesis of empirical-historical and non-reductionist approaches in Kaufmann's *oeuvre*, see Job Jindo, "Is Kaufmann's *Toledot* a 'Jewish' Project? Empirical Research Between Naturalism and Supernaturalism," in *Yehezkel Kaufmann and the Reinvention of Jewish Biblical Scholarship*, ed. Job Jindo, Benjamin Sommer, and Thomas Staubli (Fribourg and Göttingen: Academic Press and Vandenhoeck & Ruprecht, 2017), 71–88.

questionable interpretations of history is, in the eyes of many readers, merely a collection of literary artifacts, not scripture. The Bible as illuminated by historical scholarship shrank into a motley accumulation of historically dependent, culturally relative textual scraps.

After such knowledge, what faithfulness remains possible? For many today, historical scholarship exposes biblical truths as contrived, deceptions, mere vanities. In the following, I attempt to provide a rejoinder to this perspective.

RESPONDING TO THE CHALLENGE

In my book, *Revelation and Authority*, I describe what I call a participatory theology of revelation. Building on thinkers like Rosenzweig, Heschel, and Jacobs, and acknowledging the findings of biblical criticism, the participatory theology sees the Pentateuch as the result of a dialogue between God and Israel. According to this approach, the Pentateuch not only conveys God's will but also reflects Israel's interpretation of, and response to, that will.

We may contrast the participatory theology with a more well-known view of revelation, which I term "the stenographic theory of revelation." According to the stenographic theory, God dictated all the words of the Pentateuch to Moses, and Moses recorded God's words without altering them, so that all the words of the Pentateuch are God's. The participatory theory, however, understands the wording of the Pentateuch as a joint effort involving both heavenly and earthly contributions, or even as an entirely human response to God's real but non-verbal revelation. We might rephrase the difference between these two theologies, the participatory and the stenographic, by recalling the title of a chapter in Heschel's masterwork, *Torah min Hashamayim*: "הנביא שותף או כלי" ("Is the Prophet a Partner or a Vessel?").[12]

The participatory theology is not surprised to notice both inaccuracies and self-contradictions in the Torah, for it does not regard the

---

12. Abraham Joshua Heschel, *Torah min Hashamayim B'aspaqlariyah shel Hadorot*, 2 vols. ed. Dror Bondi (Jerusalem: Koren/Maggid, 2021), 2:670–714; English translation: *Heavenly Torah as Refracted Through the Generations*, ed. and trans. Gordon Tucker (New York, NY: Continuum, 2005), 478–501.

specific wording of the Torah as written by God. Rather, those words were formulated by a variety of prophets, sages, and scribes from ancient Israel who were recording their own perceptions of revelation or the perceptions of revelation recounted to them by their ancestors. The words of the Torah were written down when prophets, sages, and scribes received the revelation, interpreted it, and translated it from what may have been a non-linguistic divine communication into human language. The Pentateuchal sources, J, E, P, and D, reflect historical memories of a series of events in Israel's past. The human perceptions that formed these memories varied from the beginning. This is especially true of the texts that describe the revelation at Mount Sinai, an event that went beyond the categories of human cognition, as the verse immediately after the Ten Commandments – וכל־העם ראים את־הקולת (literally, all the people had seen the sounds, Exodus 20.18a) – already intimates.[13] Some Israelites were more oriented toward the aspect of the experience of the holy that Rudolph Otto refers to as the *fascinans*.[14] The memories of these Israelites, who were drawn into the mystery of revelation, underlie the J account, in which the Israelites at Sinai were inclined to rush towards the mountain where God had appeared (ויאמר ה' אל־משה רד העד בעם פן־יהרסו אל־ה' לראות ונפל ממנו רב/ "Yhwh said to Moses, 'Go down; warn the people not to break through towards Yhwh and see, lest many of them die,'" Exodus 19:21). Other Israelites at Sinai were more oriented toward what Otto called the *tremendum*.[15] They were frightened by the overwhelming nature of the revelation and moved back, away from the mountain (וירא העם וינעו ויעמדו מרחק, Exodus 20:18b). Out of their memories developed the E and D accounts of revelation, which emphasize the fear of the people gathered at Sinai. In this case, it's possible that both sets of historical memories are accurate. But other differences among the sources, no doubt, result from errors of memory and transmission.

---

13. On the exegetical and philological implications of these pregnant words, see my discussion in *Revelation and Authority*, 40–41 and notes.

14. Rudolf Otto, *The Idea of the Holy: An Inquiry Into the Non-Rational Factor in the Idea of the Divine and Its Relation to the Rational*, trans. John W. Harvey (London: Oxford University Press, 1923), 31–41.

15. Otto, *Idea of the Holy*, 12–24.

The editors of the Pentateuch, then, combined multiple, sometimes conflicting memories and interpretations of the history of their ancestors to produce what came to be known as the Five Books of Moses. There are three features we should note about their editorial method.

First, the anthology they produced was highly distinctive in its ancient context. To be sure, there are many other texts that ancient Near Eastern scribes created by combining already existing sources or by supplementing an already existing source.[16] But in none of those cases – I think, for example, of the various editions of the Babylonian *Epic of Gilgamesh* and of the creation story known as *Enuma Elish*, many of whose diverse sources can be identified from earlier Babylonian literature – is the edited text full of the blatant repetitions and self-contradictions that we find again and again in the Pentateuch. In these other texts, the final version was redacted so that it reads somewhat smoothly, even if a few small bumps appear here and there.[17] The Pentateuch's bumps, on the other hand, are ever-present and produce far more serious discontinuities in the plot. The editorial method of the Pentateuch, in short, is unique.[18]

Let me move to a second feature of the Pentateuch's method of combining disparate sources. In presenting us with multiple, overlapping accounts of a given event that frequently differ on various details, the

16. See *Empirical Models for Biblical Criticism*, ed. Jeffrey Tigay (Philadelphia: University of Pennsylvania Press, 1985), esp. chs. 1 and 5. On the composition of the Gilgamesh Epics, see further A.R. George, *The Babylonian Gilgamesh Epic: Introduction, Critical Edition, and Cuneiform Texts*, 2 vols. (Oxford; New York: Oxford University Press, 2003), 1:3–54. On the ritual text Maqlu's development from a process of combination and supplementation, see Tzvi Abusch, *The Witchcraft Series Maqlû* (Atlanta, GA: SBL Publications, 2015), 4–6, 16–17, 29–36.
17. On the tendency towards harmonization and expansion in the evolution of multiply- authored texts in the ancient Near East, see David Carr, *The Formation of the Hebrew Bible: A New Reconstruction* (New York, NY: Oxford University Press, 2011), 90–98.
18. On this unique method of compilation, see the brilliant treatment in Baruch Schwartz, "The Torah – Its Five Books and Four Documents," [Hebrew] in *The Literature of the Hebrew Bible: Introductions and Studies*, ed. Zipora Talshir (Jerusalem: Yad Ben-Zvi Press, 2011), 211–25, and Joel Baden, *The Composition of the Pentateuch: Renewing the Documentary Hypothesis* (New Haven, CT: Yale University Press, 2012), 221–26.

Pentateuch bequeaths us a theory of truth – or of truth as humans are able to perceive it. According to P, Noah took two of every animal onto the ark; according to J, Noah took two of some and seven of the others. Now, it can't be both! Either he took all animals in pairs, or he took some in pairs and others in groups of seven. The Torah does not tell us which report is correct; it provides both accounts of what happened without assigning preference to either one. This predilection for including mutually exclusive approaches to an issue is not only found in the Torah's narratives; we can note it in the Torah's laws, too. Either, as the Levites who wrote Deuteronomy 16 would have it, we must boil the Passover offering (Deuteronomy 16:5–7):

לא תוכל לזבח את־הפסח באחד שעריך אשר־ה׳ א־להיך נתן לך: כי אם־אל־המקום אשר־יבחר ה׳ א־להיך לשכן שמו שם תזבח את־הפסח בערב כבוא השמש מועד צאתך ממצרים: **ובשלת** ואכלת במקום אשר יבחר ה׳ א־להיך בו ופנית בבקר והלכת לאהליך:

> You may not slaughter the Passover offering in any of the places that Yhwh your God is giving to you. Rather, at the place that Yhwh your God chooses so as to make His name present – there you shall slaughter the Passover offering, in the evening, at the time that you left Egypt. **Boil it** and eat it in the place Yhwh your God chooses, then turn back in the morning and go to your tents.

Or, as the priests who wrote Exodus 12 would have it, we must roast it (Exodus 12:8):

ואכלו את־הבשר בלילה הזה **צלי־אש** ומצות על־מררים יאכלהו:

> They should eat the meat at night – **roasted in fire**, with unleavened bread and bitter herbs, they should eat it.

So – roast, or boil?[19] One might want to try somehow to do both – roast it and then boil it, or vice versa; but the priests who wrote Exodus insist that we can *only* roast it (Exodus 12:9):

---

19. It is important to realize that Biblical Hebrew בשל means "to boil, cook in water." See George Adam Smith, *The Book of Deuteronomy* (Cambridge: Cambridge University Press, 1950), 211, as well as the judicious discussion in S.R.

אַל־תֹּאכְלוּ מִמֶּנּוּ נָא וּבָשֵׁל מְבֻשָּׁל בַּמָּיִם כִּי אִם־צְלִי־אֵשׁ רֹאשׁוֹ עַל־כְּרָעָיו
וְעַל־קִרְבּוֹ:

Do not eat it raw, or **boiled in any way in water, but roasted** in
fire: its head and legs and inner parts.

Clearly, the priests who wrote Exodus 12 knew about the practice of
those wayward Levites recorded in Deuteronomy 16, and they warn us
not to follow that errant ritual system. What is striking is that the compilers of the Pentateuch include both laws, and they give us no indication
of which law we're supposed to follow, how we should decide between
them, or whether we should try (in spite of the priests' strictures) to
harmonize them, and, if so, how we might go about constructing the
harmonization.

Of course, in some cases, the versions of a story that the Pentateuch
preserves – though they may be divergent – need not contradict one
another: for example, some Israelites at Sinai may have been drawn
toward the mountain while others moved away from it in fear. In fact,
it's entirely likely that there were Israelites who were simultaneously
attracted and repelled. Similarly, the differences between the two creation stories in Genesis 1–3 include thematic points which, though
different, need not result in inconsistency: God can be transcendent and
magnificent, as in Genesis 1, but God can simultaneously be immanent
and intimate, as in Genesis 2. In Genesis 1, humanity, created in the image
of God, is exalted, but in Genesis 2, humans are made from mud and
dust, to which they will return. Both perceptions of human nature can
be accurate. In other cases, however, the compilers of the Pentateuch
present us with mutually incompatible versions of a single legal practice
or historical memory without hinting to us which one is right, or whether
we should somehow blend them together.

Driver, *Deuteronomy*, 3rd ed. (Edinburgh: T.&T. Clark, 1902), 193–94. The rendering of this verb in Deuteronomy 16:7 as "cook" in NJPS, RSV, and NJB seems
intended to soften the contrast with Exodus 12:8. LXX's καὶ ἑψήσεις καὶ ὀπτήσεις
at Deuteronomy 16:7 ("you will boil and roast") attempts to acknowledge the
presence of וּבִשַּׁלְתָּ in Deuteronomy while adding a second verb to harmonize with
Exodus 12:8. The presence of the two verbs in the LXX rendering of Deuteronomy 16:7 is itself evidence of the fact that the two verbs refer to different means
of cooking.

A third feature of the Pentateuch's editorial method is often overlooked, but it is especially crucial. The Pentateuch's compilers do not attempt to hide the fact that the text is more an anthology than a book. I say this first of all because the self-contradictions and repetitions that result from the compiling of the sources are brazenly obvious: the verses stating that Noah took two of each animal onto the ark (Genesis 6:19–20, 7:8–9, 7:15) appear only a few lines away from the verses saying that he took two of each unclean animal but seven of the ritually pure ones (7:2–3, and cf. 8:20, which explains that the additional clean animals were offered as sacrifices). According to some verses, Ishmaelites brought Joseph to Egypt (Genesis 37:25–27, 28b), while others in the very same context maintain that Midianites brought him there (37:28a, 36). This same tendency is also evident in legal passages which, while at a greater distance from each other, address the same ritual, criminal, or civil issue, as the case of the Passover offering makes clear.

Furthermore, the way the Pentateuch begins makes this text's anthological character clear to anyone familiar with the norms of narrative art in the ancient Near East (that is to say, to the original audience of the Pentateuch). Texts belonging to a particular genre often follow certain conventions, especially in their opening lines. Epics in the Western literary tradition, for example, typically open with an invocation to the muses: this is the case in works as early as the *Iliad* and *Odyssey* of Homer and the *Theogony* of Hesiod, and as late as John Milton's *Paradise Lost*. We find something analogous in ancient Near Eastern creation stories. Listen to the opening lines of two Babylonian creation epics, *Enuma Elish* and *Atrahasis*. The former begins:

> At the time when, up there, sky had not been named,
>> and, down here, strong and stable earth had not been called
>> by any term,
> And Apsu, the primeval one, the progenitor,
> And Ti'amat, the creator, who gave birth to all,
> Had mixed their waters together,
> But neither pastures nor thickets had been formed,
> At the time when no gods had been brought forth,
>> None was called by name, no destinies were decreed,
> Gods were born then, within them;

> Laḫmu and Laḫamu were brought forth, were called by
> name.

Atraḫasis, in turn, opens as follows:

> At the time when the gods were human –
>> They did the labor, they bore the burdens,
>> Great was the workload of the gods,
>> The travail was heavy, the drudgery too much! –
> The great Anunnaki forced
> The Igigi to work seven-fold.

Both of these poems commence with an unusually long and complex sentence that has a distinctive syntactic structure. Each opening sentence consists of:

- first, a subordinate temporal clause,
- then, a parenthetical clause describing the pre-creation situation,
- and, finally, the opening sentence's main clause.

This lengthy and rather complex syntax mirrors the plot of these creation stories, which describe how the cosmos moved from chaos to order.[20] Given the many well-studied points of contact between Genesis 1 and *Enuma Elish*,[21] it is no surprise to find this same syntax in Genesis 1:1–3:

> At the beginning, when God created sky and earth – the earth having been a muddle and a jumble; only darkness on the surface of deep; God's wind was hov'ring on the surface of the water – God said, "There should be light," and there was light.

What is fascinating, however, is that this unusual sentence structure appears in Genesis a second time, just a column or a page later, starting at Genesis 2:4b:

---

20. In *Enuma Elish* the sentence structure is rendered more elaborate by an additional temporal clause and an additional parenthetical comment in lines 7–8.
21. The extensive parallels have long been noted. See the still-useful listing of parallels in Alexander Heidel, *The Babylonian Genesis: The Story of Creation*, 2nd ed. (Chicago, IL: University of Chicago Press, 1942), 128–30, and, more recently, Kenton Sparks, "'Enūma Elish' and Priestly Mimesis: Elite Emulation in Nascent Judaism," *JBL* 126 (2007): 629–32.

At the time when Yhwh God made earth and sky – no field-growth was yet on earth, and no field-grass had yet sprouted, because Yhwh God had sent no rain to the earth, and there was no human to work the soil; but groundwater would well up from the earth and moisten all the topsoil – Yhwh God fashioned the human, dust from the soil. He blew into his nostrils the breath of life, and the human became a living, breathing person.

We encounter the ancient Near Eastern convention for an opening sentence of a creation narrative not only in Genesis 1 but also in Genesis 2:4.[22] The Torah, in short, begins; and then, a column or a page later, it begins again. By doing so, the Torah makes clear what sort of a work it intends to be: a compendium that embodies numerous viewpoints and competing teachings. The Torah never tries to hide its composite nature. On the contrary, with its two beginnings, the Torah announces from the outset: I shall provide you not with one narrative voice but with several. The Torah is about counterpoint, not just melody.

This realization underscores the claims of the participatory theology: It encourages us to read the Torah not as the work of a single, divine, infallible Author but as a series of interpretations of, and reactions to, divine revelation and, thus, a record of debate. Sometimes more than one opinion is right; however, as several of the cases we have discussed show, sometimes one version of a narrative or a law precludes the validity of another – at least one of the accounts or legal directives recorded must be faulty. This should not surprise those readers committed to the participatory theology, for such readers realize that the Torah's

---

22. One might debate whether, in *Atraḥasis* and in Genesis 1, the parenthetical middle clause is missing (that is to say, whether the structure is two-part rather than three part). Because this is the case in both a Babylonian and a biblical example, the parallel remains strong either way. For the two-clause structure in Atraḥasis, see Stephanie Dalley, *Myths from Mesopotamia* (Oxford: World's Classics, 1991), 9 and 36n1, and Benjamin Foster, *Before the Muses: An Anthology of Akkadian* Literature (2nd. ed.; Bethesda, MD: CDL Press, 1996), 1:161. For the two-clause structure in Genesis 1:1–3, see Rashbam's commentary on these verses. For a defense of the three-clause reading in Genesis 1:1–3, see Rashi, along with most modern commentators. For a defense of the three-clause reading in Atraḥasis, see W. G. Lambert and A. R. Millard, *Atra-Ḥasīs: The Babylonian Story of the Flood* (Oxford: Clarendon Press, 1969), 41–42 and 146ff.

authors were human beings. The fact that they were responding to a real revelation of the divine did not make them immune to human error.

Of course, those who are well-read in the Jewish tradition are quite familiar with this sort of text. Works of rabbinic literature constantly provide us with multiple opinions on a given issue. To find an example, we need go no further than the Mishnah's very first paragraph, which discusses the obligation to recite the *Shema* prayer every evening. The Mishnah opens by asking what, precisely, constitutes "evening" – that is, when may we recite the evening *Shema*? It answers that we may recite the evening *Shema* starting at nightfall, and it provides three possibilities regarding the latest time one may recite the evening *Shema*. Rabbi Eliezer rules that one may fulfill this obligation only within the first third of the nighttime. A group known as the sages, however, proposes midnight as the latest time. Finally, Rabban Gamliel concludes that the evening *Shema* may be recited up until dawn (see m. Berakhot 1:1). In presenting more than one answer to a question, the first paragraph of the Mishnah is a good introduction to the Mishnah as a whole. In this case, the Mishnah does go on to tell us which answer is correct (until dawn), but elsewhere the Mishnah presents divergences of opinion without settling them. Debates, divergences, and dissent are are even more common in the Talmuds, which greatly intensify the already impressive level of multivocality found in the Mishnah. Similarly, classical rabbinic collections of biblical interpretation such as Midrash Rabbah typically advance numerous, sometimes conflicting, readings of biblical verse, each one introduced with the words דבר אחר – "another word." Judaism is not apologetic about its sacred literature's penchant for providing several viewpoints that contend with each other. As Mishnah Avot 5:17 tells us, each of these controversies is a מחלוקת לשם שמים, an argument for the sake of heaven. Classical Jewish thought teaches that we bring glory to God when we exchange ideas about the Torah, when we contend with ideas and opinions that differ from our own, and when we listen to those other ideas and consider them seriously. Indeed, rabbinic Judaism regards this dialectical process of learning through discussion, debate, and disagreement as a form of worship – a form of worship which is, in some ways, even more important than conventional prayer.[23]

---

23. On the relative place of prayer and study as forms of worship in rabbinic

The work of biblical criticism shows us that Judaism's love of varied opinions does not start with the rabbis. It can be traced back to the two beginnings of the Torah itself. By announcing from its opening narratives that it will provide more than one approach to a subject, the Torah identifies itself as what we might call a prototypical rabbinic text. Indeed, we might even say that, in its opening two chapters, the Book of Genesis creates rabbinic Judaism.

It is crucial to notice, however, that the classical rabbinic texts and the proto-rabbinic text that is the Torah sponsor debates that have unmistakable limits. The opening paragraph of the Mishnah allows us to discuss when, exactly, we are required to recite the *Shema* every evening, but it does not countenance the possibility that we might decide to skip this obligation once in a while. The same tractate of the Mishnah assumes that there is flexibility in the exact phrasing of our daily prayers within a set structure that the tractate lays out. But the tractate never imagines that any of us can make up our own structure for these services, or that we might forego reciting them daily. Similarly, Genesis 1 and Genesis 2 disagree about what exactly was created when, and about the precise character of the relationship between Creator and created. But no text in the Torah would allow us to entertain the possibility that more than one deity created the world, or that there is no Creator God at all. The priests who composed Exodus 12 and the Levites who composed Deuteronomy 16 disagree about how, precisely, to perform the sacrificial ritual of Passover. But they agree that it must be performed each year: failing to do so, or, for example, inventing some other ritual for Passover that one could perform instead of the פסח offering are not an acceptable option in either text.

FLAWED SCRIPTURE

Let me bring together the various ideas I have been sketching out. According to what I call the participatory theology of revelation, God

Judaism, see Benjamin Sommer, "Dialogical Biblical Theology: A Jewish Approach to Reading Scripture Theologically," in *Biblical Theology: Introducing the Conversation*, ed. Leo Perdue (Nashville, TN: Abingdon Press, 2009), 29–32, with further references there.

revealed the divine will to Moses, to the prophets, and, at Sinai, to the whole nation Israel. God may have revealed this will in a manner that is beyond language – indeed, beyond all normal forms of perception and the categories of understanding associated with them. Moses, the prophets, the sages, and to some degree the whole nation Israel translate this supralingual revelation into the specific narratives and laws we find in the Five Books of Moses, the rest of the Bible, and the entirety of Jewish tradition.

In short, prophecy involves a good degree of translation.[24] Now, the idea of prophecy as translation has an important corollary that requires attention, even though the champions of this idea in Jewish thought have tended not to admit it explicitly: no translation is perfect. At best, a translation can approach the meaning of the original, but it can never precisely match it. This is true when translating from one human language to another and all the more true when translating a supralingual divine communication into human language. Scripture and tradition, as products of this act of translation, reflect how we human beings have understood God's self-revelation – and how we and our forebears, אנו

---

24. On this understanding of biblical prophecy in rabbinic and medieval Judaism, see esp. Menahem M. Kasher, *Torah Sheleimah*, 48 vols. [Hebrew] (Jerusalem: Beit Torah Sheleimah, 1979), 19:328–79; Heschel, *Torah*, 2:670–714 (=*Heavenly*, 478–501); Moshe Greenberg, "Jewish Conceptions of the Human Factor in Biblical Prophecy," in *Studies in the Bible and Jewish Thought* (Philadelphia, PA: Jewish Publication Society, 1995), 405–20; Alan Cooper, "Imagining Prophecy," in *Poetry and Prophecy: The Beginnings of a Literary Tradition*, ed. James Kugel, Myth and Poetics (Ithaca, NY: Cornell University Press, 1990), esp. 34–43. On this theme in the Bible itself, see Benjamin Sommer, "Prophecy as Translation: Ancient Israelite Conceptions of the Human Factor in Prophecy," in *Bringing the Hidden to Light: The Process of Interpretation. Studies in Honor of Stephen A. Geller*, ed. Diane Sharon and Kathryn Kravitz (Winona Lake, IN: Eisenbrauns, 2007), 271–90. On the extension of this role of prophet as translator to Moses in modern Jewish thought, see Sommer, *Revelation and Authority*, 106–9. On the extension of this role to Moses in Maimonides' *Guide*, see Lawrence Kaplan, "'I Sleep, but My Heart Waketh': Maimonides' Conception of Human Perfection," in *The Thought of Moses Maimonides: Philosophical and Legal Studies*, ed. Ira Robinson, Lawrence Kaplan, and Julien Bauer (Lewiston, NY: E. Mellen Press, 1990), 130–66, esp. 161n50; Micah Goodman, *The Secrets of The Guide to the Perplexed*, [Hebrew] (Or Yehudah: Dvir, 2010), 169–87; Sommer, *Revelation and Authority*, 80–89.

ואבותינו, have misunderstood it.[25] Such misunderstandings are inevitable when the transcendent becomes immanent. The great theorist of religion Wilfred Cantwell Smith points out that when one contemplates this paradoxical mission of scripture,

> one... discovers – and this is decidedly healthy – that the particular form through which one's own group was being introduced to transcendence was in fact a particular, human, finite form; flawed, like everything human; mediating transcendence yet in perilously earthen vessels... We human beings – each of us individually and all of us corporately – live in what I am calling the double context of mundane and transcendent: a mundane that is shot through with transcendence, a transcendent that we apprehend, although in always mundane – and often distorted, sometimes even demonic, always improvable – ways.[26]

The distortion inevitably present in scripture need not pervert the divine will,[27] but intellectual honesty and religious humility require us to

---

25. Non-Jewish thinkers have recognized that what I call the translation theory entails the imperfection of prophecy. See the discussion of Karl Barth, Emil Brunner, and Frederick Watson in H.D. McDonald, *Theories of Revelation: An Historical Study 1860–1960* (London: George Allen and Unwin, 1963), 252–53, 257, and 278, as well as Harold H. Rowley, *The Relevance of the Bible* (London: James Clark, 1942), 28. On Scholastic precursors to this idea, see McDonald, *Theories*, 255n1. The theme of scripture's fallibility – and of tradition as a revelatory response to this fallibility – is developed by David Brown, *Tradition and Imagination: Revelation and Change* (Oxford: Oxford University Press, 1999), 54–55, 159, 165–66, 366, 374–75, and Ward, *Religion*, 25, 92 (cf. 44).
26. Wilfred Cantwell Smith, "Thoughts on Transcendence," *Zeitschrift für Religions- und Geistesgeschichte* 42 (1990): 41 and 49.
27. Here we arrive at the crucial difference between the participatory theology of Rosenzweig and Heschel and the understanding of revelation in the work of Martin Buber: for the latter but not the former, this perversion is inevitable. Steven Kepnes, "Revelation as Torah: From an Existential to a Postliberal Judaism," *Journal of Jewish Thought and Philosophy* 10 (2000): 213–16, describes all three of these thinkers as viewing Torah and law as a phenomenonalization of the noumenal experience that is revelation. For Buber, Kepnes shows, this phenomenonalization (or, as I term it, translation) debases the original I-Thou experience of revelation into an I-It relationship. For Rosenzweig and Heschel, the

recognize that sometimes it does. This fact explains the existence of the troubling texts in scripture, texts that we feel cannot have been written by a God who is just or merciful, much less a God who is both. I can only understand Deuteronomy 25:17–19's call to kill all Amalekite men, women, and children as stemming from a gross misunderstanding of divine will. In that passage Israel's perception of the divine demand that Israel defend itself and that it bring malefactors to justice was distorted and exaggerated by human perception into a law of indiscriminate vengeance.

The theory of truth that underlies the Torah, then, reminds us of the incomplete nature of our own perceptions, as well as of the incomplete or flawed nature of Torah itself. God's will may be perfect, but humanity's understanding of God's will can only be imperfect. As a result, we are best served by an anthology of these imperfect perceptions, which affords us the wisdom of the crowd that is the Jewish people or כלל ישראל. With this conclusion, a key distinction emerges between the stenographic theology of revelation and the participatory one. For the stenographic theory, specifics of the law (and, to a lesser extent, Judaism's theological and ethical beliefs) either came directly from heaven or follow from interpretations based on the precise wording of a text whose every letter, vowel, and cantillation mark were penned by God. If the specifics of halakhah come directly from God or are a single exegetical step removed from God, then the extent to which human authorities can change these specifics will be limited. To be sure, one of the details of the halakhic system is that Jews are to follow the rulings of each generation's sages,[28] and thus the possibility of modest change within the system exists within the stenographic theory, but sages committed to

---

phenomenonalization need not function in so negative a way. See also Norbert Samuelson, *Revelation and the God of Israel* (New York, NY: Cambridge University Press, 2002), 175, and Alexander Even-Chen, *A Voice from the Darkness: Abraham Joshua Heschel between Phenomenology and Mysticism* [Hebrew] (Tel Aviv: Am Oved, 1999), 82–84 and 183, both of whom critique Buber for regarding the introduction of content to the contentless revelation as a step towards idolatry or anthropomorphism. See further Yehoyada Amir, *A Small Still Voice: Theological Critical Reflections* [Hebrew] (Tel Aviv: Yedi'ot Aharonot, 2009), 179–80.

28. This principle is rooted in rabbinic exegesis of Deuteronomy 17:8–11. See Menachem Elon, *Jewish Law: History, Sources, Principles*, trans. Bernard Auerbach and Melvin Sykes (Philadelphia, PA: Jewish Publication Society, 1994), 237–38,

that theory are likely to alter the system only with the greatest hesitancy. Furthermore, if, as an adherent to the stenographic theory, one is sure that the details of the law one observes come from heaven, then one may believe one's actions correspond precisely to the will of God. This belief risks fostering an extraordinary spiritual confidence, which can easily devolve into arrogance. There is nothing more dangerous than a human being who thinks he knows exactly what the deity wants – and nothing more lacking in the humility that our created status should engender. Evidence abounds demonstrating the correlation between certainty regarding God's will and tendencies toward arrogance, inflexibility, intolerance, and even religiously motivated violence.[29]

Attitudes toward halakhic change and religious certainty that flow from the participatory theory of revelation will be entirely different. As Louis Jacobs has pointed out, this sort of theology leads to an observance that is less scrupulous and more flexible, though no less committed and consistent.[30] A person who regards the specifics of the halakhic system as the product of Israel's attempts to translate a divine command will feel obligated to observe those specifics, but she will also be aware that it is possible that the translation occasionally errs. As a result, religious practice among Jews committed to a participatory theology should avoid engendering the arrogance that can mar observance among some people committed to a stenographic approach. And yet, here too lurks a danger. The virtue of observance that is unsure of itself, taken to an extreme, leads to the sin of non-observance. Empirical evidence for this assertion is, alas, as abundant as evidence of the dangers that result from theological certainty.[31]

279–80, 481–85; Joel Roth, *The Halakhic Process: A Systemic Analysis* (New York, NY: Jewish Theological Seminary, 1986), 115–16, 125–27.

29. For examples of such empirical evidence, check the newspapers during whatever week you are reading this. You'll find some.

30. Cf. Louis Jacobs, *Principles of the Jewish Faith, an Analytical Study* (New York, NY: Basic Books, 1964), 299–300. See also Arnold Eisen, "Re-Reading Heschel on the Commandments," *Modern Judaism*, 9 (1989): 16–17.

31. For an example of such empirical evidence, see *A Portrait of Jewish Americans: Findings from a Pew Research Center Survey of U.S. Jews* (Washington, D.C.: Pew Research Center's Religion & Public Life Project, 2013), available at https://www.pewforum.org/2013/10/01/jewish-american-beliefs-attitudes-culture-survey/.

The question of the law's malleability also appears in a new light when seen from within the participatory theology. If the specifics of Jewish systems of religious observance were, from the outset, part of Israel's response to divine will, then it is entirely appropriate that today the nation Israel and its sages should strive to hear God's will more clearly; having done so, they will be able, indeed required, to alter details of the halakhic system accordingly. If משה רבינו, our sage Moses, created specifics of the law through acts of interpretation or translation, then his successors can continue that work. Doing so by moving the halakhic system in new directions not contemplated by Moses is no act of disloyalty towards him. On the contrary, imitating Moses's work of translation is an appropriate tribute to the humble servant of God who hoped that all Israelites could attain the status of prophets (Numbers 11:29).

The frank acknowledgment that the Torah is a multivocal human document, more an anthology than a book, frequently prone to contradict itself and at times prone to err, does not have to preclude us from accepting it as a sacred text. But it does tell us that truth is something we strive for more than something we can possess. Seen in this light, the Torah, the Scroll of Guidance, points us towards truth, but does not bring us all the way there. The Torah leaves us more in the position of Moses, looking towards a promised land, than Joshua, confidently entering it; and Moses, not Joshua, is the prototypical sage of the Jewish people.[32] This תורת משה – this Torah associated with Moses rather than with Joshua – cautions us regarding the dogmatism, overconfidence,

---

32. Thus, it is vital to realize that the Torah consists of five books ending with Deuteronomy and not of six books ending with Joshua, as may once have been the case according to the speculation of some biblical scholars. On the fateful nature of Judaism's decision to accord the highest canonical status to the Pentateuch and not to a Hexateuch, see James Sanders, *Torah and Canon* (Philadelphia, PA: Fortress Press, 1972), 27–28, 52, and David Frankel, *The Land of Canaan and the Destiny of Israel: Theologies of Territory in the Hebrew Bible* (Winona Lake, IN: Eisenbrauns, 2011), 25–29. Because the Pentateuch is more sacred and authoritative in the Jewish canon than is the rest of scripture, promise takes a central place in the shaping of Jewish identity, while fulfillment is secondary. It is no coincidence that the hymn of the Zionist movement and later of the State of Israel is entitled (rather Pentateuchally) התקוה, "The Hope," not (Hexateuchally) ההגשמה, "The Consummation" or הניצחון, "The Victory."

and self-righteousness that religions not infrequently engender. The Torah's multivocality and, yes, its self-contradictions and errors, guide us towards cultivating the epistemological humility that should be the foundation of religious consciousness and practice. ‎כֵּן יְהִי רָצוֹן.

The Torah, Our *Chavruta*:
(Re)Constructing Truth in Sacred Text

RACHEL ADLER

Our understanding of what constitutes a sacred text, as well as our understanding of how we engage with such a text, are distinguishing features of Judaism. Rabbinic Judaism posits two sources of revelation: Written Torah and Oral Torah. The twentieth-century scholar Shimon Rawidowicz argues that the rabbinic concept of Oral Torah embeds interpretation into revelation itself.[1] Interpretation, then, is not a secondary process to find out what a sacred text *really* means; indeed, rabbinic interpretation tends to deny that texts have a single correct meaning. Sacred texts are sacred not because they teach one timeless truth, but because they are inexhaustible in their truth-telling potential. We can return to them again and again, drawing new insights each time.

ESTABLISHING TRUTH

That sacred texts are unlimited in their ability to give new insights does not mean that their interpretation lacks ground rules or that their meaning is utterly indeterminate. On the contrary, the rabbis have explicit rules regarding interpretation, summarized in The Thirteen Rules of Rabbi Yishmael, which are recited daily during the preliminary morning service in Orthodox liturgy.[2] Moreover, as R. Eliezer Berkovits ar-

---

1. Simon Rawidowicz, "On Interpretation," *Proceedings of the American Academy of Jewish Research* 26 (1957): 83–126.
2. Louis Finkelstein and Biblioteca Apostolica Vaticana, "Baraita D' Rabbi Yish-

gues, *sevarah,* reason or plausibility, is itself a powerful and dispositive criterion for establishing truth.[3] But these are not the only possible interpretive rules. In their essay "Women and Interpretation of the Torah" in the introductory materials for *The Torah: A Women's Commentary,* editors Tamara Cohn Eskenazi and Andrea Weiss survey the (largely overlooked) history of women's interpretation of Bible, and the various commentaries which follow in this volume attest to a diverse variety of interpretive methodologies.[4] Still other interpretive frameworks might emerge if interpreters strategized to facilitate greater inclusion. For example, the modern philosopher Seyla Benhabib offers a method for preventing rules that have become obstructive from bringing the processes of legal change to a grinding halt – a real problem for a legal process that relies on an ancient interpretive system conceived in patriarchal cultures.[5] Benhabib argues for establishing metadiscourse – a discussion about existing discourse rules – among all those concerned in a rule-bound project, including previously excluded participants. If rules can be renegotiated, rules that function to inhibit or suppress truth and justice can be amended. If Judaism's laws were amended to allow negotiation about the laws themselves, many discriminatory regulations about women's status and communal participation might be renegotiated.[6]

---

mael," *Torat Kohanim: Al Pi Ketav Yad Romi,* Vat. Ebr. 66 (New York, NY: Beit Hamidrash Larabbanim Be'Amerikah, 1956). The Thirteen Rules originate as a baraita, a Tannaitic text not included in the Mishnah. This baraita was originally appended to the beginning of the Sifra, the halakhic midrash on the Book of Leviticus. An accessible translation with explanation of these rules of talmudic exposition can be found in Phillip Birnbaum, *Ha-Siddur Ha-Shalem* (New York, NY: Hebrew Publishing Company, 1949), 41–46.

3. Eliezer Berkovits, *Not In Heaven: The Nature and Function of Halakha* (New York, NY: Ktav, 1983), 3–32.

4. Tamara Cohn Eskenazi and Andrea L. Weiss, eds. *The Torah: A Women's Commentary* (New York, NY: Women of Reform Judaism/URJ Press, 2008), xxxvi–xl.

5. Seyla Benhabib, "The Generalized and Concrete Other: The Kohlberg-Gilligan Controversy and Moral Theory," in *Situating the Self: Gender, Community and Postmodernism in Contemporary Ethics* (New York, NY: Routledge,1992), 148–77. When rule makers engage in meta-discourse while excluding other interested parties, however, they may legislate their own axiological visions into law, leaving the disenfranchised parties even worse off than before.

6. For examples, see Rachel Biale, *Women in Jewish Law: The Essential Texts,*

Why Truth Matters

But why should the interpretation of texts *matter*? And why should truth matter? Texts and the truths that texts communicate matter *because* truth is not an abstract ideal for us to contemplate. What we *believe to be true* with all our hearts, with all of our being, and with all our might moves us to act in the real world. A believed "truth" can impel one man to mow down people at prayer with an AR-15. It can move doctors and nurses to treat a racist who would like to kill them. Every day we demonstrate with our actions the truths that we hold.

In Hebrew, the linguistic roots Alef Mem Nun (AMEN) and Alef Mem Tav, (EMET) derive from a single archaic root.[7] Words derived from AMEN have meanings associated with trustworthiness, skill, and artistic integrity. Words derived from EMET involve truth and truthfulness. These constellations of words suggest that truth, trustworthiness, and integrity are deeply intertwined in Hebrew, *and* that these terms do not refer to abstract absolutes. They are values actively lived out in interpersonal relations and the public sphere, embodied by human beings in human societies. Our enacted values are rooted in overarching ideals whose most perfect embodiment is Godself.

In the Tanakh, *emet* is often paired with another value. *Emet*, truth, is paired with *ḥesed*, compassion, twenty-three times. The pairing *ḥesed v'emet*, compassion and truth, is often translated as a hendiadys, a figure of speech in which two words joined by the word "and" express a single idea – for example, "nice and warm" or "good and plenty." But is *ḥesed v'emet* a hendiadys? Compassion and truth can easily be at odds with one another. Those who claim they are telling others the unvarnished truth often cause pain. On the other hand, acting with compassion at

Their History and Their Relevance for Today (New York, NY: Schocken, 1995), and Rachel Adler, "Here Comes Skotsl: Renewing Halakhah," in *Engendering Judaism: An Inclusive Theology and Ethics* (Philadelphia, PA: Jewish Publication Society, 1998), 21–59.

7. *A Hebrew and English Lexicon of the Old Testament*, ed. Francis Brown, S.R. Driver, and Charles A. Briggs, (Oxford: Clarendon Press, 1968), s.v. "*emet*," 52–54. See also *Theological Dictionary of the Old Testament*, vol. 1, ed. G. Johannes Botterweck and Helmer Ringgren, trans. John T. Willis (Grand Rapids, MI: Eerdmans,1974), s.v. "*aman*," "*emunah*," "*amen*," and "*emet*," 292–303.

the expense of truth breeds lies and allows us to evade realities which must be confronted in order to be addressed responsibly.

The Sacred Pairing

Combining compassion and truth is delicate and difficult. Yet these are attributes joined together in the Bible's most profound revelation about the nature of the Divine. In Exodus 33:18, Moses asks God, "Let me behold your Presence." In Exodus 34:6–7, God responds by revealing to Moses the most about Godself that a human could comprehend. From this revelation the rabbis and post-rabbinic commentators derive the Thirteen Divine Attributes, recited in services for the Days of Awe and the Festivals. The recitation of the Attributes begins with the words, "Adonai, Adonai, a God, merciful and gracious, patient, abounding in compassion (*ḥesed*) and truth (*emet*)."[8]

Of the twenty-three biblical appearances of the pair *ḥesed v'emet*, four refer directly to these as divine attributes,[9] another nine use the terms in the context of swearing an oath or conferring a blessing on others,[10] or as a means of invoking divine compassion and truth as protection.[11] Three uses, all in Proverbs, portray *ḥesed v'emet* as constituting wise conduct for those who wish to live righteously, or as recommended behavior for a king.[12] Finally, in God's indignant complaint in Hosea 4:1, the order of the two terms is reversed: "Hear the word of Adonai, O people of Israel! For Adonai has a case against the inhabitants of this land, because there is no *emet* and no *ḥesed*, and no knowledge of Adonai in the land."[13] Other common partners for *emet* are *shalom* (peace)

---

8. b.Yoma 86a. The rabbis make the argument that results in the retributive ending of Exodus 34:7 being omitted from the recital. For a short history of the Thirteen Attributes, see Reuven Hammer, *Entering the High Holy Days: A Complete Guide to the History, Prayers and Themes* (Philadelphia, PA: Jewish Publication Society, 2005), 125–27.

9. Exodus 34:6; Psalms 86:5, Psalms 89:15, Psalms 25:10.

10. Genesis 24:49, Genesis 47:29; Joshua 2:14.

11. 2 Samuel 2:6, 2 Samuel 15:20; Psalms 61:8, Psalms 85:11; Proverbs 14:22; Genesis 24:27; Psalms 57:4; Genesis 32:11; Psalms 115:1, Psalms 40:11–12.

12. Proverbs 3:3, Proverbs 16:6, Proverbs 20:28.

13. Robert Alter, *The Hebrew Bible. Volume 2. Prophets: A Translation with Commentary* (New York, NY: W.W. Norton, 2019), 1212. In his translation of this verse,

and *mishpat* (justice).[14] Both in interpersonal relations and in public affairs, truth is to be balanced with concerns about its human impact. That is why it is supplemented by the values of compassion, justice, and peace. Widespread untruth is a symptom of social collapse. The prophet Jeremiah laments, "One cheats another; they will not speak *emet*; they have trained their tongues to speak lies" (Jer 9:4).

Truths – Relative and Universal

Many (post)moderns, because they are relativists, are skeptical about truth claims. Not only do relativists deny the existence of absolute truths, they believe that so-called truths are merely what particular individuals or cultures happen to believe. Relativists believe that people can differ about the meanings of true and untrue, moral and immoral. Given that cultures differ in their prevailing beliefs and customs, do any overarching values exist? And can there be truths that are not abstract and immutable but, instead, adaptable to changing social contexts?

If it is a demonstrable fact that cultural values differ, how is it possible to outlaw and condemn behaviors a particular culture tolerates? This was a challenge the Nuremburg Tribunal judges confronted.[15] Defenders of Nazi war criminals argued that, because Jews and Roma were not categorized as fully human in Nazi culture, those who participated in their murder could not be held morally accountable. In this particular culture, extermination of those regarded as non- or sub-human is considered a moral good. Other cultures may disagree, but should not be judgmental about a different culture's norms. However, the Nuremburg verdicts and the charter of the United Nations instead took the stance that, beyond cultural variations, there are overarching definitions of humanity and of what is owed to human beings. Many religions, including our own Judaism, attribute full humanity to marginalized groups, including outsiders and low status insiders. The way we live out these values, however,

---

Robert Alter translates *ḥesed* as "trust," arguing that the term may also mean loyalty in a covenant or relationship.

14. Ezekiel 18:8–9; Zechariah 7:9; Psalms 19:10, Psalms 111:7: *mishpat/emet*. 1 Kings 5:4; 2 Kings 9:22; 1 Kings 20:19: *emet veshalom*.

15. Richard L. Rubenstein and John K. Roth, *Approaches to Auschwitz: The Holocaust and Its Legacy* (Atlanta, GA: John Knox Press, 1987), 246–53.

continues to evolve. In various modern societies, concepts of human rights and equal political representation challenge status-based political systems, and change perceptions of who is fully human. Arguably, values of truth and compassion exist in all cultures. What must keep evolving is to whom these values apply. Who is entitled to truth and to compassion? Who is entitled to be treated as a full human being? Throughout human history our species has far too often chosen to dehumanize others rather than to accept them. Many indigenous tribes' name for themselves means "The Human Beings," although the colonialists who enslaved and massacred them certainly did not perceive them as such.[16] As we experience the wave of xenophobic, racist, antisemitic, and misogynistic terrorism and policy-making that has washed over this country, we must conclude that all of us need to work harder to extend our definition of who qualifies as fully human.

Overarching values and broad definitions continue to be tested. Some argue, for instance, that child marriage, domestic violence, and female genital cutting are legitimate cultural variations; some Western embassies have even refused sanctuary to women and girls seeking escape from realities such as these. However, as feminists point out, allowing a dominant class within any culture the unilateral power to determine cultural rules is to ally *against* those whom the culture disadvantages: slaves, women and LGBTQ+ people, among other marginalized and disenfranchised groups.[17]

The notion of shared overarching values is universalistic. Universalism reasons that since all humans share certain characteristics, certain obligations should apply to all. A Jewish articulation of this value is the Seven Mitzvot of the Children of Noah, a set of basic ethical rules all human societies should follow.[18] Another is found in Mishnah Sanhe-

---

16. David Livingstone Smith, *Less Than Human* (New York, NY: Griffin 2012), 58–59.

17. See, for example, Nafiseh Ghafournia, "Culture, Domestic Violence and Intersectionality: Beyond the Dilemma of Cultural Relativism and Universalism," *International Journal of Cultural Studies* 11, no. 2 (March 2014): 23–29. Carolyn Fluehr-Lobban, "Cultural Relativism and Universal Human Rights," *AnthroNotes* 20, no. 2 (Winter,1998): 1–5, 16–18.

18. b. Sanhedrin 56a–57a, 74b–75a.

drin 4:5, which teaches, "A sole human being was first created to teach that if one destroys a single human soul, Scripture charges that person as if they had destroyed an entire world. One who saves a single human soul, Scripture credits as if they had saved an entire world." These are universalist values, yet they are embedded in the law and stories of a particular tradition. Even when we believe that truths are universal, we can only express them through our own community's stories and images. Stories, images, and metaphors are always particular rather than generic – just as we cannot speak Capital L Language, but only English or Hebrew or Urdu.

Locating New Truths

Truths are conveyed not merely through language but also through specific genres: not only through straightforward reportage but also through stories, midrashim, poetry, and other art forms. A genre's conventions shape how it can convey its truths. Genesis 2–3, for example, draws generically upon animal fable. If you complain that the story cannot be true because snakes do not speak Hebrew, you have missed the point. The story's truths do not concern herpetology. Regarding revelation, Abraham Joshua Heschel cautions us about how misunderstanding genre can lead to misreading. He writes,

> "We must not try to read chapters in the Bible dealing with the events at Sinai as if they were texts in systematic theology. Its intention is to celebrate the mystery...rather than to penetrate or to explain it. As a report about revelation, the Bible itself is *a midrash*.[19]

By using the term "mystery," Heschel means that revelation is *ineffable*. He describes it as "something...human language will never be able to portray."[20] My own students are often shocked by Ezekiel's vision of the heavenly court, populated by creatures reminiscent of customers in the barroom scene of the first Star Wars movie. I tell them that the most important word in Ezekiel's account is not even a word but a particle, *k,*

---

19. Abraham Joshua Heschel, *God in Search of Man* (Philadelphia, PA: Jewish Publication Society, 1955), 185.
20. Heschel, *God*, 185.

meaning "like," "similar to," "evocative of." The prophet cannot articulate what he saw, only what it was *sort of like*.

In sacred texts, truths often come in stories. Stories are *specific* in their relation to time and place. They are populated by characters to whom we respond as if we knew them personally, upon whose motivations we speculate. Stories move us in ways bare facts do not. The headline "Eleven Killed in Pittsburgh" shocks us, but we grieve only after we learn who the dead were, when we see the particular faces and hear the particular stories of those eleven particular Jews who came early to make the Shabbat *minyan* one October morning in 2018. Because stories move us, it is important that stories have integrity, even fictional stories. Elie Wiesel famously said, "Some events do take place but are not true; others are – although they never occurred.[21]

As Heschel insists, some truths can only be expressed in the enigmatic, multi-resonant language of metaphor, because they are truths toward which we are *pointing* rather than concrete facts anyone might observe. Any statement we make about God is metaphorical. It is an effort by the finite to represent the infinite. As such, it is always incomplete. That is why any statement about God needs to be supplemented by a heterogeneous multitude of other metaphors. Every individual metaphor is powerful, because its vividness and the feelings it evokes reach deep into us in a way a statistic does not.

There *are* empirical truths – facts – that can be proven by observation or replicable experiments. Things fall down and not up. Fire will burn your hand. Jewish tradition, however, also affirms truths that cannot be perceived with the senses or measured. The difference between empirical facts and ineffable truths is that facts are descriptive, whereas all ineffable truths have normative implications. Facts can tell us what something is and, sometimes, what caused it to be that way. But facts do not tell us what to do about the reality they describe. A philosophical argument has raged for centuries about whether one can derive an "ought" from an "is." You will be relieved to hear that I'm not getting into that. From my perspective, a fact or an "is" can't tell you what you "ought" to do unless you specify what your goals are. Do you want to clean up the

---

21. Elie Wiesel, *Legends of Our Time* (New York, NY: Avon, 1968), viii.

planet or make a billion dollars as quickly as possible? Different goals lead to different actions. But ineffable truths will *always* lead you into commitments to *ethical* action.

Holding Ourselves and our Torah Accountable

Heschel, Martin Buber, and Emmanuel Levinas all assert that truths arise within relationships. Buber distinguishes the objectifying I-It relation, in which we view the other as a utility, from the I-Thou relation, which is a communion between individuals or between an individual and God.[22] But the modern Jewish philosopher who most closely links revelation, relationships, and actions is Emmanuel Levinas.

Most philosophers assume that the starting point of philosophy is epistemology and its inquiries: what is knowledge and how do we know things? In contrast, Levinas argues that the starting point of philosophy must be ethics, and the starting point of ethics is in the face of the other.[23] By *other*, he means any other person we encounter. By *face*, Levinas means what is distinctively "not-me" in that other: a being I'll never completely understand, who is a whole other universe I did not create. For Levinas, the face of the other contains both a trace of God – the *tselem Elohim*, or divine image – and a trace of the commandment to love my neighbor. The face of the other brings me revelation. Its first revelatory words are *Lo tirtsaḥ* – "You shall not murder."[24]

The Levinasian other commands me, not with superior power, but with her nakedness in the world, her potential destitution, her status as a widow, an orphan, a stranger.[25] The other calls me to answer for myself, and consequently grounds my freedom in my responsibility.[26]

---

22. Martin Buber, *I and Thou*, trans. Walter Kaufman (New York, NY: Charles Scribner's Sons, 1970).

23. Emmanuel Levinas, *Totality and Infinity*, trans. Alphonso Lingis (Pittsburgh, PA: Duquesne University Press, 1969), 150.

24. Emmanuel Levinas, *Difficult Freedom: Essays on Judaism*, trans. Seán Hand (Baltimore, MD: Johns Hopkins University Press,1990), 8.

25. Levinas, *Totality and Infinity*, 150.

26. Emmanuel Levinas, *Entre Nous: On Thinking of the Other*, trans. Michael B. Smith and Barbara Hernshaw (New York, NY: Columbia University Press, 1998), 74.

I am unique and I matter, precisely *because of* my responsibility to give what only I can give. Not only were the events at Sinai revelation, but *every conversation* is a revelation – a revelation because I cannot predict what the other will say. An other, human or divine, can surprise me, teach me what I did not know. Encountering an other delights me *and* reminds me that that I am *limited*. Precisely because I am not one with and the same as the other, I am able to be *in relationship* and I am able to be *surprised*. If everything was already in my own head and under my own control, no one could ever reveal to me what I did not already know. For Levinas, revelation is not preposterous. It is the alternative to egomania or solipsism. Because truths are *embodied* and sometimes painful, revelation impels action. Ultimately, what revelation reveals to us is our obligation.

If we believe that all ineffable truths propel us toward action, it is handy to have a genre in which truths must constantly confront social and behavioral change and readjust so that we can live them out with integrity. Such a genre in Judaism is *halakhah*: either classical *halakhah* – which itself contains both liberal and highly illiberal iterations – or *halakhah* as movements and thinkers interpret and transform it. The Responsa literature attests to the fact that legal truths have readjusted for hundreds of years. What does not change is the Torah's commands: "You shall love your fellow person as yourself" (Lev 19:18), "Justice, justice you shall pursue" (Deut 16:20), "You shall do what is right and good in the sight of God" (Deut 6:18), and "You shall love the stranger" (Deut 10:19). What does change is how we implement those responsibilities in specific social contexts. Determining these readjustments is the task of our law, our *halakhah*.

In his book *Revelation and Authority*, Benjamin Sommer demonstrates that the notion of an Oral Torah unfolding through Israel's engagements with the texts is present not only in rabbinic, interpretative text, but also in the Tanakh.[27] He calls this the "participatory theology of revelation." Rather than rabbinic texts being radically disjunctive from the Tanakh, he argues, they are in continuity with one of its two theories. This allows

---

27. Benjamin D. Sommer, *Revelation and Authority: Sinai in Jewish Scripture and Tradition* (New Haven, CT and London: Yale University Press, 2015).

him to explain *why* biblical books are not edited to be internally consistent or to all reflect a single consistent version of truth.

Maḥloket – halakhic dispute – does not *disconfirm* truth. Rather, it is part of a larger, more complex truth. Allow me to illustrate with a story from Tractate Berakhot 27b–28a. In this narrative, Rabban Gamliel II, head of the Sanhedrin, tries to suppress *maḥloket* by expelling R. Yehoshua b. Ḥananyah, champion of minority positions. Even scholars who disagree with Yehoshua leap to his defense. They fire Rabban Gamliel, replacing him with Eliezer ben Hyrkanos. An explosion of halakhic creativity ensues. Scholars are invited in who were rejected under Gamliel's entrance requirements. Tractate Eduyyot, concerning witnessing, is formulated. Rabban Gamliel apologizes to Yehoshua but recovers only three quarters of his former authority. Eliezer ben Hyrkanos retains the rest.

The story affirms that *maḥloket* – dispute – is the very engine that drives Judaism. Minority opinions have value because truth transcends single answers. It embraces contradictions and complexities. Aggadah, rabbinic narrative interpretation, prizes this approach to truth. Midrashim pile up heaps of interpretations, proclaiming *davar aḥer! davar aḥer!* – another interpretation, and another. Although these may contradict one another, they need not be reconciled. All the interpretations are valued as alternative perspectives. Each may shine forth to us as truth in some context or other.

How, then, should we engage with Torah, with written Torah and Oral Torah, this dual sacredness of contentious written texts and interpretive dialogues unfolding across time? Steven Kepnes argues that Martin Buber's dialogic hermeneutics treats the sacred text as a *thou* rather than as an *it*.[28] This notion certainly does resonate with the practices of our tradition. When we finish a chapter of Talmud, we bid it farewell, calling the chapter by its name and promising it *hadran alakh*, "we will return to you." If interpretation arises out of *relationship* with the text, I'd say we should call Torah our *chavruta*, our study partner. Since the rabbinic period, Jewish textual study has been interactive. It *is* possible,

---

28. Steven Kepnes, *The Text as Thou: Martin Buber's Dialogical Hermeneutics and Narrative Theology* (Bloomington: Indiana University Press, 1992).

as the rabbis acknowledge in Berakhot 6a, to learn Torah alone, noting that even a solitary learner has a companion: the *Shekhinah*. But, they add, "the words of two are written down in the book of remembrance. The words of one are *not*." Torah learned alone is not dialogic and is therefore not transmissible.

The *viability* of revelation depends on dialogue, on *mahloket*, on old words and obligations re-encountered in new contexts. This dual Torah is not an authority that dictates from beyond time. If Torah is our *chavruta*, then, just as we must be accountable to our *chavruta*, our *chavruta* must be accountable to us. This is why we have the legal principle *derakheiha darkei noam*: "Her ways are ways of pleasantness."[29] Given more than one possible way to determine a ruling, one must choose the ruling that is *noam* – the one that does not make the Torah ugly, hurtful, or burdensome.[30]

Accountability becomes an issue whenever the boundaries of participation expand. Historically, interpretation and lawmaking have been restricted to a cisgendered masculine elite.[31] Women, nonbinary, and LGBTQ+ people have had to talk their way into the conversation of Jewish tradition. As these groups bring their lived experiences into our learning, hurts and injustices perpetrated through interpretation come to light. In bringing forth justice where justice was lacking we bring

---

29. Proverbs 3:17. The rabbis apply this verse as a legal principle in which decisions that promote "ways of pleasantness and peace" are preferred over those that permit or promote enmity, oppression, or pain. See b. Sukkah 32a, b. Gittin 59a–b.
30. See Berkovits, *Not In Heaven*, 28–39, for an extended discussion of this legal principle.
31. Sexuality and gender are performed differently in different historical contexts and settings, but, in traditional Jewish cultures, persons identified as male have had monopolies on advanced Jewish education and on authority. Eve Kosovsky Sedgwick in her book, *Between Men: English Literature and Male Homosocial Desire* (New York, NY: Columbia University Press, 1985), 1–27, coined the term "homosocial" to describe social environments that revolve exclusively around the needs and wishes of men. In rabbinic culture sexuality followed different rules than in our own, but some would argue that narratives like that of the Amoraim R. Yochanan b. Napcha and R. Shimon ben Lakish (b. Bava Metzi'a 84a) or that of the Tanna Ben Zoma who refused to marry (b. Yevamot 63b) suggest the possibility of more than one sexual orientation among the rabbinic masculine elite.

forth new truths from our inexhaustible texts. As more of the people Israel engage our *chavruta*, the Torah, and hold her and one another accountable, new revelation emerges from old wounds. I once wrote,

> We must keep asking Torah to speak to us in human language, this crude jargon studded with constraints and distortions, silences and brutalities, that is our only vessel for holiness and truth and peace. We must keep teaching each other and our *chavruta*, the Torah, all that it means to be human... Human owns no perfect, timeless texts because human inhabits no perfect, timeless contexts.[32]

In this violent time, when our lives can be emperilled by the fears of others, it is easy to become consumed with fear ourselves. But fear is the enemy of truth, and especially of those truths that cannot be empirically proven. Yet, according to our tradition, these are precisely the truths that matter most. They comprise a *torat ḥayyim* – a Torah of life, a living Torah. "She is a tree of life to all who hold fast to her."

---

32. Rachel Adler, "In Your Blood, Live: Re-visions of a Theology of Purity," *Tikkun* 8, no. 1 (January/February 1993).

Section 2

Tefilat Emet: Liturgical Truth

Truth in Liturgy: When Prayer Doesn't Quite Capture Our Intent

Dalia Marx[1]

At the end of the recitation of the *Shema*, the core declaration of Jewish faith, the prayer leader announces: ה׳ אֱלֹהֵיכֶם אֱמֶת (The Eternal, your God is **true/truthful**).[2] The following blessing, which, in traditional Ashkenazi worship, concludes the *Shema* liturgy in the morning, repeats the word "truth" six more times,[3] adding up in a staccato-like manner

---

1. I would like to thank Joshua Garroway and Wendy Zierler, the organizers of the HUC-JIR symposium, "These Truths We Hold: Judaism in an Age of Truthiness" (November 2018). Also, shortly before the submission of the final essay, I found the recently published essay by our teacher, Rabbi Lawrence Hoffman, "How Liturgy Tells the Truth" (*CCAR Journal*, [Spring 2019]: 150–63), a revised version of which appears in the next chapter of this book. Rabbi Hoffman's paper is not discussed here, but I was happy to find out that some of my conclusions are similar to his.

2. These words were added to the public recitation of the *Shema* liturgy by the medieval German pietists (*Ḥasidei Ashkenaz*), who paid great attention to the number of the words in each prayer. This addition brings the number of words to 248, and this number corresponds with the number of the positive commandments (b. Makkot 23b) as well as, according to tradition (m. Ohalot 1:8), the number of limbs in the (male) human body The words אֵל מֶלֶךְ נֶאֱמָן (God is a faithful king) were also added, immediately before the recitation of "Shema Yisrae'l," in order to reach that number. The word *ne'eman* (faithful) shares the same etymology as *emet* (truth); see more on this below.

3. In traditional Sephardic prayer books, the word *emet* is repeated eight times. In Liberal prayer books, the text is often trimmed to avoid what seem to be verbal repetitions.

and serving as affirmation of the covenant between the Eternal and
Israel[4]:

אֱמֶת וְיַצִּיב [...] הַדָּבָר הַזֶּה עָלֵינוּ לְעוֹלָם וָעֶד.

אֱמֶת אֱלֹהֵי עוֹלָם מַלְכֵּנוּ [...]

אֱמֶת וֶאֱמוּנָה, חֹק וְלֹא יַעֲבֹר.

אֱמֶת שָׁאַתָּה הוּא ה' אֱלֹהֵינוּ וֵאלֹהֵי אֲבוֹתֵינוּ [...]

אֱמֶת אַתָּה הוּא אָדוֹן לְעַמֶּךָ [...]

אֱמֶת אַתָּה הוּא רִאשׁוֹן וְאַתָּה הוּא אַחֲרוֹן [...]

True and steadfast [...] is this matter for us for all eternities.
True it is the eternal God is our Ruler [...]
True and trustworthy it is, a matter that cannot be transgressed.
True that You are the Eternal our God and God of our Ancestors
[...]
True it is that You are a sovereign to Your people [...]
True, You are the first and You are the last [...][5]

This repetition of the word "true" again and again serves as a covenantal affirmation of what was just said, namely, the *Shema* unit, comprised of three biblical passages (Deut 6:4–9, 11:13–21 and Num 15:36–41)
and encased by liturgical blessings. It stresses the importance of the
concept of truth in the Jewish faith as well as the importance of its
expression in worship.

The parallel blessing in the evening recitation of the *Shema* also
invokes truth, but in a different tone: אֱמֶת וֶאֱמוּנָה כָּל זֹאת וְקַיָּם עָלֵינוּ כִּי
הוּא ה' אֱלֹהֵינוּ וְאֵין זוּלָתוֹ וַאֲנַחְנוּ יִשְׂרָאֵל עַמּוֹ (**True** and faithful [lit. truth and
faithfulness] is all this, and accepted by us, for He is our God and there
is none else, and we are Israel His people).[6] Like the blessing recited in

---

4. Reuven Kimelman, "The Shema Liturgy: From Covenant Ceremony to Cor-
onation," in *Kenishta*, ed. Joseph Tabory (Ramat Gan: Bar-Ilan University Press,
2001), 9–105.

5. Since Reform liturgy is based on the Ashkenazic rite, the texts cited here are
taken from the Ashkenazic prayer book, unless otherwise stated.

6. Perhaps the evening liturgy stresses faithfulness (*emunah*) because people
are more likely to experience existential anxiety in the dark, when the created
world is less visible.

the morning, it serves as a covenantal pledge at the end of the *Shema* liturgy. According to Rashi:

> The blessing "True and steadfast" is all about the loving-kindness [*ḥesed*] that (God) had for our ancestors, for He delivered them out of Egypt and opened the sea for them and caused them to pass, while the blessing "True and faithful" is referring also to the future events, for we are hoping that He shall fulfill his promise and faithfulness for us to redeem us. (Rashi on b. Berakhot 12a)

These two references to truth in the liturgy, Rashi says, acknowledge the divine acts of lovingkindness that happened in the past and express confidence in the bestowal of future gifts, respectively. Even that which is yet to come can be *emet*.

WHAT IS EMET?

I will treat the term "truth" as it is popularly understood, namely as describing a proposition in accordance with a reality of some kind. The reader will most likely note that the term "truth" refers on occasion also to authenticity, integrity, and sincerity, which are not perfectly synonymous but belong to the same semantic field and for our purposes are often inseparable. Truth in itself is a multifaceted concept and is especially complex when it intersects with issues of worship and faith. Should we relate to truth in prayer in the same way in which we relate to truth in other types of speech? When searching for truth, in what ways is prayer unique? Can one lie when praying and still consider this prayer? In other words, is sincerity a necessary condition for prayer? Is there an essential difference between the search for truth and integrity in Jewish prayer in traditional as opposed to in liberal Judaism? Are there different kinds of truths – for example, historical, theological, and social truths – that are manifested in prayer? And, if this is the case, is there a truth that governs all others, a truth that encompasses and transcends all these fragmentary "truth" statements? I will tentatively address these questions below.

Before we further delve into the concept of אמת (truth) in Jewish liturgy, let us consider its etymology. The root of the word is א.מ.ן.[7] the word אמונה (faith) is also derived from it, as is the response to hearing a blessing, אָמֵן (amen), by which one expresses affirmation of the content of the blessing and allegiance to the praying community.[8] The fundamental connection between faith and truth is expressed in Rabbi Joseph Karo's *Shulḥan Arukh*: "And they should respond 'amen' after every blessing [...], with the intention to direct [the following] in their hearts: 'the blessing that was recited is truth, and I believe in it'" (*Oraḥ Ḥayyim* 124:6).

While the question "what is truth?" occupies an essential place in every sphere of human experience and knowledge, it is especially crucial when discussing religious worship. When we read biblical or rabbinic texts, we may appreciate their poetic, cultural or intellectual value, even if we don't necessarily believe that they represent "truth" for us. But when one prays, when one lifts the eyes in concentration and *kavvanah* – in deep intentionality – and recites words of a prayer, these words must bear truth of some sort, or else the prayer becomes empty and void. Yet, despite this (or, perhaps, because of this), the definition of truth in the context of liturgy remains especially difficult and elusive.

I shall treat *emet* as a central concept in Jewish liturgy later in this essay. Before doing so, however, I must first address whether speaking the truth is a necessary characteristic of prayer. Is it really a prayer if it is not true? Can a prayer that does not embody and reflect the truth still be referred to as prayer?

CAN ONE PRAY A LIE?

The Talmud specifies the three main liturgical genres: praise, petition, and thanksgiving (b. Berakhot 34a). Only utterances of praise can easily be deemed true or false, as they describe either an existing or hoped-for

---

7. That is why conjugations of the word *emet* have a dagesh in the letter ת, replacing the נ that was omitted due to assimilation of the two consonants נ and ת, for example in the word אֲמִתִּי (truthful, real).

8. See Numbers 5:22; Deuteronomy 22:16–26; 1 Kings 1:36; Isaiah 65:16; Jeremiah 11:5, 28:6. In an explicitly liturgical, biblical, context one finds אָמֵן in the conclusion of the Book of Psalms 41:11, 72:19, 89:53, 106:48, as well as in Nehemiah 5:13, 8:6; and 1 Chronicles 16:36.

reality. Petitions and thanksgiving, on the other hand, fall into the category of performative speech.[9] They cannot easily be examined in terms of their truthfulness or falsehood; rather, it is their felicity – to use John L. Austin's terminology – which is of relevance.[10]

The sages of the Talmud asked how our prayer should reflect the truth in the most refined and exact manner. The following talmudic discussion raises this fundamental issue, relating to a single phrase in Avot, the first blessing of the 'Amidah. The phrase refers to the Eternal as "הָאֵל הַגָּדֹל הַגִּבֹּר וְהַנּוֹרָא" (The great, the mighty, and the Awesome God), citing Moses's speech (Deut 10:17). It appears again in the Hebrew Bible twice with minor yet meaningful changes, first in the words of the prophet Jeremiah (Jer 32:18) and then again in Daniel (Dan 9:4). Each of these subsequent texts lacks a word from Moses's threefold description: Jeremiah lacks the epithet "awesome" and Daniel lacks "mighty." Although these utterances were not initially meant to be used in the liturgy, Rabbi Yehoshua understands the change from Moses's "original" phrase as reflecting changing historical realities and a theology revised accordingly:

TALMUD BAVLI, YOMA 69B[11]	בבלי, יומא סט, ע"ב
For Rabbi Joshua ben Levi said: "Why were they called 'men of the Great Assembly'?" Because they restored the crown to its original splendor.	דאמר רבי יהושע בן לוי: למה נקרא שמן "אנשי כנסת הגדולה"? שהחזירו עטרה ליושנה.
Moses had come and said: "The great, the mighty, and the Awesome God" [Deut 10:17].	אתא משה, אמר: "הָאֵל הַגָּדֹל הַגִּבֹּר וְהַנּוֹרָא" (דברים י, ז).

9. One may argue that the truthfulness of liturgical requests and utterances of thanksgiving may also be judged; however, our discussion will concentrate mainly on those indicative liturgical expressions dealing with the divine and with experienced reality.

10. John L. Austin, *How to Do Things with Words. The William James Lectures Delivered at Harvard University in 1955*, ed. J.O. Urmson & Marina Sbisà (Oxford: Clarendon Press, 1962), 14. In fact, praise is also a speech act, but it is an indicative expression, describing (or constating) a reality.

11. Another version of this tradition can be found in y. Berakhot 7:3 (55b).

Jeremiah came and said: "Aliens are destroying His Temple. Where are, then, His awesome deeds?" Hence, he omitted [the word] "Awesome."[12]

אתא ירמיה ואמר: נכרים מקרקרין בהיכלו, איה נוראותיו? לא אמר "נוֹרָא".

Daniel came and said: "Aliens are enslaving his sons. Where are His mighty deeds?" Hence, he omitted the word "mighty".

אתא דניאל, אמר: נכרים משתעבדים בבניו, איה גבורותיו? לא אמר "גִּבּוֹר".

They [the Men of the Great Assembly] came and said: "On the contrary!" Therein lie His mighty deeds that He suppresses His wrath, that He extends His long-suffering to the wicked. [13] Therein lie His awesome powers: For but for the fear of Him, how could one single nation persist among the [many] nations?!

אתו אינהו ואמרו: אדרבה, זו היא גבורת גבורתו שכובש את יצרו, שנותן ארך אפים לרשעים; ואלו הן נוראותיו – שאלמלא מוראו של הקדוש ברוך הוא היאך אומה אחת יכולה להתקיים בין האומות?!

But how could our Rabbis [Jeremiah and Daniel] abolish an ordinance established by Moses?!

ורבנן היכי עבדי הכי ועקרי תקנתא דתקין משה?!

Rabbi Eleazar said: Since they knew that the Holy One, blessed be He, is true, they would not ascribe false [things] to / lie about Him.

אמר רבי אלעזר: מתוך שיודעין בהקדוש ברוך הוא שאמתי הוא, לפיכך לא כיזבו בו.

Rabbi Eleazar praises Jeremiah and Daniel for their determination to speak truth about God: "Since they knew that the Holy One, blessed be He, is true, they would not ascribe false [things] to / lie about Him." Rabbi Yehoshua, on the other hand, applauds the ancient authorities (Men of the Great Assembly) for restoring the "original" phrase in the

---

12. The midrash refers to Jeremiah 32:18: "The great, the mighty God, the God of hosts is His name."

13. The midrash refers here to Daniel 9:4: "The great and awesome God who keeps His covenant and mercy with them that love Him and keep His commandments."

liturgy, even though it did not reflect historical reality and the diminished circumstances of the Jews.

This short text reveals two approaches to truth in the liturgy. According to Rabbi Eleazar, prayer should reflect reality, at least as we experience it. If a liturgical epithet for God no longer applies, it needs to be revised. Thus, Daniel and Jeremiah are willing to revise the "original" text to make prayer more accurate or suitable for their contemporary situation. The second approach is that of the Men of the Great Assembly, who retained Moses's phrase even in the face of a differing historical reality. The midrash praises them as those who "restored the crown to its original splendor," having found a way to read the praises in a metaphorical way and ascribe contemporary and relevant meaning to old words. However, the midrash also praises Jeremiah and Daniel, who lived in a time of disaster, namely that of the destruction of the First Temple, and knew that God was true, so "they would not ascribe false [things] to Him." As is often the case in the Talmud, the argument is left without clear resolution, leaving it to future readers to decide which truth they choose to accept, the truth of historical circumstances or the philosophical truth as first expressed in the text.

TALKING TRUTH IN LITURGY

While it is generally agreed upon that prayer ought to be truthful and that it lacks meaning if it is not, it is not always clear what we mean by "truthful." Indeed, several measures of truthfulness can be adduced in relation to prayer: historical, theological, ideological, philosophical, and aesthetic. One may also reflect on liturgical truthfulness by contemplating the tension between the personal, communal, and more general truths embedded in the liturgy. One can attempt to evaluate the integrity of the liturgical text and the sincerity of what is expressed in it.

Unsurprisingly, these different truths are often in tension, even in contradiction with each other. We will thus consider here two cases revealing tensions between different manifestations of truth and sincerity in Jewish liturgy. The first has to do with the evaluation of historical events and the second with the integrity of the text itself.

Time of Perfect Love or Disloyalty:
The Israelites' Sojourn in the Wilderness

The siddur is often referred to as the "life journal" of the Jewish people, as that which holds all its joys and sorrows, fears and hopes.[14] It is thus worthwhile to examine which historical events found their way into this liturgical life journal and which did not merit inclusion.[15] But even those events that are often mentioned in the siddur receive varying treatments. An example of this phenomenon is the different liturgical evaluations of the forty years of the Israelites' sojourn in the wilderness. In some instances, the wilderness sojourn is presented as time of special nearness and grace, as in the citation from Jeremiah in the additional service (*Mussaf*) of Rosh HaShanah: "Thus said the Eternal: I remember the devotion of your [Israel's] youth, the love of a bride; how you followed Me in the wilderness, land unsown" (Jer 2:2). Quite a different depiction of the same period appears in the opening psalm in *Kabbalat Shabbat*, the ceremony welcoming Shabbat, which reads "For forty years was I wearied with that generation, saying: It is a people that do err in their heart, and they have not known my ways" (Ps 95:10).

The different estimations of the Israelites' forty years of sojourn on their way to the promised land may not be a matter of truth and falsehood – yet how does one reconcile these differences? What actually happened in the wilderness? Even if we set aside questions relating to the historicity of these events as they are depicted in the Bible, we have a confusing literary depiction of that period. The ramifications of these different versions are vital to our understanding of this nascent era in the history of the Israelites and of the nature of their relationship with

---

14. Jakob J. Petuchowski, *Prayerbook Reform in Europe: The Liturgy of the European Liberal and Reform Judaism* (New York, NY: World Union for Progressive Judaism, 1968), 22–23.

15. A salient example concerns the mentioning of the two major events that shaped Jewish history in the twentieth century: the Holocaust and the establishment of the State of Israel. See on this Dalia Marx, "Memorializing the Shoah," ed. Lawrence Hoffman, in *May God Remember: Memory and Memorializing in Judaism* (Woodstock, NY: Jewish Lights, 2013), 39–62.

God.[16] And yet, identifying historical accuracy in the liturgy remains a complex task.

Textual Integrity or Selective Truth: The Thirteen Attributes of the Divine

Jewish prayers often cite other texts: the books of the Bible, rabbinic literature, even other prayers.[17] One may ask, if citation represents the cutting and pasting of a portion of text – be it a phrase, a verse, a paragraph, or an entire psalm – whether the cited text maintains the integrity of the original. In other words, when a text is taken out of its original context, does it (and can it) preserve its contextual meaning, its integral truth, or does it become a new creation altogether? An example of the tension between the integrity of the cited text and the new context that cites it concerns the thirteen attributes of the Divine, recited in the liturgy for the High Holidays:

וַיַּעֲבֹר ה' עַל־פָּנָיו וַיִּקְרָא ה' ה' אֵל רַחוּם וְחַנּוּן אֶרֶךְ אַפַּיִם וְרַב־חֶסֶד וֶאֱמֶת: נֹצֵר חֶסֶד לָאֲלָפִים נֹשֵׂא עָוֹן וָפֶשַׁע וְחַטָּאָה וְנַקֵּה

And the Eternal passed by before him, and proclaimed: "The Eternal, the Eternal, God, merciful and gracious, long-suffering, and abundant in goodness and truth, keeping mercy unto the thousandth generation, forgiving iniquity and transgression and sin . . . " (Exod 34:6–7)[18]

---

16. While American Reform liturgy incorporated Jeremiah's positive description of the Israelites in the wilderness as included in the Rosh Hashanah liturgy (*Mishkan Hanefesh for Rosh HaShanah*, 265), the editors chose to omit the second part of the psalm, thus avoiding the harsher parts. Most likely, this omission was made not in response to questions of historical accuracy but because of the unpleasant sentiments in that text. The current American Reform Siddur, *Mishkan T'filah* (2007), continues the path of the previous Siddur, *Gates of Prayer* (1975), including only the first, pleasant part of the text. Other Reform siddurim, such as the Israeli Reform siddurim *Ha'avodah Shebalev* (1982) and *Tfillat HaAdam* (2020), cite the text in its entirety.

17. Michael Marmur, "Why Jews Quote," *Oral Tradition*, 29/1 (2014): 5–46.

18. While the Talmud refers to this list as the "Thirteen Attributes," there are several ways to count them. Several biblical passages provide variations of the attributes of the Divine (among them: Num 14:18; Jonah 4:2; Micah 7:18–20).

In many synagogues, the recitation of the thirteen attributes is considered to be an especially moving moment in the service, and most worshippers seem unbothered by or unaware of the fact that the liturgical text cites only the loving and merciful aspects of the divine, omitting the harsh words of the final part of verse 7: "לֹא יְנַקֶּה פֹּקֵד עֲוֹן אָבוֹת עַל־בָּנִים וְעַל־בְּנֵי בָנִים עַל־שִׁלֵּשִׁים וְעַל־רִבֵּעִים" ("and that will by no means clear the guilty; visiting the iniquity of the ancestors upon the children, and upon the children's children, unto the third and unto the fourth generation").

It appears that the rabbis creatively carved out from the Torah text only what was relevant for them – the portion portraying the compassionate aspects of the divine – pasted it in the liturgy, and omitted the rest. This practice reflects a significant sense of ownership over Scripture, but is it *true to* the original text? By modern scholarly standards, the rabbinic selection of some verses and omission of others would be viewed as dishonest, as it reflects (and in this sense is "true to") a particular rabbinic agenda: that of presenting God as forgiving and merciful at times when Jews needed forgiveness and mercy. The theological "truth" the rabbis sought to convey, however, stands in tension with textual sincerity and integrity.

These two examples, the first dealing with different depictions of historical events and the second with sincerity in the use of scriptural passages in the liturgy, attest to the complexity of liturgy's attempt to express theological truth while simultaneously maintaining a commitment to textual integrity.

TRUTHFULNESS AND INTEGRITY
IN TRADITIONAL LITURGY

Reciting the fixed prayers was considered by the rabbis a fulfilment of a religious duty (and is still deemed as such by many contemporary Jews). However, this does not mean that these prayers were merely texts to be mechanically intoned daily (or weekly) and at designated times. The words of the prayers were meant to embody and convey meaning – to embody and convey truth. Jews were and remain concerned about their duty to say the truth when pouring out their heart to the divine.

We saw this in the abovementioned talmudic discussion regarding the proper and accurate manner to address the divine. The complexity of considerations regarding the truthfulness of liturgical utterances is an issue often discussed in classical Jewish sources. A famous example is a question asked of Maimonides (1138–1204) by "Ovadia the convert," who wanted to know if he was allowed to join the congregation in saying, "Our God, and God of our ancestors" at the beginning of the 'Amidah, knowing that his ancestors were not Jewish. Maimonides concluded that a convert can use the same liturgical language as everyone else, even when the utterance seems to contradict their personal biography.

Rabbi Joseph Qafih (1917–2000), who researched Maimonides' work and restored the early version of his unprecedentedly comprehensive legal work, *Mishneh Torah*, maintains, based on early manuscripts of his commentary on the Mishnah (Bikkurim 1:4), that Maimonides initially did not approve of converts reciting this statement about Jewish ancestry. However, when asked about the matter by a specific convert – Ovadia – he came to recognize the sensitive position of this individual who had decided to join the Jewish people and did not want to add to the difficulties he faced. Therefore, he ruled that converts should recite the same text as ethnic Jews.[19] In other words, even in such cases where an utterance contradicts simple, biographical truth, Maimonides acknowledged that truth is a complex matter and that one needs to take a plethora of matters into consideration when searching for it.

However, other authorities were reluctant to allow converts to use a phrase that contradicted the simple truth.[20] Still others tried to retrofit the truth reflected in the phrase "Our God, and God of our ancestors," to the reality of the convert. Rabbi Reuvein Margolies (1889–1971), for example, maintained, based on a midrash (b. Shabbat 146a; Num. Rabbah 13:16), that the souls of all converts were present at Sinai; thus, and when a person decides to convert, it only retroactively reveals their original Jewish soul. Therefore, converts should be treated (and should

---

19. Ari Isaac Shvat, "Can a Convert Say, 'Who Did Not Create Me A Gentile?'," *Thumin* 15 (1995): 434–45 [Hebrew].

20. For the various opinions on this matter in the halakhah, see Shvat, "Can a Convert" [Hebrew]; Dalia Marx, "Converts and Prayers" (forthcoming).

pray) as though they were Jews by birth.[21] Recently, it has been suggested that some Jews by choice may want actively to acknowledge their choice to become Jews through the liturgy, in which case a special framing of the prayer would not be an act of exclusion but one of self-assertion.[22] Either way, the case of Ovadia the convert shows that Jewish legal authorities have long been attentive to questions relating to the need for truthful expression in prayer and have acknowledged that truth can mean more than one thing.

TRUTHFULNESS AND INTEGRITY IN REFORM PRAYER

The search for truthfulness in prayer emerges with particular intensity in the context of the Reform movement, or, more broadly, in liberal Judaism. Emerging in response to modernity and the Enlightenment, Reform Judaism has placed truthful expression at the center of its ideological and theological agenda.[23] This commitment is attested to first and foremost by the liturgy Reform Judaism has created. Indeed, at the heart of Reform innovation was an effort to make the liturgy relevant and truthful.[24] That said, Reform thinkers often were bolder and more

---

21. Margolies arrives at this from the talmudic phrase "a convert who converted" (גר שנתגייר, b. Yevamot 22a), instead of "a gentile who converted." See Shvat, "Can a Convert," 440.

22. Marx, "Converts and Prayers."

23. See, for example, the statement in the first declaration of principles of the Reform movement, (Pittsburgh, 1885): "We recognize, in the modern era of universal culture of heart and intellect, the approaching of the realization of Israel's great Messianic hope for the establishment of the kingdom of truth, justice, and peace among all men." The CCAR commentary from October 27, 2004, on the newest Reform platform (Pittsburgh, 1999) reads:

> Truths: The plural suggests the Reform view that within Torah can be found a plethora of truths, but because Torah reflects God's word mediated through human transcribers (Moses or anonymous scribes), not all of Torah may register as true in every age. The revelation of all that is true in Torah awaits the coming of the messianic age.

https://www.ccarnet.org/rabbinic-voice/platforms/article-commentary -principles-reform-judaism/.

24. Dalia Marx, "Reform Liturgy: Then and Now," in *A Life of Meaning: Embrac-*

direct in their theological writings than in their liturgical creativity;[25] they understood that traditional expressions might be important to the praying community and thus were often cautious about applying thoroughly radical changes to the liturgy. In some instances, it seems, however, that the classical reformers treated the prayer book as if it were a legal document that held worshippers accountable with each liturgical utterance.[26]

Classical reformers insisted that the liturgy authentically reflect not only their understanding of reality (as communicated in the statements we referred to above as "praise") but also their contemporary desires and wishes. This latter commitment has persisted over the years in Reform communities, a classic example being the ever-changing liturgies regarding Zion and Zionism. Classical reformers omitted supplications for the ingathering of the exiles, the return to Zion, and the rebuilding of Jerusalem, and de-emphasized references to Zion as the birthplace of the Jewish people.[27] Rabbi Abraham Geiger (1810–1874), the most influential Reform rabbi in Europe,[28] explained the changes he had made in the Siddur he edited in 1854 regarding the supplications for a return to Zion as follows:

> Jerusalem and Zion are places from which instruction went forth, and memories are attached. But as a whole, they are to be celebrated more as a spiritual idea – as the nursery of the Kingdom of God – than as a certain geographical locale connected with a special divine providence for all times.[29]

---

ing *Reform Judaism's Sacred Path*, ed. Dana Evan Kaplan (New York, NY: CCAR Press, 2018), 349–68.

25. See David Ellenson, *After Emancipation: Jewish Religious Responses to Modernity* (Cincinnati, OH: Hebrew Union College Press, 2004), 203–13.

26. For examples, see Marx, "Reform Liturgy: Then and Now."

27. Jacob J. Petuchowski, *Guide to the Prayerbook* (Cincinnati, OH: Hebrew Union College Press, 1967), 44–45; *idem, Prayerbook Reform in Europe* (New York, NY: World Union for Progressive Judaism, 1968), 277–97.

28. Michael Meyer, *Response to Modernity: A History of the Reform Movement in Judaism* (Detroit, MI: Wayne State University Press, 1995), 88–99.

29. Abraham Geiger, *Israelitisches Gebetbuch* (Breslau, 1854), vi (cited from Petuchowski, *Prayerbook*, 278–79).

Geiger's statement reflects the unbridled optimism and positivist approach of many early reformers, who believed that humanity was on the verge of reaching a messianic brave new world of universal enlightenment and justice. Over the course of the first half of twentieth century, however, with the First World War, the rise of Nazism, the Second World War, and the Holocaust, this view gradually receded. The acknowledgment of Zion as the birthplace of the Jewish people as well as a valid site of Jewish longing began to feel more and more authentic, and Reform liturgy changed accordingly.[30] Thus, contemporary Reform prayer books reincorporate many liturgical phrases pertaining to Zion that were omitted from earlier Reform liturgies.

Other changes made in Reform prayer books were intended to remove statements that seemed to contradict scientific or empirical truth.[31] The second paragraph of the *Shema* (Deut 11:6–22), for example, is omitted from many Reform siddurim for several reasons,[32] one of them being a rejection on the basis of scientific understanding of the Deuteronomic notion that a lack of rain and thus famine (Deut 11:17) could be attributed to Israelite disobedience. Today, however, as awareness of the ecological ramifications of our deeds and the need for communal responsibility continues to evolve, some Reform rabbis and leaders have begun to reincorporate the second portion of the *Shema,* reading this passage more metaphorically as relating to communal accountability and the consequences of our actions.[33] Israeli Reform siddurim tend to choose a dif-

---

30. Regarding the evolution of the approach to Zion and Israel in Reform liturgy, see Dalia Marx, "Zion and Zionism in Reform Prayerbooks," in *The Fragile Dialogue: New Voices of Liberal Zionism,* ed. S.M. Davis and L.A. Englander (New York, NY: CCAR Press, 2017), 155–74.

31. In the second platform of the Reform movement (Columbus, 1937), we find the following: "Judaism welcomes all truth [...] The new discoveries of science, while replacing the older scientific views underlying our sacred literature, do not conflict with the essential spirit of religion" (CCAR website, https://www.ccarnet .org/rabbinic-voice/platforms/article-declaration-principles/).

32. See Eric Caplan, *From Ideology to Theology: Reconstructionist Worship and American Liberal Judaism* (Cincinnati, OH: Hebrew Union College Press), 2002, 62–63, 114–15, 190–91.

33. The newest major American Liberal prayer book, *Mishkan Hanefesh: The Machzor for Yom Kippur* (2015) incorporates the second portion of the *Shema* in

ferent approach, keeping the traditional text from Deuteronomy 11 but juxtaposing it with an alternative reading from Deuteronomy 30:15–20, a passage stating that the punishment for idolatry would be exile rather than famine (Deut. 30:18), which seemed a more rational response to Israel's disobediences.[34] However, in the light of the environmental crisis, more and more people find the original second portion of the *Shema* apt and meaningful.

The example of the *Shema* illustrates newly found willingness to relate to liturgical language as metaphorical in nature, to understand the truth it holds symbolically, and to seek out the core truths embedded within it which are among the most central features of contemporary liberal Judaism.[35]

*　*　*

When reflecting upon Jewish liturgy, some passages may seem outdated, meaningless, or even outrageous. Some, many contemporary Jews (myself included) find, can no longer be recited with integrity – for instance, those which promote gender inequality or those which refer to people of other faiths and races as inferior. I believe that we should denounce such utterances as abominations.[36] However, other statements can be revisited, reread, and newly understood in metaphorical-midrashic ways, allowing for a richer reading of the liturgy than in the past.

Hebrew and English (34–35) as well as in English alone (190), explaining in the commentary that it is possible to "interpret the passage more naturalistically, as a dire prediction of the consequences of human arrogance."

34. *Haʿavodah Shebalev* (1982) and *Tfillat HaAdam* (2020).

35. Lawrence Hoffman, "Re-imagining Jewish Worship," *CCAR Journal* 49/1 (2002): 77.

36. For example, *Tfillat HaAdam: An Israeli Reform Siddur* (2020), which I was privileged to co-edit with Rabbi Alona Lisitsa, does not contain the exclusionary phrases at the beginning of *'Aleinu LeShabeah*. Instead of praising God for "not [making] us as the nations of the lands nor [placing] us as the families of the earth," *Tfillat HaAdam* reads, based on some previous liberal versions, that we praise God "who gave us a Torah of truth [or, truthful Torah] and implanted eternal life within us." We also included alternative versions of *'Aleinu LeShabeah* by Marcia Falk and Dan Pratt, which celebrate the beauty of the world and our responsibility to maintain it.

The tension between these two options is a healthy and creative one; we should not shy away from it, but, rather, actively engage with it.

I believe that we should advocate for Jews of the more traditional streams to follow the leads of Jeremiah and Daniel, who insisted on speaking truth when addressing the divine and therefore dared to revise, replace, or even omit passages or phrases in the liturgy – because, just like Jeremiah and Daniel, we know that "the Holy One, blessed be He, is true," and we want to address God sincerely and truthfully. At the same time, we should recommend worshippers of the liberal streams of Judaism to look toward the example provided to us by the "Men of the Great Assembly," who acknowledged the importance of the prayer text and thereby allowed themselves to read seemingly challenging liturgical passages in a metaphorical or symbolic way.

May we merit to fulfill this supplication:

וְטַהֵר לִבֵּנוּ לְעָבְדְּךָ בֶּאֱמֶת!

(Purify our hearts to worship You truthfully!)

How Liturgy Tells the Truth[1]

Lawrence A. Hoffman

JUDAISM AND TRUTH

Jews like to imagine that we are a religion of "deed, not creed," as the old saw goes – not like Christians, where belief is what matters most. But we, too, have liturgical statements of truths that, presumably, worshipers are asked to believe. These statements concern not only God (theology) but human nature (anthropology) and the universe (cosmology) as well. Notable examples include *Yigdal* (Maimonides' Thirteen Principles), *Adon Olam* (a God both distant and intimate), the tag line of *Avinu Malkeinu* (our own doctrine of grace, for "we have no deeds to save us"), and the everyday *Shema* and its Blessings, crediting God with creation, revelation, and redemption. The original topic of the third blessing of the *Shema*, said founding liturgist Ismar Elbogen (1874–1943), was actually not redemption – that was added later – but "truth" (*emet v'yatziv, emet ve-emunah*). It was Judaism's great affirmation that the *Shema* and its two introductory blessings are, in fact, "true!"[2]

In the pre-modern world, content-driven liturgical emendations had been made from time to time, but this was usually not a result of issues

---

1. This is an expansion of an earlier version of this paper, dedicated to the memory of Rabbi Aaron Panken, z"l, which appeared in the *CCAR Journal* (Spring, 2019): 150–63. The current version benefits from the careful reading by this volume's editors: Drs. Joshua Garroway and Wendy Zierler, to whom I am grateful.
2. Ismar Elbogen, *Jewish Liturgy: A Comprehensive History* (German original, 1913; English trans., Raymond P. Scheindlin, Philadelphia, PA: Jewish Publication Society, 1993), 21; for original discussion see, Elbogen, *Studien zur Geschichte des jüdischen Gottesdienstes* (Berlin: Meyer und Müller, 1907).

of belief but, rather, because the content of a prayer was perceived to be politically dangerous: for example, the famous line in *'Aleinu: sheheim mishtachavim l'hevel v'rik...* ("they bow down to worthlessness and emptiness..."). With modernity, however, issues of belief came more and more to matter, not just because of Enlightenment mentality, but because newly translated prayer books showed worshipers what they were really saying. Offensive material was sometimes overlooked *de facto*, such as, for instance, the concluding lines to *Birkat HaMazon*, which include Psalm 37:25, *Na'ar hayiti...lo ra'iti...* ("...I have never seen the righteous abandoned and their children seeking bread"). "The custom," says Seligman Baer (1825–1897), "is to say these verses silently." His rationale is pastoral – "lest poor people present be embarrassed"[3] – but it seems clear that this troubles him morally as well.

Baer felt constrained to offer halakhic justification: "We have already concluded with *Oseh shalom*," so the offending verses are "extraneous to the blessing formula [*matbe'a birkat hamazon*]." Reform Jews back then worried less about halakhic restraint. "In our days," said Abraham Geiger (1810–1874), referring to *'Aleinu*, "Israel is far from...self-satisfaction and delusion...We can say with conviction, 'Thou hast chosen us for thy holy law,' but not 'Thou hast chosen us from among all nations, Thou hast elevated us above all tongues.'"[4] Geiger's rationale became standard, even among those not normally considered "Reform": Philadelphia's Marcus Jastrow (1829–1903), for example, praised God simply for "removing us from idolatry and superstition and [bringing us] to the knowledge of light and truth."[5]

Kol Nidrei provides a particularly enlightening example of the complex ways in which embarrassing prayers have been emended in modern Judaism. In nineteenth-century Germany, its apparent absolution of Jewish promises was associated with the *more judaico*, the demeaning practice of demanding a specific "Jewish oath" in court, whereby Jews swore to fulfil their promises (despite what *Kol Nidrei* seemingly implies). Tellingly, the very first (!) rabbinic conference (Brunswick, 1844) voted

3. *Seder 'Avodat Yisra'el* [*The Baer Siddur*] (1864), 562.
4. Gunther Plaut, *The Rise of Reform Judaism* (New York, NY: World Union for Progressive Judaism, 1963), 157–58.
5. *'Avodat Yisra'el*, pt. 1 (Philadelphia, PA, 1914), 125.

to abolish it. In fact, however, it had already been removed from services in several synagogues, and not just by reformers: even Samson Raphael Hirsch (1808–1888), the leading German advocate of modern Orthodoxy, had done away with it![6] Another solution, if congregants insisted on the melody, was to substitute alternative lyrics – frequently in vain, however, because cantors, who could not easily fit new words to the old melody and were loath to deliver the prayer poorly, would sing the original anyway.[7]

The North American *Union Prayer Book* (1894) replaced it with a hymn, "Day of God," based on a longer original ("O Tag des Herrn") by German reformer Leopold Stein (1810–1882).[8] Only with the Newly Revised Edition of 1940 was *Kol Nidrei* restored – almost. After several stormy meetings on the subject, the chairman of the committee responsible for preparing the book, Rabbi Solomon Freehof (1892–1990), chose to include it, placing it just below an English "Reader's Prayer" about vows, but articulating an altogether different petition than the one expressed in *Kol Nidrei*: "[May] all the resolutions that we make [to repent and depart from sin] be acceptable before Thee, and may we be given strength to fulfil them." When the book appeared, however, and committee members noticed the inclusion of *Kol Nidrei*, Freehof was accused of acting in bad faith (or, at least, of having experienced a serious memory lapse). The committee had apparently voted to *exclude* the prayer! As a result, a second edition of the *machzor* was hastily prepared without it. But repaginating the book was an expensive operation, so the new version expanded the spacing in the Reader's Prayer at the top of the page (to fill the empty space left by *Kol Nidrei*'s removal below it); and added the bracketed instruction, "(The *Kol Nidre* chant)".[9]

---

6. Jakob J. Petuchowski, *Prayerbook Reform in Europe* (New York, NY: World Union for Progressive Judaism, 1968), 337.

7. Petuchowski, *Prayerbook Reform*, 340.

8. Composed four years before the Brunswick conference; see Stein's own footnote to the prayer reproduced (in English translation), by Petuchowski, *Prayerbook Reform*, 339. Wise's *Minhag America* included it in the original German and English translation.

9. *Union Prayer Book, Newly Revised.* (New York, NY: Central Conference of American Rabbis, 1962), 130. See correspondence housed in the American Jewish

Many congregations were already performing *Kol Nidrei* instrumentally, without the words, but now, the liturgy called for it at least to be chanted (without, of course, translation).

When the words of *Kol Nidrei* finally returned (in the 1975 *Gates of Prayer* siddur), the old Jewish Oath had become a thing of the distant past. Still, worshippers had to deal with the fact that virtually none of them believed what the text implies: that God punishes us for unfulfilled vows but annuls such vows and cancels the punishment if we say the right formula. We say it, says the accompanying meditation, because "we identify with the agony of our forebears who had to say 'yes' when they meant 'no'" – an oblique reference to the putative connection between *Kol Nidrei* and forced conversion of Jews throughout time. The potential moral objection to even wanting God to pardon unfulfilled vows was addressed by the modified translation, "Let all our vows...be null and void *should we, after honest effort, find ourselves unable to fulfill them.*"[10]

Other progressive liturgies in use today "translate" with similar modifying caveats: "All vows and oaths we take...we hereby publicly retract *in the event that we should forget them*" (North American Conservative

---

Archives, including a letter dated February 7, 1946, from Samuel Cohon (professor at Hebrew Union College) to Robert Gordis (chairman of the Conservative movement's Joint Prayer Book Commission, then preparing its forthcoming *Sabbath and Festival Prayer Book* of 1946) explaining that *Kol Nidrei* "was inserted by a member of the committee without the knowledge of the rest and was immediately disowned by the other members. While it is too late to withdraw the first printing from circulation, the next printing which appeared only a few weeks later omits the text." Other letters make it clear that the "guilty party" was Solomon Freehof, and the chief complainer, Cohon himself, who had composed an alternative text in Hebrew and thought it should have appeared instead of the original Aramaic (letter by Cohon to Freehof, April 8, 1945). Two days later (April 10, letter back to Cohon) Freehof assures Cohon that according to the minutes kept by the committee's secretary (Isaac Marcuson, the rabbi in Macon, Georgia), the committee had rejected Cohon's alternative. Freehof describes the cost factor that mitigates against resetting the entire volume, and explains, "The Kol Nidre in Aramaic or in Hebrew is never recited anyhow, it is sung by the choir. Hence, if we decide to change it, no one will know the difference after a year or so when the first printing gradually is swamped by later printings."
10. *Gates of Repentance* (New York, NY: CCAR Press, 1999), 152.

Movement, 1972);[11] "May we be absolved from... the duties and promises *we cannot keep*, the commitments and undertakings *which should never have been made... Though all promises to our fellowman stand, may God annul the empty promises we made in our foolishness to Him alone, and shield us from their consequences*" (British Reform Movement, 1985);[12] "All vows... and promises that we vow or promise *to ourselves and to God... we hereby retract*" (North American Conservative, 2010).[13]

Still other liturgies handle the problem with exculpatory commentary: "Although we may have theological hesitations regarding Kol Nidrey's annulment of vows, these pale in comparison to the fulfilment of our one shared commitment to be here together" (Reconstructionist, 1999);[14] "*Kol Nidrei* applies to obligations a person undertakes in relation to God... This annulment has nothing to do with obligations to other human beings" (North American Reform *Mishkan HaNefesh*, 2015)[15] – an explanation going back to Moses Gaster's classic Sefardi liturgy of Great Britain [1904], "This solemn absolution of vows.... Does not in the least possible degree affect the promises or vows entered into between man and man."[16]

Prayers do not need to have adverse political or moral implications to be troubling to us, however. Sometimes their words just strain credulity, like the promise of "resurrection" (*mehayeh hametim*) in the second blessing of the 'Amidah. Isaac M. Wise (1819–1900) still included *mehayeh hametim*, with, however, the moderating translation, "who granteth perpetual life after death" – a guarantee of eternality, albeit not necessarily resurrection. His contemporary, David Einhorn (1809–1879),

11. *Machzor for Rosh Hashanah and Yom Kippur*, ed. Jules Harlow (New York, NY: United Synagogue of Conservative Judaism, 1972), 353

12. *Forms of Prayer for Jewish Worship III, Prayers for the High Holydays* (The Reform Synagogues of Great Britain, 1985), 273.

13. *Mahzor Lev Shalem* (New York, NY: The Rabbinical Assembly, 2010), 205.

14. *Kol Haneshemah: Prayerbook for the Days of Awe* (Wyncote, PA: Reconstructionist Press, 1999), 694.

15. *Mishkan HaNefesh, Machzor for the Days of Awe* (2 volumes) (New York: CCAR Press, 2015), 18.

16. *The Book of Prayer and Order of Service According to the Custom of the Spanish and Portuguese Jews Based Principally on the Work of the Late Rev. D.A. De Sola*, ed. Moses Gaster (London: Oxford University Press, 1904), 13.

ended the prayer with *notéa betokheinu ḥayeiʿolam*, and a literal German translation (*unsterbliches Lebens eingepflanzt*) – which was rendered by Emil Hirsch (1851–1923), Einhorn's father-in-law, in his 1896 English edition, as "dispenser of life eternal." Ever since, Reform Jews have gone back and forth among strategies, the ultimate vacillation being the current practice of using *meḥayeh hakol* (as in the *Gates* liturgies)[17] but bracketed alongside *meḥayeh hametim* for those who can manage it.

These examples, however, are just the collective tip of a larger iceberg: the growing proportion of our liturgy that people cannot easily believe anymore. Geiger still thought God chose Israel as a uniquely precious people, but many Jews today find that proposition less convincing: not because they deny that Israel is their people (most, in fact, are rather proud of this), and not because they lightly dismiss covenantal responsibility (most Jews like that idea, too), but because it seems arrogant to call themselves "chosen" – and apologetic, then, to say, "But other people are chosen too, you know." In the 1970s, when the committee on *Gates of Repentance* sat down with Chaim Stern's original manuscript for the Yom Kippur *Avodah* ("From Creation to Redemption") the members got stuck on his line, "God chose us." The substitution "We chose God" was suggested, and the committee ultimately settled for a compromise, "God chose us; we chose God. There is a mystery here that reason cannot solve, nor cynicism deny."[18] Fair enough. But we can hardly editorialize in the English of every prayer that bothers us.

Other examples are legion, most notably, perhaps, our ubiquitous prayers for healing. Do we really believe that God personally intervenes to heal the sick? Why this sick person but not that one? Yet we pray for healing anyway, and we do not think we are dissembling.

The issue of truth extends even to less emotionally-laden liturgical passages, like the blessings surrounding the *Shema* that I mentioned earlier. The doctrines of creation, revelation, and redemption come with less angst than do the words of *ʿAleinu* and *Mi Shebeirach*, but a God of creation, revelation, and redemption is not all that different from a

---

17. *Meḥayah metim* occurs normally in the body of the blessing as well, and there, the *Union Prayer Book* already substitutes *meḥayeh hakol*.
18. *Gates of Repentance*, 429. Details of discussion are my personal recollection, as a member of the committee.

God who chose Israel and who heals the sick: these positions are all of a piece, in that a good proportion of modern, university-educated, and thoughtful worshippers do not actually believe them – even if they don't actively disbelieve them either. They more or less avoid the issue of belief by treating the content of these passages as standard prayer book rhetoric rather than as factual claims about the way things are – claims that would be apt to induce cognitive dissonance because they fly in the face of science, on one hand, and of everyday raw experience, on the other.

And there we have the nub of the issue. Truths about the universe are backed up with mathematics, scientific discourse, and empirical demonstration; liturgical truths are not. If we wish to maintain them as true, we need a different conception of truth.

We have largely ignored the issue of liturgical truth. We let poetic translations and alternative readings paper it over, with consequences that were already becoming apparent in the 1970s, as *Gates of Repentance* was being written. The original manuscript provided two parallel services, one with traditional translation and the other with creative alternatives. In experimental trials, however, nearly every congregation chose the latter, leading the committee to fear that an entire generation might never encounter what the traditional liturgy says. The final volume, therefore, mixed and matched the two: one service with a true translation of the *Shema* and Its Blessings, but creative English for the *'Amidah*; the other, just the reverse. Whichever version you choose, you get at least half of it with traditional English.

The problem continued with *Mishkan T'filah*, where a committee was charged with supplying "true" translations on the right-hand pages. In practice, however, worshippers may sing or chant the right-page Hebrew originals, but when it comes to the English, they prefer the left-page creative alternatives. The right-page "true" translations are in prose; we are taught to divide prose into fiction or non-fiction; prayer can hardly be fiction; so worshippers see it as non-fiction, which is to say, it must pass the test of truth, and now we are back where we started. Whether they are presented with the "traditional"-translation version of *Gates of Repentance* or the "true" translations on the right-hand pages of *Mishkan Tefila*, congregants prefer to read the alternatives because they have trouble with the truth-value of what the traditional prayers contend.

What we are prepared to see as "true" depends on what has long been called a "plausibility structure," a range of possibilities determined primarily by the social networks that sustain us, the socialization processes those networks have, the media those networks consult, and so on.[19] As "true statements of belief," *Mishkan Tefila*'s right-side translations may indeed meet the approval of rabbinic translators, whose "plausibility circle" is other rabbis and cantors, socialized to appreciate nuanced theological interpretations of traditional religious claims. The plausibility structure of average worshippers, however, is much less forgiving. The right-side literal translations run distinctly counter to what most worshippers are likely to "believe." By contrast, the left-side passages were chosen precisely because they already comport with contemporary belief systems. Alternatively, they are cast as poetry, which people are trained to read as harboring meaning below the surface. Poetry masks hard-to-take theology, whereas the prose translations on the right force questions of belief upon us.

Congregants rarely ask outright how this inherited liturgy still tells truths, but the liturgical keepers and purveyors should, and toward that end, we need a rationale of liturgical hermeneutics, an intellectually competent explanation of how liturgy "means."

HOW LITURGY TELLS THE TRUTH

Truth has traditionally been conceived as pictures of reality: pictures that correspond "truly" to what they picture, as opposed to falsehoods that do not. The picture a sentence provides must "correspond" to what is "really" out there. Until the rise of science, "out there" included metaphysical realities like angels and heaven and even God; with modernity, however, scientifically-minded critics denounced such metaphysics as imaginary. Their critique entered late nineteenth- and early twentieth-century philosophy as Logical Positivism: the doctrine that the truth or falsity of a sentence depends ultimately on empirical evidence.

Logical Positivism goes back to physicist Ernst Mach's *Science of Mechanics* (1883), and was institutionalized in the 1920s, when the Vi-

---

19. Peter L. Berger, *The Sacred Canopy* (New York, NY: Doubleday, 1967; Anchor ed., 1969), 45.

enna Circle, a fellowship of Weimar-era thinkers led by physicist and philosopher Friedrich Albert Moritz Schlick (1882–1936), was formed. Schlick held the truth of a sentence to be dependent on its *actual verifiability in experience.* His claim was modified by others, such as A.J. Ayer, for example (1910–1989), who demanded only that a sentence provide *a probable* [!] *condition of verifiability.* Karl Popper (1902–1994) changed "verifiability" to the less stringent "falsifiability": a sentence need only be *potentially falsifiable.* In a book written during World War 1,[20] Ludwig Wittgenstein (1889–1951) provided the conceptual backdrop for the positivists' claim. Sentences constitute verbal "pictures" of reality; the picture is either accurate (true) or inaccurate (false). We call this doctrine the "Correspondence Theory of Truth."

But Wittgenstein never was an orthodox positivist. The positivists' demand that a sentence be at least theoretically falsifiable led them to the absurdity of excluding some of the most important things that people feel called upon to say – affirmations about religion, ethics, and art, for example, which positivists reduced to mere personal preference ("Beethoven's music is brilliant" just means "I like Beethoven"); or to outright nonsense ("God is good" is no more true or false than "All the unicorns in the room are angry"). But people still made aesthetic judgements and talked about God, convinced that they were having meaningful conversations, and Wittgenstein was not willing to call this delusional.

In his later work, therefore,[21] he turned to the many ways in which people normally talk, and arrived at the metaphor of "language games." Language does more than describe "scientifically" justifiable truths. It does many different things, each of them a "game" with its own rules, its own criteria for success. Sentences about religion, art, and ethics were

---

20. Ludwig Wittgenstein, *Tractatus Logico-Philosophicus,* trans. C.K. Ogden (London: Kegan Paul, 1922). [First published in German as "Logisch-Philosophische Abhandlung" *Annalen der Naturphilosophie* 14 (1921)].

21. Most significantly, in a book written by Wittgenstein but only as a draft, and then edited and published posthumously by his students, G.E.M. Anscombe and R. Rhees. Ludwig Wittgenstein, *Philosophical Investigations* (New York, NY: Macmillan Publishing Co., 1953).

not meaningless; they just had their own rules – their own way of being meaningful – that needed surfacing.

Wittgenstein's understanding of religion is of distinct importance as we turn to the truths of liturgy, but first, we should return briefly to the core idea behind the correspondence theory of truth – the claim that language provides pictures of the universe, and that "true" sentences correspond in "picture-perfect ways" to the reality they describe. Even for empirical phenomena, that claim is not altogether accurate. In matters of science, the only proper descriptor of the physical universe is mathematics: if the math works out, the universe must be "like that." By contrast, the verbal pictures that we draw may correspond to the human *experience* of things, but not to the things themselves. The tables, rocks, and ice cubes that we call "solids," for example, are actually made of atoms, which are mostly empty space between particles, not solidity at all.[22] The lesson we should take away about language and its pictures is, therefore, more subtle than the correspondence theory might lead us to believe.

Any particular verbal picture of reality presupposes a larger *conceptual* picture (or frame) that a given sentence presupposes. Philosopher Hilary Putnam (1926–2016) puts it well: whenever we try to describe something, he says, we run the risk of being "in the grip of inappropriate conceptual pictures."[23] Arguments revolve around words; they occur, however, because we erroneously locate those words within conceptual frames that are inappropriate.

If we apply this insight to liturgy, we see that our usual problem with prayer book sentences is that we are working from the wrong set of conceptual pictures. We falsely assume, for example, that the word "God" is like other nouns and then believe or disbelieve sentences about God with the wrong conceptual framework in mind. When atheists prove the picture of God to be wrong, we reject their argument, because we didn't mean that kind of thing in the first place.

Wittgenstein insisted that religious talk be judged according to its

---

22. Discussed in Hilary Putnam, *The Many Faces of Realism* (LaSalle, IN: Open Court Publishing, 1987), 3–4.

23. Hilary Putnam, *Jewish Philosophy as a Guide to Life: Rosenzweig, Buber, Levinas, Wittgenstein* (Bloomington: Indiana University Press, 2008), 11.

own rules of usage and not be confused with the altogether different "game" of science. "God loves Israel," for example, cannot be true in a scientific sense. The positivists were right on that score. It could not, that is, be "empirically demonstrable" (Ayer), or even "potentially falsifiable" (Popper). Religion simply isn't that sort of thing. To imagine otherwise is to be confused by rival conceptual pictures, the pictures that constitute the way we think. Wittgenstein's examples include the belief that illness is punishment:

> Suppose someone is ill and he says, "This is punishment," and I say, "If I'm ill, I don't think of punishment at all." If you say, "Do you believe the opposite?" – you can call it believing the opposite, but it is entirely different from what we would normally call believing the opposite.
>
> I think differently, in a way. I say different things to myself. *I have a different picture.*[24]

Sentences are language games. Different language games presuppose different pictures.

Religion, Wittgenstein held, is not an objective picture of some reality "out there" so much as it is a set of existential reflections, immersion in what Putnam aptly called "a deep-going way of life."[25] Religious discussions are not scientific debates about a theory of the universe; they are a dialogue between two different people discussing their own respective ways of life. Religion, I suggest, might usefully be described as *the practice of speaking in a register that does justice to the entirety of the human condition.*

A particularly interesting case involves narratives that are central to religious identity but not necessarily historically true, like "Israel received Torah at Sinai" or "Jesus died for our sins." Wittgenstein came from Jewish stock – his grandparents were Jews by birth – but in his own depressive states, haunted by existential issues of death and meaninglessness, he had come across *The Gospel in Brief*, by Tolstoy, who had suffered similarly. The Jesus story was not "based on historical

---

24. *Wittgenstein: Lectures and Conversations on Aesthetics, Psychology and Religious Belief*, ed. Cyril Barrett (Berkeley, CA: University of California Press, nd), 55. (Italics added.)
25. Putnam, *Jewish Philosophy*, 11.

truth," Wittgenstein knew, but nonetheless, he was inclined "to believe in Christ's Resurrection," because:

> Faith is faith in what my heart, my *soul* needs, not my speculative intelligence … The whole planet cannot be in greater anguish than a single soul. The Christian faith – as I view it – is the refuge in this ultimate anguish.[26]

We might say that liturgy doesn't provide objectivized truths so much as it immerses us in an alternative set of pictures, a "deep-going way of life." If the immersion feels comfortable, we apply its pictures to our lives in process, and start making sentences about it with others who live there. If not, we go elsewhere for the stories we conceive about ourselves.

Chris Stedman, for example, now a humanist chaplain at Harvard University, grew up as a nominal Methodist in a largely secular home. When a childhood friend invited him to attend her seder, he was so intrigued that he began to imagine himself converting to Judaism. "As I sat there, plate and meal before me, I did my best to conjure up an image of myself in this story," he recalls, "but to my great surprise, I could not.… Though this was a beautiful story, it was not my story."[27]

Sentences do not just portray reality, then; they sometimes provide us with pictures of existential truths: pictures that define our lives against the backdrop of a broader story. The Haggadah's narrative is not necessarily something people believe to be scientifically true – indeed, they may believe it to be historically false. But Jews rehearse it annually as a set of existential truths about who they are, and Chris Stedman could not do that.

Sentences do other things as well. In 1955, for example, J.L. Austin (1911–1960) introduced the notion of "performative" sentences, those that create truths just by being said: weddings, for example, where saying the right thing in the right way makes people "married."[28]

---

26. Quoted by Malcolm, *Wittgenstein*, 17. From Wittgenstein's *Vermischte Bemerkungen*, ed. G.H. von Wright (Frankfurt am Main: Suhrkamp, 1977). Published in English as *Culture and Value*, trans. Peter Winch (Chicago, IL: University of Chicago Press, 1980).
27. Chris Stedman, *Faitheist* (Boston, MA; Beacon Press, 2012), 29–30.
28. J.L. Austin, *How to Do Things with Words*, ed. J.O. Urmson (Cambridge, MA: Harvard University Press, 1962) (based on lectures at Harvard, 1955).

Speaking doesn't so much *say* something, therefore, as it *does* something; we should properly be talking about speech *acts*, not speech *utterances*, in which the proper measuring rod for them all is whether they turn out well, whether they deliver, whether they do what they intend, whether (in Austin's terminology) they are "felicitous."

It is not entirely clear what makes sentences claiming to represent objective reality felicitous. A minimalist understanding reduces them to the function of pointing. Such sentences "truly" describe the universe by directing our attention to it and prompting us to compare it to what the sentences say: the sentence "Snow is white" is true if, and only if, snow is actually white.[29] Alternatively, the truth of such sentences may be judged by the extent to which they explain the behavior of ourselves and the universe in which we live,[30] a criterion that is echoed in the pragmatic theory of truth, according to which such sentences are more or less true based on the extent to which they allow us pragmatically to operate in the universe.[31] Most of us blithely assume a popular version of the first option: "Snow is white" is true if, and only if, snow is actually white.

Liturgical sentences about theology ("God is good"), religious anthropology ("We are made in God's image") and religious cosmology ("The world to come is without oppression") sound like "Snow is white," but they do different things; they become felicitous in different ways. Liturgical sentences become felicitous in ways other than being "true" the way "Snow is white" is true. They may enact a transformation (*"Harei at mekudeshet li..."* ["You are sanctified to me..."] at weddings); they may also, among other things, name ("We are Israel..."), hope ("On that day..."), promise ("We shall overcome"), commit ("All Jews are responsible for one another"), and remember ("We were slaves to Pha-

---

29. The so-called "deflationist" theory of truth, associated with Gottlob Frege (1848–1925) and Alfred Tarski (1901–1983). Cf. Frederick F. Schmidt, *Truth: A Primer* (Boulder, CO: Westview Press, 1995), 123–44; Roger Scruton, *Modern Philosophy: An Introduction and Survey* (New York, NY: Penguin: 1994), 109–11; Bernard Williams, *Truth and Truthfulness* (Princeton, NJ: Princeton University Press, 2002), 63–64.

30. Schmidt, *Truth*, 149–62.

31. The pragmatic theory of truth, associated, primarily, with William James (1842–1910), John Dewey (1859–1952), and (more recently) Richard Rorty (1931–2007).

raoh in Egypt"). Each of these is a speech act with its own criteria for felicitousness.

Felicitousness is contextual. In weddings, for example, if the couple is at a carnival and the rabbi is dressed like a clown, we might properly wonder if they are really married. Overly politicized or preachy prayers that browbeat us as congregants into feeling guilty and then make promises on our behalf (like, "We shall never forget injustice!") may fall flat (become infelicitous) because, among other things, we are made to feel forced into promising without prior personal commitment to what the promise is; and because the promise is being made in what we consider an inappropriate milieu. We came to pray, not to be harangued. The context seems wrong, not unlike a wedding at a carnival with a rabbi-clown.

In the case of existential truths (Putnam's reflections on a "deep-going way of life"), liturgy shapes pictures of lives in process, like a child's game of connecting the dots. The child's dots, however, are numbered points on a page, and the picture is predetermined. Life's dots are the points of our experience that we connect however we wish. Existential felicitousness depends on the way the liturgical sentences paint a picture of the person we think we authentically are. If we rattle them off as merely someone else's definition of ourselves – if, that is, we cannot or will not internalize them as what we really think we are or want to be – we suffer what Jean Paul Sartre famously described as "bad faith."

In all such cases, sentences become felicitous when they are said and heard against the backdrop of apt conceptual pictures – and, indeed the very word "picture" suggests a further approach to the way liturgy "means": aesthetics.

TRUTH AND ART

One benefit of an aesthetic analysis is that it goes beyond words and sentences to encompass other modes of "saying something": music, for instance, which is so central to worship. Considerations of space allow me only to outline a single example of what I have in mind: the difference between "representation" and "expression."

From the Renaissance until the advent of Modernism, Western pictorial art generally sought to represent reality in ever-more-accurate ways. Modern art, however, increasingly abandoned the goal of faithful *representation*, shifting its orientation instead to artistic *expression*: Robert Motherwell's "automatic drawing," for example, an attempt to suspend conscious control so as to get at what lies buried in the artist's unconscious; or Jackson Pollock's "drip paintings," which picture nothing at all. When artist Hans Hoffman complained to Pollock that even artistic abstraction ought to be derived from nature, Pollock responded, "I am nature."[32] This shift was so monumental that, in his advocacy of Abstract Expressionism, critic Clement Greenberg (1901–1994), went so far as to declare representational art dead.[33]

But expression need not be totally self-referential, and representation can be what does the expressing. Great representational art too, after all, has "expressed" such deeper realities as serenity, evil, nobility, and so on. For a modern example, think of *Nighthawks*, Edward Hopper's 1942 depiction of a lonely diner: the image *represents* the diner realistically enough but *expresses* the patrons' loneliness far better than any verbal description might. Art can represent while also expressing what lies below or behind the representation.

The "truth" of *Nighthawks* lies in its expression, not its representation. Even less can the truth of abstract art be found in its similitude to the real thing – not to mention the truths of totally nonrepresentational media like music. While the truth of a simple picture may lie in what it represents, the truth of an artistic one lies in what it expresses.

Cartoons too both represent and express. We break out laughing when we see one, not because of the representation alone, but because of the human truth that the representation expresses. A *Far Side* cartoon, for example, portrays dinosaurs smoking cigarettes: so much for the picture's *representation*, which alone means little. The caption, however, *expresses* the point: "The real reason the dinosaurs perished," from which we further deduce a contemporary lesson on the dangers of smoking.

So too with theatre. Every performance of Hamlet *represents* the same dramatic script – we know the story. But we don't turn down

---

32. Arthur C. Danto, *What Art Is* (New Haven, CT: Yale University Press, 2013), 13.

33. Clement Greenberg, "Avant Garde and Kitsch," *Partisan Review* 6:5 (Fall, 1939): 34–49.

tickets to its newest revival on the grounds that we have seen it before, because we know that diverse productions *express* its dramatic truths differently; when it reappears in a new staging, we see it again, to recollect realities that have grown dim with time and need to be recaptured in the immediacy of artistic expression. So, too, do we attend High Holy Day services year after year, not because we do not know what *Kol Nidrei* sounds like, but because we want to hear it again, at the right calendrical moment, and in its proper setting, to rediscover the truths it expresses. When worship merely *represents* the liturgy (we read through the prayers properly enough) but does not *express* the truths behind it, we properly decide not to come back. The artistry of worship leaders lies in their ability to *express* the liturgy's truths, not just *represent* the words and music as so many markings on a page.

The best artistic parallel to liturgy may be opera, what Wagner considered a *Gesamtkunstwerk* ("a complete work of art") in that it integrates all the arts into a larger expressive whole. Liturgy is like opera, a "complete work of art" with music, speech, poetry, drama, and architectural setting. The very word, "opera," arose in the seventeenth century as the Italian for "work," just as "liturgy" is from the Greek *leitourgia*, meaning "work" as well, the public work, in ancient times, of sacrificing to please the gods. Opera and liturgy are parallel *works* – complete *works* of art.

We have seen how religious truths were rejected by Logical Positivism, a doctrine that goes back to the triumphalist days of science in the late nineteenth century. Simultaneously, however, there were those who sought to *save* religious truths through the arts. In 1875, poet and literary critic Matthew Arnold advanced the cause of world culture generally ("the best that has been thought and known in the world") as religion's successor; and in 1888, Richard Wagner connected art and religion expressly – and memorably. "It is reserved to art," he said, "to salvage the kernel of religion, inasmuch as the mythical images which religion would wish to be believed as true are apprehended in art. . . . Art reveals the concealed deep truth within them."[34]

---

34. From Richard Wagner, *Die Religion und die Kunst* in *Gesammelte Schriften und Dichtungen*, 2nd ed., vol. 10 (Leipzig 1888), 211. Translation by Roger Scruton, *Beauty* (Oxford: Oxford University Press, 2009), 188.

Wagner's historical consciousness is suspect, as we know from his views on Jews. Knowing also how Wagnerian opera was coopted by the Nazis, we should at least acknowledge that as much as art tells truths, it may also lead people astray. The beauty of scientific truth claims is precisely their built-in capacity (à la Popper) to be proven false. By definition, truth claims of art do not have that capacity – if they did, they would be science. But the same is true of other non-scientific sources of truth, including religion. Religion, ritual, and art combine in liturgy, which is a religious ritual embedded in an art form, the same art form experienced with opera.

The point at issue here, however, is whether liturgy even can tell truths, and if so, what those truths are like. On those points, Wagner is correct in seeing different degrees of power across forms of art, the most complete (in terms of its expressive power) being opera, to which I best liken the performance of liturgy. He is correct also in seeing how religious claims that look suspect to scientifically trained minds can yet seem apt when expressed through art – in our case, the art of liturgy performed as worship.

A closing anecdote from Wittgenstein is in order. Even in his early positivist period, he had come to believe in the power of the arts to convey the truths that are beyond descriptive sentences. "There are, indeed, things that cannot be put into words," he maintained. But if they cannot technically be "said," how would we know them? Wittgenstein's enigmatic answer is "they *make themselves manifest*. They are what is mystical."[35] The word "mystical" has so many implications for us today that it is hard to know with certainty what Wittgenstein meant by it back in 1921, the year his *Tractatus* was published. At the very least, however, he had in mind those language games that may not properly be said to *represent* reality, but that somehow *express* it. These expressed truths "make themselves manifest."

And thus, the anecdote: when invited once to address the Vienna Circle, Wittgenstein refused to limit his remarks to the positivist rules of his audience. Trying to express the deeper truths that "make themselves manifest," he read them poetry!

---

35. Wittgenstein, *Tractatus Logico-Philosophicus* 6:522. Italics Wittgenstein's.

The materialist objection to our various prayer-claims (healing, redemption, and so on) fails because it attacks only the representational quality of the sentences in question and not the expressive quality that liturgical performance shares with the other arts.

SUMMARY

Our response to liturgical skeptics should concede that many liturgical claims are indeed false – but only when viewed in the context of the wrong conceptual pictures. If religion speaks in a register that does justice to the human condition, liturgy recalibrates that register as art – an artistic reflection on the stream of life we find ourselves negotiating, a set of existential truths that make us who we are.

Judaism does have truths that matter, but these truths are not representational. When worshipers question what prayers say, they are having trouble with what the prayers represent. But even when prayers seem just to *represent*, they more accurately *express* – because prayer is the ritual art form where expression matters most.

Religious language expresses a great deal: deeper aspects of reality that we find useful to name; states of affairs according to which we promise, hope, and commit our lives; and so forth. It even creates new realities, such as marriage, and enacts other transformations across the rest of the human life cycle. Its compelling language is designed to do justice to the entirety of the human condition, to the point where its expressive truths become our existential truths as well.

Jewish liturgy presupposes its own conceptual picture: of lives in struggle but lives worth living; of a God who calls us to service, and who even reaches out a hand as the gates of *N'ilah* close and a final shofar blast announces the rebirth for which we yearn.

People in antiquity and the Middle Ages, perhaps, saw this as an adequate representational picture of metaphysical reality. It has been a very long time since we could see it that way. It is still, however, Judaism's age-old *expression* of the human condition. The extent to which we can construct the art of worship to do justice to that condition is the litmus test of whether and how our liturgy can be true.

Section 3

Sefat Emet: Telling the Truth

A Jewish Ethic of Truth Based on the Responsa of Rabbi Haim David Halevi

DAVID ELLENSON

INTRODUCTION AND CONCERNS

Concerns over the issues of truth-telling and lying have gained center stage in America over the past two decades. As the Harvard ethicist Sissela Bok pointed out in the preface to the 1999 reissue of her justly acclaimed *Lying*, the "debate about the moral issues of lying and truthfulness came to a head in 1998 as the charges and countercharges surrounding the Clinton White House were televised the world over in breathless detail." In an August 17th speech that year, President Clinton stated with seemingly "utter sincerity" that he had "misled" the public, his family, and his colleagues when he had denied, earlier on January 26, 1998, "with the same seemingly utter sincerity," that he had never had sexual relations with Monica Lewinsky. As Bok points out, "Together, the two conflicting statements brought a human face and a human voice to the center of the debate about what constitutes lying..."[1]

The concerns over truth-telling and lying raised by the actions of President Clinton at that time have only intensified in the present moment, and the conduct of President Trump is surely a major cause for the attention this issue now commands. As *The Washington Post* reported, President Trump made 2,400 false or misleading claims in his first 400 days in office.[2] To be sure, there is nothing particularly novel about this,

---

1. Sissela Bok, *Lying: Moral Choice in Public and Private Life* (New York, NY: Second Vintage Books Edition, 1999), xv–xvi.
2. Cited by Donald A. Effron in, "Why Trump Supporters Don't Mind His Lies,"

and Presidents Clinton and Trump hardly hold a monopoly among public figures over uttering falsehoods or misleading statements. After all, as Hannah Arendt once wryly observed, "No one has ever doubted that truth and politics are on rather bad terms with each other."[3]

Whether there are more lies today than in the past may be an open question. However, the public is certainly more aware of them due to social media platforms and greater societal shifts towards openness and accountability. Discussions surrounding the corrosive effects of lying on societal integrity and individual and group self-respect have unquestionably become considerably more frequent.

In this paper, I would like to examine how Jewish textual tradition addresses the issues of truth and deceit by examining the halakhic writings of Rabbi Haim David Halevi (1924–1998), the late Chief Sephardic Rabbi of Tel Aviv-Yafo. His legal writings and textual commentaries – particularly his responsa collection, ʿAseh Lekha Rav – directly address issues of truth and deceit. It is my view that his words on these topics provide for a nuanced and textured understanding of the moral considerations surrounding these issues and present a representative halakhic approach to these matters. In looking at his writings on this topic, my hope is that the contours of a "Jewish ethic of truth" based on his responsa might begin to emerge.

THE WRITINGS OF RABBI HALEVI ON "TRUTH AND LIES"

Every Jewish schoolchild who learns the daily morning service knows from a young age that the three paragraphs of the *Shema* end with the proclamation, "*Adonai Eloheikhem emet* – Adonai, your God is truth." Also, in Yoma 69b, the Talmud states, "The seal of God is truth." Furthermore, the preeminent modern moral philosopher, Immanuel

---

The New York Times (April 28, 2018, p. SR6 of the NY edition). As of April 29, the number of Trump lies has reached 10,000. See https://www.washingtonpost.com /opinions/no-president-trump-your-family-separation-policy-is-not-remotely -humane/2019/04/29/63d189ce-6aae-11e9-be3a-33217240a539_story.html?utm _term=.03b56cf96616.

3. Effron, "Why Trump Supporters, " SR6.

Kant, in his famed 1797 response to Benjamin Constant, "The Supposed Right to Lie," held that it was an absolute moral duty never to lie. It seems only logical, then, to many of us, that confidence in the integrity of personal relationships and public life can emerge only when the commitment to truth is absolute.

An initial responsum R. Halevi wrote on this topic would indicate that he also saw these matters as being "clear-cut" and that a commitment to truth could brook no compromises. A case came before him where the academic pressures students faced led some students to cheat on their examinations. Asked to issue a ruling on such behavior, R. Halevi was unequivocal in his moral condemnation of such actions. The student who posed this question to R. Halevi stated that he was a student in a Torah institution that placed great emphasis on truth and honesty. Consequently, examinations were not taken under the supervision of teachers. Rather, students were honor-bound not to cheat on their exams. However, it appeared that some students did not live up to this responsibility. The student then posed the following questions to R. Halevi: what exactly is the prohibition against copying on an exam? Is copying from another genuinely a prohibition? What if a friend allows another to copy his paper? Is this a "severe" or "light" lie? How should all this be understood?[4]

R. Halevi responded by saying that the answers to all these questions were clear from the very first sentence the student questioner wrote – "Great emphasis is placed here on the subject of truth – *Dagesh rav musam kan 'al nos'ei ha'emet*." R. Halevi then stated that all persons are told in Psalm 15 that they "should dwell in God's tent and live on His holy mountain." As King David says, a person should "walk uprightly, work righteousness, and speak truth in his heart" (15:2). The prominent medieval biblical exegete Rabbi David Kimḥi, in his commentary on this verse, observed that "one should not only speak the truth orally, but even his thoughts should express truth." Furthermore, R. Halevi stated, Ibn Ezra taught the greatness associated with truth and honesty when he stated, "*Vehu kol ha'adam* – and this is the essence of what it is to be human."

---

4. Haim David Halevi, *'Aseh Lekha Rav*, 5:59.

According to the Talmud (Shabbat 31a), on the day of judgment a person will be asked, "Did you negotiate in truth and integrity?" In addition, the *Shulkhan 'Arukh* (*Oraḥ Ḥayyim* 156) rules explicitly that one must always negotiate in truth. R. Halevi observed that, while these moral guidelines are directed at business dealings, they apply to all areas of life. Judaism requires that a person act with faithfulness in dealing with others.

R. Halevi therefore ruled that the prohibition against lying and deception was operative even when not applied to honor exams. A student who copies from another is simply and clearly lying to his teachers. Such behavior can only be morally-religiously condemned, and such a lie unequivocally constitutes a "serious violation (*issur ḥamur*)" of Jewish law. Indeed, it is so deserving of censure that "our rabbis taught in Ketubot 85a that one should distance oneself from even the appearance of a lie." *Miḥzei shekira*, the specter of a lie, is absolutely forbidden. In this case, where "we speak of an 'honor exam,' in addition to the lie that injures this student and his character, the student undermines and defrauds the very education he is supposed to be receiving."

As for the individual who permits his peer to copy his work either from "embarrassment" or from a desire to maintain relations with a friend, R. Halevi stated that this student "also transgresses a prohibition, for he is 'abetting the hands of a sinner.'" Judaism holds that such deception is plainly and simply unacceptable. Consequently, R. Halevi urged the student to "choose the path of uprightness that King David chose: 'The way of falsehood remove from me, ... I have chosen the way of faithfulness'" (Psalm 119:29–30).

Despite the apparent moral absolutism that R. Halevi displayed in this responsum on the matter of truth-telling and lying, other responsa in his halakhic compendium, *Aseh Lekha Rav*, indicate that he held a more multi-layered attitude on this issue. In a second case, he was asked about the ethical propriety of a teacher who published a fictitious calendar of examinations that she did not intend to give. The teacher said she did this to see how her students would react to the pressure. The students were angry over this and protested. Rabbi Halevi was asked whether the teacher was right when she did this, even if "we assume that her purpose was educational." The students and their principal asked directly, "Is it permitted to lie for such a purpose?" Indeed, they asked this question because they recognized that in some instances Jewish tradition did allow "truth" to be outweighed by other considerations. After all, they wrote to Rabbi Halevi, Jewish tradition did teach that "truth may be superseded for the sake of peace." However, they asked, should such a knowingly false announcement be permitted even for an ostensibly "educational purpose?" Furthermore, they wanted to know "why truth should be overruled even for the sake of peace." After all, "is not the truth 'the seal of God' and do we not walk in its ways?...Do we not have to aspire [always] to the absolute truth?" [5]

Rabbi Halevi responded clearly and directly to the question about whether the teacher was correct or had justifiable moral-religious grounds for issuing her false statement to the students about the fictitious examination schedule. He said no. He stated that what the teacher did was not right even if her intention was educational. R. Halevi declared that an instructor should never employ lies or deceitful means as a pedagogical tool no matter what the aim. He emphatically restated and emphasized that what the teacher had done was absolutely forbidden even if one were to concede that the teacher was well-intentioned.

However, Rabbi Halevi did not let the matter rest there, turning to the second and what he clearly regarded as the more interesting part of the query posed to him. He acknowledged that "the seal of God is truth. Are we not therefore required to aspire to absolute truth [in every instance]?" Given this, how could even "peace" ever take precedence over "truth"?

In response to this question, Halevi conceded at the outset that Judaism does indeed teach that "peace is so elevated a value that it is given priority even over truth," and provided prooftexts to support this contention. He cited Genesis 50:16–17, where the brothers of Joseph, then Viceroy of Egypt, sent a message to him, saying, "Your father gave this command before he died: 'Say to Joseph, please forgive the transgression of your brothers and their sin...'" Of course, as Rashi and

---

5. Haim David Halevi, 'Aseh Lekha Rav, 4:62 – "Sheker meta'amim hinuḥiyim umadua' mutar lesha'ot mipenei hashalom – A lie for educational reasons and why it would be permitted for the sake of peace."

numerous biblical commentators on this passage have noted, in saying this the brothers lied because Jacob offered no such command. However, the Talmud, R. Halevi noted, justified this falsehood in Yevamot 65b. There, the rabbinic text states, "And Rabbi Ila'a said in the name of Rabbi Elazar who spoke in the name of Rabbi Shimon, 'It is permitted a person to depart from the truth in a matter that will bring peace, as it is stated [in Genesis 50:16–17], 'Your father commanded before he died...' Jacob never issued this command, but his sons falsely attributed this statement to him in order to preserve peace between them and Joseph." R. Halevi further observed that Midrash Rabbah on Genesis 50:16 took the same position on the matter that Yevamot 65b did when the great Rabbi Shimon ben Gamliel is quoted as saying, "Great is peace that even the tribes spoke falsely (*devarim beduyim*) to bring about peace."

While these texts seemingly provide a clear justification for offering "white lies" for the sake of peace, R. Halevi observed that the example of Joseph and his brothers might not actually provide such a rationale. After all, these specific texts in Yevamot and Midrash Rabbah might well be construed in a different way. The conduct of the brothers may well have been motivated by prudential concerns, not moral sensibilities. It may have been that the brothers lied only because they feared the revenge Joseph might have exacted against them for the sin they committed against Joseph when they sold him into bondage. They may have falsified the truth for this reason, and not for the sake of peace. If this were so, these prooftexts cited for legitimating such behavior would not constitute justification for the argument that "peace" takes priority over "truth."

R. Halevi therefore turned to the Jerusalem Talmud (Pe'ah 1:1) for confirmation of this position. There, Rabban Shimon ben Gamliel said explicitly, "Scripture spoke words of falsehood to create peace between Joseph and brothers, when it was written, 'And he [Jacob] commanded...' (Genesis 50:16–17). Yet, we do not find that Jacob issued any command." This meant that R. Shimon ben Gamliel, as R. Halevi explained, understood the brothers had lied about what Jacob had said. R. Halevi concluded, "The proof does not come from the brothers themselves, but from the Torah which reported the lies that the brothers spoke. From this we learn that such an action is permitted." It is the Torah itself that sanctions the telling of falsehoods for the sake of peace.

R. Halevi then went on to explicate further texts discussed in the Yevamot passage on this matter. He pointed out that Rabbi Nathan, like Rabban Shimon ben Gamliel, also stated that "it is a commandment" to lie for the sake of creating peace, citing 1 Samuel 16:2 as an additional prooftext in support of this position. There it states, "And Samuel said, how can I go [anoint David the son of Jesse as King]. If Saul hears, he will kill me. And God said, take a heifer with you [as a pretext] and say, 'I have come to sacrifice before the Lord.'" In short, God told Samuel to lie and engage in subterfuge to hide what he intended to do – to anoint David as King – from Saul. From this, the Talmud concluded, "So great is peace that even the Holy One, blessed be He, lied for its sake" (Yevamot 65b).

The Sephardic sage then stated that the Talmud continued by referring to yet another biblical text where God "lies." As Yevamot 65b states, "It was taught in the school of Rabbi Yishma'el. Great is peace, as even the Holy One, blessed be He, departed from the truth for it. As, initially, it is written that Sarah, when told by God that she would become a mother, said of Abraham, 'And my lord [Abraham] is [too] old' (Genesis 18:12), and cannot sire a child. However, in the end it is written that God told Abraham that Sarah said [of herself], 'And I am old' (Genesis 18:13). God adjusted Sarah's words to spare Abraham hurt feelings that might lead Abraham and Sarah to quarrel."

The lesson R. Halevi derived from this was that "the seal of God is truth and, if we are capable, it is always necessary for us to aspire to absolute truth." However, such truth does not exist in the earthly realm in which we live. Therefore, "all the examples from the Torah cited above teach us that if we tell the truth in a world of lies (be'olam hasheker), it will only cause arguments [and strife]." It is therefore sometimes "better to lie for the sake of peace." After all, "what benefit is there in in telling the truth if the argument that will likely ensue in its wake will only cause destruction and murder. Even God, in dealing with His creatures who live in this reality, chooses to act in a deceptive way "for the sake of peace."

R. Halevi then reinforced this notion that the reality of the world sometimes necessitated deceptive acts by turning to the biblical passage where Jacob lied to Esau to save his life. In Genesis 33:14, Scripture relates that Jacob said to Esau, "Let my lord pass over before his servant and I will journey on gently, according to the pace of the cattle... and the children until I come unto my lord in Seir." However, in Genesis 33:17, it states that Jacob journeyed not to Seir, but Succoth, as it is written, "And Jacob journeyed to Succoth, and built himself a house." As Rabbi Abahu observed (Genesis Rabbah 78:14), Jacob, fearing that Esau sought to slay him, was justified in deceiving Esau to save his life. As a result, the Talmud (in 'Avodah Zarah 25b) stated that Jacob, fearing that Esau would murder him, was correct in deceiving Esau so that he could save his life. Furthermore, R. Halevi concluded that Jacob was permitted to lie to avoid the harm he believed Esau intended.

To be sure, these ancient rabbinic sages were not completely comfortable with Jacob behaving in this manner. They acknowledged that while Jacob was not completely candid with Esau, they cited another verse, from Obadiah 1:21, "Deliverers will go up on Mount Zion to govern the mountain of Esau," to argue that Jacob did intend to go to Seir in the future. In this way, they softened the "lie" that Jacob told to his brother. It seems that the rabbis of the Talmud, even when a lie was required to save a life, were still not completely comfortable with such an act.

R. Halevi then repeated his claim that even though every attribute Jacob possessed was "truth," Jacob was nevertheless ultimately permitted to act deviously for his own rescue. His behavior was morally sanctioned because humans are destined to live in an imperfect world of lies (be'-olam hasheker). From this, R. Halevi concluded, "He who wishes to act in accordance with absolute truth is likely to cause injury to himself and others, and therefore it is permitted to shade the truth for the sake of peace."

The Sephardic Chief Rabbi of Tel Aviv-Jaffa then cited several more classical Jewish sources to provide additional support for his argument that a lie can be countenanced ethically-religiously for the sake of peace. In the final passage of the Laws of Hanukkah in the Mishneh Torah, Maimonides wrote, "Great is peace for God's name can be blotted out to create peace between a husband and his wife.... For the entire Torah was given to bring about peace within the world, as Proverbs 3:17 states, 'Its ways are ways of pleasantness, and all its paths are peace.'" In addition, the Sifre, in its commentary on Numbers 6:26, states, "Great is peace for the name of the Holy One, blessed be He, is peace." From these and other sources, R. Halevi concluded that "while the seal of God is truth, His Name is Peace. Therefore, it is no surprise that in a time of distress that we do not seize the seal of God, but rely on his holy or Great Name." In sum, "all of the Torah was given for the sake of peace in the world."

R. Halevi further contended that at the very moment God created the world, God planted this hierarchy of values into the very nature of the universe. He quoted the famous midrash contained in Genesis Rabbah, Parshah 8:5, where it states, "R. Simon said: When the Holy One, blessed be He, came to create Adam, the ministering angels formed themselves into groups and parties, some of them saying, 'Let him be created,' whilst others urged, 'Let him not be created.' Thus, it is written, Mercy and Truth are met together, Righteousness and Peace have kissed each other (Psalm 135). Love said, 'Let him be created, because he will dispense acts of love'; Truth said, 'Let him not be created, because he is compounded of falsehood'; Righteousness said, 'Let him be created, because he will perform righteous deeds'; Peace said, 'Let him not be created, because he is full of strife.' What did the Lord do? He took Truth and cast it to the ground (Daniel 8). Said the ministering angels before the Holy One, blessed be He, 'Sovereign of the Universe! Why do You despise Your seal [which is truth]?'"

R. Halevi culminated his argument by citing work of nineteenth-century Rabbi Yitzhak Zev Yadler, who, in his *Tiferet tsiyyon* commentary on this midrash, wrote that because the angels are pure spirit and are not involved in the material world, it was impossible for God to explain to them that even the righteous (*tzadikim*) on occasion must lie. The discomfort R. Halevi felt with this position was painfully apparent in the final observations with which he completed this responsum. He emphasized that truth must remain the foundation of the entire Torah, and approvingly cited Malachi 2:6, which states, "The law of truth was in his mouth, and unrighteousness was not found in his lips; he walked with Me in peace and uprightness." Nevertheless, he reluctantly and, it seems, painfully acknowledged that a lie must sometimes take precedence over truth.

Elsewhere in *'Aseh Lekha Rav*, R. Halevi repeated the position that the nature of the physical world on occasion demanded misleading and dishonest behavior.[6] He turned in this instance to a reported interaction between Isaac and Rebecca in Genesis 27:46 to support this stance. There it was written, "Rebecca said to Isaac, 'I am disgusted with my life because of the Hittite women. If Jacob marries a Hittite woman... from among the native women [where we live], what good will life be to me?'" In asserting this concern to Isaac as a cause for sending Isaac away from their home among the Hittites, Rebecca, R. Halevi maintained, "hid the truth with her words." She failed to tell Isaac that her ostensible concern about Jacob marrying a Hittite woman was only an excuse that concealed her genuine fear. "She did not," R. Halevi wrote, "tell Isaac that Esau was furious [with Jacob] and intended to kill him after their father's death. This," he stated, "was the real reason she wished to send Jacob to Padan Aram." In short, Rebecca "lied" to her husband to conceal her true motive for casting Jacob out of their home. R. Halevi then stated that "such an act is not forbidden in and of itself, for is it not permitted to lie" for what R. Halevi understood to be for "the sake of peace" in the home and in the family. Further, if such behavior could be deemed appropriate for "the sake of peace," then it was certainly permissible not "to reveal the entire truth" for the sake of avoiding enmity and discord in cases such as this. While R. Halevi argued that this stance was a morally acceptable one in this instance, he issued the same caveat about it that he had in the responsum cited above. Such behavior, he concluded, could only be approved in the "lower world," the earthly world in which humans dwell. In the "world above," which is the realm of absolute truth, it could never be countenanced. It appears that, for R. Halevi, Judaism allows for an ethic of discretion on the question of "truth-telling" in the oft-murky universe in which persons exist. [7]

CONCLUDING THOUGHTS

Millions today would agree with Judge Susan Webber Wright when she contended, in the judgment she rendered on President Clinton on August 12, 1998, that his untruthful conduct eroded public trust in the

---

6. '*Aseh Lekha Rav* 5, p. 60.
7. '*Aseh Lekha Rav* 5, 60.

government. In her ruling, which found him guilty of contempt of court, she wrote, "It is simply not acceptable to employ deceptions to obstruct the judicial process... Sanctions must be imposed, not only to redress the President's misconduct but to deter others who might consider emulating the President... by engaging in misconduct that undermines the integrity of the judicial system." [8]

However, as an opinion piece in *The New York Times* titled "Why Trump Supporters Don't Mind His Lies," written by London Business School Professor Donald Effron, suggests, large numbers of the public have a high tolerance for deceptions and fabrications. [9] Effron himself, in an academic study published in 2018 in the *Personality and Social Psychology Bulletin*, offers insight into why this is so. [10] He points out that there is a psychological proclivity to believe that even when a claim is false, *if* it could be true, then it may not be deemed unethical for a politician to utter it. Thus, when Trump retweeted a false video showing a Muslim migrant committing an assault, Sarah Huckabee Sanders defended him saying, "Whether it's a real video [or not], the threat [from such migrants] is real." Kellyanne Conway also addressed Trump's problematic claim about the size of the crowd at his inauguration, saying that inclement weather may have kept people away. Lest one think that only Republicans are inclined in such directions, Effron found that a majority of those opposed to Trump continued to believe that an untruth told about Trump – that the President had removed a bust of Dr. King from the Oval Office – was "true" or at least "morally tolerable," even when reliable reports indicated that this was a misrepresentation. This was because they felt the report reflected what they regarded as a "real truth" about Trump and his attitudes towards Dr. King and issues of race. [11]

---

8. Bok, *Lying*, xvii.
9. See Effron, "Why Trump Supporters Don't Mind His Lies."
10. Daniel Effron, "It Could Have Been True: How Counterfactual Thoughts Reduce Condemnation of Falsehoods and Increase Political Polarization," *Personality and Social Psychology Bulletin*, vol. 44:5 (2018): 729–46.
11. Effron, "It Could Have Been True." The study revealed that if the falsehood could have been true, it was regarded as "less unethical" to tell it. That is, when it confirmed one's political views, a falsehood was tolerated or even applauded. There is a lower standard for tolerating falsehoods we find politically appealing

To be sure, there are other philosophical and sociological grounds for sanctioning "untruths" in certain contexts. As Bok, citing the work of psychiatrist Willard Gaylin, argues, "brutal, needless, or uncaring truth-telling can wreak" considerable "harm." Telling the truth can sometimes "violate fundamental standards of respect and concern," and "judicious lying" may in some instances be a preferable way for persons to operate. Or, as the doctor in Mark Twain's short story, "Was it Heaven? Or Hell?," puts it to two sisters, "Haven't you got sense enough to discriminate between lies? Don't you know the difference between a lie that helps and a lie that hurts?" [12] While truth-telling is surely prized, Bok nevertheless contends that there ought to be alternatives between "lying or constant, no-holds-barred truth-telling." In short, she believes there should be moral "room for discretion." [13]

This paper has shown that Rabbi Halevi and the Jewish tradition echo the sentiments and judgments of Professor Bok. "Judicious lying" is seemingly preferred in instances where "brutal truth-telling will wreak harm." Nevertheless, such deception is permitted only for the sake of promoting "peace" and preventing "enmity" among persons. At the same time, the rabbis, even when they tolerate deceit or justify actions that reflect a lack of complete candor, display a palpable sense of discomfort with such behavior. A "law of truth" always remains the ideal, and Judaism adopts a cautionary stance that absolutely circum-scribes the instances and situations where a lack of commitment to a "law of truth" can be sanctioned. In instances where falsehood can

---

than for those we find unappealing. Thus, Effron concluded, even when partisans agree on facts, "they can come to different moral conclusions about the dishonesty of deviating from those facts." As Effron writes, "Conditional propositions – *if* circumstances had been different *then* an event would have occurred – are called *counterfactuals*. Logically, they do not render falsehoods true, but psychologically, they may make falsehoods seem less unethical." Falsehoods "that seem close to reality may seem ... justified ... " It seems many persons have a psychological and ethical proclivity to see a "lie" told in the service of a moral cause as justifiable. Or, as Effron phrases it, "Motivated reasoning affects moral judgments." Persons unquestionably "strategically construe ambiguous information as supporting" desired "conclusions."

12. Bok, *Lying*, xxiv.
13. Bok, *Lying*, xxii–xxiii.

wreak harm in personal relationships and cause damage to the public, Judaism, as presented in the legal writings of R. Halevi, regards deceit as intolerable. While Judaism allows for truth to be compromised, it can be done only for the purest and most altruistic of motives and only where salutary outcomes can be reasonably assured. Those who would seek Jewish justification for behavior that would fall short of this standard of "uprightness" should question their own motives and intent before engaging in behavior that would violate the admonition of the Psalmist to remove "the way of falsehood." In an age of polarization, Jewish tradition expresses an ethic on the subject of "truth" that is not black or white, but pragmatic and sensible; not simplistic and one-dimensional, but multi-valent and nimble. It is a vital teaching for our time.

SECTION 4

Emet Umada': Judaism, Science, and Philosophy

Science and Truth

GEOFFREY A. MITELMAN

The words "trust" and "true" are intimately related, and not just in English: *emunah*, "trust" or "faithfulness," is linked with *emet*, "truth."[1] Not only do the words *emet v'emunah* appear together immediately following the *Shema*, in b. Ta'anit 8a, the words are almost synonymous:

אמר ר' אמי אין גשמים יורדין אלא בשביל בעלי אמנה שנאמר (תהלים פה, יב) אמת מארץ תצמח וצדק משמים נשקף.

Rabbi Ami further said: Rain falls only due to faithful people, as it is stated: "Truth springs out of the earth, and righteousness has looked down from heaven." (Psalms 85:12)

Indeed, Judaism has long valued truth as being foundational to everything in the world: b. Shabbat 10a remarks that כל דיין שדן דין אמת לאמיתו אפילו שעה אחת מעלה עליו הכתוב כאילו נעשה שותף להקדוש ברוך הוא במעשה בראשית – "any judge who judges truthfully for even an hour, the verse sees him as if he were a partner of the Holy One in the creation of the world." M. Avot 1:18 has the classic citation: רבן שמעון בן גמליאל אומר, על שלשה דברים העולם עומד, על הדין ועל האמת ועל השלום, שנאמר (זכריה ח) אמת ומשפט שלום שפטו בשעריכם – "Rabban Shimon Ben Gamliel said, 'The world is sustained by three things, by justice, by

---

1. Linguist Joel Hoffman notes that while *emunah* comes from the root *aleph-mem-nun*, "*emet* seems to have a consonant dropped (because of words like *amiti*, with a *dagesh* in the *tav*), and the obvious guess for that consonant would be a *nun*. If so, *emet* comes from *ement*, which comes from the root A.M.N. with the common nominal suffix -T." From personal correspondence with the author.

truth, and by peace. As it has been stated: Speak every man the truth (*emet*) to his neighbor; execute the judgment of truth and peace in your gates'" (Zechariah 8:16). Truth is even seen as the "seal of God" based on Psalm 85:11–12: חסד ואמת נפגשו צדק ושלום נשקו: אמת מארץ תצמח וצדק משמים נשקף "Faithfulness and truth (*emet*) meet; justice and well-being kiss. Truth (*emet*) springs up from the earth; justice looks down from heaven."[2]

These verses from Psalm 85, which are used multiple times in rabbinic literature, can also help us understand why discovering "truth" can be so challenging for us imperfect human beings. The idea of "truth springing up from the earth" contrasts with the idea of an eternal, unchanging truth that simply "comes to us" through revelation from on high. We are not passive recipients of truth; rather, it is only through study and engagement with the world, and through the findings unearthed by that exploration, that we are able to attain a closer approximation of how the world really works. The idea that "truth springs up from the earth" implies that truth comes from the bottom up, rather than from the top down. It emerges when we tap the spring, so to speak – when we observe, examine, and ponder the world, and then re-observe, re-examine, and re-ponder it.

This ongoing process is known as "science," and we moderns consider it a valuable source of truth. Science, however, is not about getting us to an exact or eternal truth. Rather, science helps us become progressively less wrong, as one definition puts it. Science allows us to further refine our ideas about the natural world. Sometimes these ideas end up being totally incorrect, like the idea of the "ether" that dominated theories of light in the late nineteenth and early twentieth centuries. But sometimes even theories that are later seen to be "wrong" ultimately got us closer to a better explanation – after all, attempting to investigate the "ether" helped launch Einstein's theory of relativity.[3] Indeed, as new hypotheses, new data, and new instrumentation arise, we get closer to a more accurate representation of the world as it is, but there is no immutable scientific "truth" that holds forever. The scientific enterprise is a process, not a final result.

---

2. Bereishit Rabbah 8:5.

3. https://mathshistory.st-andrews.ac.uk/Extras/Einstein_ether/.

Even several hundred years before the scientific revolution of the sixteenth and seventeenth centuries, Maimonides understood that there is an interplay between physics and metaphysics, or between "science" and "truth," and that physics precedes metaphysics. As he explains in his introductory remarks of *Guide for the Perplexed*:

> Do not imagine that these most difficult problems can be thoroughly understood by any one of us. This is not the case. At times the truth shines so brilliantly that we perceive it as clear as day. Our nature and habit then draw a veil over our perception, and we return to a darkness almost as dense as before. We are like those who, though beholding frequent flashes of lightning, still find themselves in the thickest darkness of the night.[4]

"Truth," both in science and in Judaism, is not instantaneously discovered and eternally accurate. Rather, it is a slow-moving process, and any good scientific answer will lead to a whole host of new questions.

In his book, *Ignorance: How It Drives Science*, Professor Stuart Firestein, former chair of the Columbia University biology department, echoes this notion. Science, he asserts, advances not by giving us definitive answers, but by opening up new avenues of exploration. In a 2013 speech, he expounded upon this concept of science:

> I think what really happens in science is a model...like the magic well, where no matter how many buckets you take out, there's always another bucket of water to be had, or my particularly favorite one, with the effect and everything, the ripples on a pond. So if you think of knowledge being this ever-expanding ripple on a pond, the important thing to realize is that our ignorance, the circumference of this knowledge, also grows with knowledge. So the knowledge generates ignorance. This is really well said, I thought, by George Bernard Shaw. This is actually part of a toast that he delivered to celebrate Einstein at a dinner celebrating Einstein's work, in which he claims that science just creates more questions than it answers. Science is always wrong. It never solves a problem without creating ten more.[5]

---

4. *Guide for the Perplexed*, Moses ben Maimon, trans. M. Friedlander, 7.
5. https://www.ted.com/talks/stuart_firestein_the_pursuit_of_ignorance/transcript.

Science, in other words, is a work in progress, a fact that has become particularly clear recently due to the reality of COVID-19. Over just several months, differing – and even conflicting – information arose surrounding recommendations for protection, such as the wearing of masks,[6] the use of hydroxychloroquine,[7] and whether children can catch and spread the virus.[8] As most people are not scientists (let alone epidemiologists), laypeople were placed into a position of having to try to sort out scientific information on their own. Without the appropriate scientific training to know what was "true," people had to simply decide which sources to trust and which to ignore.

In the midst of COVID-19, Professors Mark A. Bloom, Sarah Quebec Fuentes, and Jonathan Crocker wrote an essay on "How the COVID-19 Pandemic Reveals Gaps in Science and Mathematics Instruction."[9] They highlighted the difference between how laypeople view science as opposed to how science actually works. We want science to have answers, offering us the "truth" on whatever subject we are looking for. However, it's crucial for laypeople to understand that this vision of science is not accurate:

> The claims and recommendations of science are tentative, meaning they are subject to change as further research and exploration provide more information. While some might imply this means one cannot have confidence in science, the tentative nature of science implies that scientific understanding is constantly being refined and improved to accommodate the new discoveries. For example, new hominin discoveries may necessitate a refinement of the hominin family tree, but they do not substantively change our understanding of the relationship between hominins and other primates. Rarely, do new discoveries call for a complete abandonment of previous scientific claims. For example, for decades scientists held the notion

6. https://www.ucsf.edu/news/2020/06/417906/still-confused-about-masks -heres-science-behind-how-face-masks-prevent.

7. https://www.who.int/news-room/q-a-detail/q-a-hydroxychloroquine-and -covid-19.

8. https://explaincovid.org/kids/kids-and-covid-19/.

9. https://ejse.southwestern.edu/article/view/20555.

that neural tissue, when lost or damaged, could not be regenerated. In more recent years, however, through new discoveries by cell biologists, the process of neurogenesis was discovered [...]

Establishing the current body of scientific knowledge has taken decades to be achieved. However, in the current climate with COVID-19, people want answers now. This need to have an answer and, if possible, find someone to blame for bad circumstances like the COVID-19 pandemic drives so many to accept the claims of the conspiracy theory documentary *Plandemic* (a now removed YouTube video "documentary" film) over the uncertain and changing recommendations of the Centers for Disease Control and Prevention (CDC), WHO, and other medical experts. The public has been presented science in textbooks and on websites and fail to see the "messy side" of science. If we can emphasize the process of science, recognizing the "trial and correction" cycle that scientists enact, the public might not be so surprised by the changing and uncertain recommendations of medical experts that are being communicated through press briefings and news outlets.

COVID-19 is reflective of a larger challenge we are facing in our society: how we distinguish among information that may change as new data arises, information that is well-intentioned but inaccurate, and information that is willfully distorted or deceptive.

Perhaps this is why Judaism places such an emphasis on not just truth, but on honesty as well. This is made especially clear in Leviticus 19, which contains some of the most important and well-known laws in the Torah. The Ten Commandments appear here, as do the verses, "You shall not stand by idly while your neighbor bleeds" and "You shall love your neighbor as yourself." The whole chapter is known as the "holiness code," implying that beyond just being ethical, treating people fairly is truly a sacred obligation that God demands of us. Leviticus 19:14 says, "You shall not put a stumbling block before the blind." On its surface, this *mitzvah* seems a bit ridiculous – what kind of sadist would intentionally place a barrier in front of someone who can't see?

However, the rabbis expand on this idea, reminding us that we are "blind" to many things simply because we lack certain information. Sifra

Kedoshim 2:14 takes this *mitzvah* to mean that we should not offer misleading advice "before one who is 'blind' in a certain matter":

> If he asks you: "Is that man's daughter fit for (marriage into) the priesthood?" Do not tell him that she is kosher if she is not. If he asks you for advice, do not give him advice that is unfit for him. Do not say to him "Leave early in the morning," so that robbers should assault him. "Leave in the afternoon," so that he fall victim to the heat. Do not say to him "Sell your field and buy an ass," and you seek occasion against him and take it from him. Lest you say "But I gave him good advice!" – these things are "known to the heart," namely: "And you shall fear your God; I am Adonai."

Relaying information, by its very nature, is asymmetrical – if you have it, and need to share it with someone else, you need to recognize the "blindness" of the other person in that matter, and even more so, not take advantage of them because of the additional knowledge you have.

However, as important as it is not to intentionally mislead someone, we are often unaware of what we ourselves are blind to. We may think we "know our own heart," but we have a strong tendency to lie to ourselves. As physicist Richard Feynman said about the scientific enterprise, "The first principle is that you must not fool yourself and you are the easiest person to fool."[10] Data doesn't speak for itself – it entails assumptions and interpretations, which come from us as human beings, and we can easily become blind to our own biases. Princeton psychology professor Tania Lombrozo explains that there are, in fact, two models of how we think about data and evidence, and it's not always simply about discovering truth:

> In the first view, people are like scientists. They go about the world gathering data, constructing theories and using those theories to guide their interactions with the world. As new evidence comes in, they revise their beliefs accordingly.
>
> In the second view, people are more like trial lawyers. They already know what they want to conclude (innocent or guilty, pro or con),

---

10. http://calteches.library.caltech.edu/51/2/CargoCult.htm.

and they go about seeking and construing evidence to favor that conclusion. Rather than matching their beliefs to the evidence, they match the evidence to their beliefs.

There's research to support each of these views. For instance, we know that even young children[11] conduct "experiments" and gather "data" to update their beliefs about the way the world works and that, under some conditions, adults are pretty sophisticated probabilistic reasoners.[12]

Yet, we also know that people engage in motivated reasoning: They let the conclusions they hope to reach influence their decisions. Among other things, this can contribute to confirmation bias: the tendency to seek and favor evidence that supports what one already believes.[13]

Our brains aren't designed to help us find truth; they are meant to keep us alive. There's clearly a survival value in having an accurate understanding of the world (holding onto a belief that you can fly from great heights or that saber-tooth tigers would make wonderful pets would kill you quite quickly), but there can also be a survival value in manipulation or deception. If you present yourself as trustworthy (even if you are not) then you'll be more likely to get the resources you need (see, for example, the work of behavioral economist Dan Ariely).[14] While we may speak about the sacred value of truth, on a practical level, its value is often instrumental. If it's more effective for us to lie – to others or to ourselves, whether consciously or not – we may be tempted to do so. And that's why there are *mitzvot* and *aggadot* on the importance of truth: they remind us that we are likely to be tempted to fudge the facts when it serves our aims.

"Truth" and "trust," then, are linked to power, responsibility, and authority, which is why the Torah reminds us of the tremendous respon-

---

11. http://www.alisongopnik.com/TheScientistInTheCrib.htm.

12. http://dx.doi.org/10.1126/science.1192788.

13. https://www.npr.org/sections/13.7/2016/04/11/473769249/is-the-minds-approach-more-like-a-scientist-or-a-trial-lawyer.

14. http://people.duke.edu/~dandan/webfiles/PapersPI/Dishonesty%20of%20Honest%20People.pdf.

sibility carried by those who collect, provide, interpret, and communicate specialized knowledge. Scientists, like politicians, *poskim*, and other professionals, possess proprietary knowledge. Therefore, there is always the potential danger that they will mislead others, even if only unintentionally. For such authority figures, it is less important to pursue an eternal and unchanging truth than it is to speak truthfully about the state of knowledge and ignorance at that given time. Laypeople, in turn, ought to rely on experts for information on specific topics rather than on their own personal biases, interpretations, or findings. This is why astrophysicist Ethan Siegel wrote a piece entitled "You Must Not 'Do Your Own Research' When It Comes To Science."[15]

> There is no excuse, with all the wonderful scientists and science communicators telling the truth about a whole slew of issues in our world, for people to seek out only the opinions that confirm their own biases. The best scientists in the world – even the ones who hold contrarian beliefs of their own – all agree that we should base our policies on the scientific consensus that we've achieved. When that consensus changes, evolves, or moves forward because we've learned more than we previously knew, we should correct course to follow that novel path instead.
>
> But that requires a kind of transformation within yourself. It means that you need to be humble, and admit that you, yourself, lack the necessary expertise to evaluate the science before you. It means that you need to be brave enough to turn to the consensus of scientific experts and ask, legitimately, what we know at the present stage. And it means you need to be open-minded enough to understand that your preconceptions are quite likely to be wrong in some, many, or possibly even all ways. If we listen to the science, we can attempt to take the best path possible forward through the greatest challenges facing modern society. We can choose to ignore it, but if we do, the consequences will only increase in severity.

And just as scientists converse in their own language and then try to translate their findings into language that we can comprehend – language

---

15. https://www.forbes.com/sites/startswithabang/2020/07/30/you-must-not-do-your-own-research-when-it-comes-to-science.

that can impact us, so that we may impact the world – in Judaism, the authoritative language of halakhic expertise and textual knowledge gets translated into particular responsa which communicate this knowledge in practical contexts. Indeed, when I myself was ordained, one of my professors remarked that "The only reason you have any right to speak to your community is because of your expertise. The only reason anyone will listen, though, is through the relationships you will build."

Rabbi Dov Linzer, President and Rosh HaYeshiva of Yeshivat Chovevei Torah Rabbinical School, raises this question of how and why rabbinic authority exists. As he mentions, the Torah itself doesn't give rabbis the authority to make decisions. Yes, they have studied, and yes, they have specialized knowledge. However,

> [w]e live in a world in which, for the majority, religious practice is not imposed by the state but is fully voluntary. We live in a world in which, in practice, the only power that rabbis have is given to them by the people who turn to them and those who employ them. Some may bemoan this state of affairs, but for many, it is the ideal. It helps prevent – to some degree and in most, but not all, cases – gross abuses of power. It also helps create a dynamic wherein rabbis must be attuned to the needs of the populace if they hope to have people turn to them for their rulings and leadership. Such is the nature of an authority that emerges from belief, acceptance, and choice.[16]

Truth, in other words, is a communal enterprise. We need both experts and communicators, both those who are deeply enmeshed in the minutiae of a specific milieu and those who can share that knowledge with the public in a way that facilitates their understanding and enables them to respond with action. And we must remember that if we pretend to be more knowledgeable than we actually are, then, even if this is done with the best of intentions, we are spreading falsehoods.

And this leads us back to our first point: in Judaism, truth "springs from the earth" because Judaism, like science, does not see truth as existing in the (now-known-to-be-non-existent) ether, waiting to be discovered. Truth is not static; searching for it is a long and winding

---

16. https://library.yctorah.org/2016/09/says-who-what-is-the-basis-for-rabbinic -authority/.

process, with missteps and dead ends. Furthermore, what we understand to be true at any given time is ultimately simply provisional and
is unavoidably also influenced by our own human biases, errors, and
worldviews. Therefore, we need to recognize that process, debate, and
expertise are how we can help gain a clearer understanding of the world,
and we must also encourage the responsibility to communicate the
process and results honestly. There is a reason that the Talmud doesn't
simply record the halakhic rulings of the rabbinic debates, but also
records the debates themselves, as conversations, making a point to
include the various arguments and minority opinions that led to the
discussion. Mishnah Eduyyot 1:5 even tells us why:

> ולמה מזכירין דברי היחיד בין המרבין, הואיל ואין הלכה אלא כדברי
> המרבין. שאם יראה בית דין את דברי היחיד ויסמך עליו, שאין בית דין
> יכול לבטל דברי בית דין חברו עד שיהיה גדול ממנו בחכמה ובמנין.
> היה גדול ממנו בחכמה אבל לא במנין, במנין אבל לא בחכמה, אינו יכול
> לבטל דבריו, עד שיהיה גדול ממנו בחכמה ובמנין:

> And why do they record the opinion of a single person among the
> many, when the halakhah must be according to the opinion of the
> many? So that if a court prefers the opinion of the single person
> it may depend on him. For no court may set aside the decision of
> another court unless it is greater than it in wisdom and in number.
> If it was greater than it in wisdom but not in number, in number
> but not in wisdom, it may not set aside its decision, unless it is
> greater than it in wisdom and in number.

The truth we have right now may change. The rabbis understood this
and thus allowed room for revision, recognizing that later generations
may be "greater in wisdom" – which is also the way science tends to
progress. As Isaac Newton remarked on his own insights, "If I have seen
further, it is by standing on the shoulders of giants."[17] Our knowledge
right now – both scientifically and halakhically – is the best we have in
this moment, but we also build on it, allowing "truth" to evolve based
on new information and new interpretations.

---

17. https://link.springer.com/chapter/10.1007/978-1-4471-0051-5_5.

This also means that if God is a "God of truth" (as our liturgy describes it), we can change and shift our understanding of God in the same way we can change our understanding of truth. For example, what do we know about "the earth"? If you had asked that question to people in the 1400s, they would have told you that they "knew" the earth was the center of the universe.[18] If you had asked Lord Kelvin, one of the greatest scientific minds of the nineteenth century, he would have told you that he "knew" that the earth was between twenty-four and 400 million years old.[19] And if you had asked that question to most geologists in the early twentieth century, they would have told you that they "knew" that the earth's continents were fixed in place.[20] And of course, we now realize that what all these people "knew" about the earth was completely wrong.

In one sense, the earth has been whatever the earth has been over its billions of years of history. But our *understanding* of what the earth is has changed dramatically over just a few centuries. In other words, the earth as an *actual object in reality* is different from the earth *as we know it at any given moment*. Indeed, everything science can illuminate – be it the earth, the sun, atoms, genes, the universe, or humanity – exists in these same two realms at once: the realm of reality and the realm of our current understanding. Professor Steven Goldman highlights this dichotomy in his outstanding course for the Teaching Company entitled "Science Wars: What Scientists Know and How They Know It."[21] On one hand, science is an attempt to give us clearer, better, and more accurate descriptions of the universe – a striving for a Platonic ideal. On the other hand, science is historical and temporal. New data, new instruments, new analyses and new interpretations can and will change how we understand everything around us.

To help resolve that conflict, Goldman suggests that we view things like the earth, the sun, or atoms as "scientific objects." As he explains:

---

18. https://www.universetoday.com/32607/geocentric-model.
19. https://www.americanscientist.org/article/kelvin-perry-and-the-age-of
-the-earth.
20. https://pubs.usgs.gov/gip/dynamic/dynamic.html.
21. http://www.thegreatcourses.com/tgc/courses/course_detail.aspx?cid=1235.

It is much less controversial and difficult for us to grasp that "scientific objects" are redefined as we improve, as we get more experience, as we accumulate new data, we make new experiments. We have to redefine [these objects] – we sharpen the definition or throw it out and start with a new definition. That's different from changing Reality [sic], because our intuition is that what we mean by "Reality" is something changeless...

[S]eeing scientific knowledge as about actualities ["scientific objects"] is a potentially useful way of eliminating much of the controversy from trying to understand the status of scientific knowledge and truth claims. At a minimum, scientific objects are justifiable instrumentally. What the implications of this instrumental success are vis-a-vis Reality is a separate issue.

This concept of a "scientific object" is indeed, as Goldman asserts, tremendously valuable. It helps us realize that we have to hold our beliefs about the world lightly, and, at the same time, remember that these imperfect beliefs form the very lens through which way we look at and live in the world. Along those lines, then, I propose that we can consider God a "scientific object."

To be sure, this metaphor is not suggesting God can be studied scientifically, or that if we find enough evidence we can prove (or disprove) God's existence, or that anything we don't understand yet is the result of God's handiwork. Rather, just as we shouldn't focus on the earth in Reality (because we will never understand the earth in that way) and instead focus on the earth as we understand it right now, which can change based on new knowledge, similarly, we shouldn't focus on God in Reality (because we will never understand God in that way), and instead focus on God as we understand the divine right now, which can change and grow based on new knowledge.

We hold certain beliefs, including beliefs about God – in particular, who or what God is (or is not) and how God acts (or doesn't act) in the world. But what doesn't happen often enough – whether someone is a fundamentalist, an atheist, or anything in between – is a willingness to rethink what we believe about God based on new ideas and new experiences. We need a "working definition" of God, so to speak, a theology that can change and adapt based on new data and new experiences.

Rather than saying either, "This is what God is, and I know that I am right," or "There is no God because I don't believe that there is an Omnipotent, Omnipresent, Omnibenevolent Being that created the universe and directly impacts the world today," we can instead say, "Given what I know and what I believe at this moment, this is what I believe God is and how God acts in this world. However, as new data or new experiences arise, I might need to change my outlook."

In other words, we can think of and talk about God in the same way scientists have thought of and talked about scientific objects throughout human history, holding our "truth" to be provisional. After all, just as we have been willing and able to change what we "know" about the earth, about atoms, and about the universe, we have to be willing and able to change what we "know" about God as well.

Truth is a valuable principle, but both science and the Jewish tradition remind us that all truth is provisional. It evolves, grows, and builds on past knowledge. With this overarching understanding of the dynamic and ever-provisional nature of all truth, however, also comes the ability and responsibility to take certain crucial, more specific actions. First, we need to link truth with trust, to connect *emet* with *emunah*. Trust entails more than just honesty and integrity – it also entails both a level of expertise and a recognition of limitations. Our sources of truth need to be trustworthy, and we ourselves need to strive to be trustworthy as well. Second, we need to recognize our blind spots, and create structures to minimize motivated reasoning and rationalized dishonesty. We will never be able to avoid those pitfalls as individuals, but as a society and as a species, we can slowly get better at it. Finally, we need to be willing to move back and forth between theory and practice, between data and interpretation. Most of what comprises our knowledge can be considered "scientific objects" – useful tools and heuristics that may need to be updated in the future, but only after much conversation and reflection.

Both science and Judaism remind us that truth is much more a process than a result, more a striving than an absolute. There's a reason that both religion and science celebrate *truth* rather than *certainty*. As we strive to build a world based on peace, justice, and truth, may we always remember that our "progress" doesn't mean "perfection," and that by aiming to be honest, accurate, and trustworthy, we can get closer to truth.

Reason, History, and Politics: Modern Jewish Thought on Truth*

Leora Batnitzky

Beginning with Philo of Alexandria in the first century, Jews who are also philosophers have had to concern themselves with the question of whether the truths contained in particular Jewish texts and traditions can be reconciled with the purportedly universal truth of philosophical thinking. Historically, there is no one Jewish philosophical answer to this question. And the question is not only a philosophical one, but one intrinsic to the internal workings of the Jewish tradition, including the rabbinic tradition and the biblical one that preceded it. For instance, God's promise to Abraham that his seed would become both a great nation and a blessing to other nations (Gen 12:1–3) suggests that the particular fate of the Jewish people is intimately bound to the fate of all others. This implies that it is not possible to think about the meaning of Jewish particularity as wholly separate from its universal significance. Nevertheless, thinking about truth from within the bounded field of "Jewish philosophy," as opposed to from within strictly intertextual or literary fields, for example, always means considering what constitutes truth from within at least two traditions at once: the (usually) Western philosophical tradition as well as the diverse and at times contradictory

---

* Parts of this essay were previously published as "Moses Mendelssohn and the Three Paths of German Jewish Thought," *German-Jewish Thought Between Religion and Politics: Festschrift in Honor of the Seventieth Birthday of Paul Mendes-Flohr*, ed. Christian Wiese and Martina Urban (Walter de Gruyter: Berlin and Boston, 2012), 31–41.

sources of the Jewish tradition. For this reason, questions about the meaning and nature of Jewish philosophical thinking are implicit in any attempt at such thinking. What does it mean to do philosophy from the point of view of Judaism? Is such philosophy relevant for non-Jews as well as for Jews? A bit more technically, if Jewish philosophical thinking articulates Judaism in a philosophical medium, which has more weight in this effort at translation – Judaism, or philosophy? If the answer is Judaism, how can this still be philosophy, which is usually understood as a universal means to truth? And if the answer is philosophy, how can this still be an authentic portrait of Judaism, which, however one defines it, is constituted by specific texts and traditions, not to speak of a special, if not unique, relationship with God?

In the modern period, many of these questions are not just implicit but explicit in Jewish philosophical thinking. While there are considerable debates about the proper dating and substance of the shift from pre-modern to modern Judaism, this essay defines Jewish modernity in terms of the dissolution of the political agency of pre-modern corporate Jewish communities and the concurrent shift of political agency to the individual Jew who became a citizen of the modern nation-state.[1] A fundamental question for modern Jewish thinkers, in their many varieties, is: what value, or unique truth, might there be to Judaism when Jews no longer have to define themselves as Jews, at least from the perspective of the modern nation-state? Indeed, as Daniel Frank has remarked, as an academic field that emerged only in the nineteenth century, "Jewish philosophy came into being as a disciplinary response of Jewish academics to a particular historical condition, one which threatened the very identity and being of Jewish culture. Jewish philosophy came into being as an attempt to delineate, along standard academic lines, a certain body of literature."[2] So too is "Jewish philosophy," as discussed in what follows, distinctly modern because it is inextricably bound to attempts to provide philosophical *defenses* of Judaism's unique, though not necessarily exclusive, access to truth in this modern political context.

---

1. For an overview, see Jacob Katz, *Tradition and Crisis: Jewish Society at the End of the Middle Ages* (New York, NY: Syracuse University Press, 2000).
2. *History of Jewish Philosophy*, ed. Daniel Frank and Oliver Lehman (New York, NY: Routledge University Press, 1997), 2.

Understood within this framework, the German Jewish philosopher Moses Mendelssohn (1729–1786) is undoubtedly the father of modern Jewish philosophy. Jews and non-Jews alike knew him as the "Socrates of Berlin."[3] But it is important to underscore, however, that despite his fame, Mendelssohn, like all other Jews, had no civil rights, as it was only in 1812 that Jews were declared citizens of the Prussian State. So even though Mendelssohn may have been the "Socrates of Berlin," his physical existence remained precarious. And because the Jewish community was subject to collective punishment for the behavior of individual Jews, Mendelssohn's relation to the non-Jewish world brought implications not just for himself and his family but for the entire Jewish community. Nevertheless, as a contemporary of Thomas Jefferson, Mendelssohn lived and wrote at a time in which philosophers and others were in the process of imagining what a modern nation-state might look like.

In 1769, Mendelssohn was forced to publicly defend his loyalty to Judaism, as well as his reasoning, given his enlightened views of philosophy and religion, as to why he should remain a Jew and not convert to Christianity. Simply put, Mendelssohn's Christian interlocutors could not understand how, given his demonstrated philosophical acumen, Mendelssohn did not recognize the truth of Christianity. While it was the Swiss clergyman John Casper Lavater who delivered this challenge, many Berlin theologians of the Enlightenment were deeply troubled by the fact that Mendelssohn did not seem to be taking steps towards conversion. Mendelssohn's reply to Lavater, his now classic *Jerusalem: Or on Religious Power and Judaism* is among the most eloquent Enlightenment pleas for religious toleration and for the separation of church and state. Mendelssohn argued that Judaism does not conflict with reasoned enlightenment because it is a religion with no dogmas and therefore neither contradicts nor makes any particular claim to philosophical truth.[4] Judaism, instead, centers on legislation that was revealed to and continually reinterpreted by a particular people. As such, for Mendelssohn, Jewish particularity is intrinsic to the meaning of

---

3. For more on Mendelssohn, see Shmuel Feiner, *Moses Mendelssohn: Sage of Modernity* (New Haven, CT: Yale University Press, 2010).
4. Moses Mendelssohn, *Jerusalem: Or on Religious Power and Judaism*, trans. Allan Arkush (Hanover and London: Brandeis University Press, 1983).

Judaism but it does not conflict with either reasoned enlightenment or the possibility of a civil society. Put somewhat differently, Jews could be assured that Judaism was true for them but for non-Jews, or Christians, Judaism's truth posed no threat.

Mendelssohn's arguments about Judaism and truth, to which we will turn in more detail below, did not fare well with subsequent Jewish thinkers and philosophers who accused him of two things: first, of narrowing the bounds of Jewish life only to Jewish law and, second, of offering an argument for Judaism motivated not by internal Jewish concerns and resources but rather by his need to defend Judaism in order to appease non-Jews, a type of argument sometimes referred to as an "apologetic." A particularly harsh indictment of Mendelssohn on these two counts comes from the Hebrew writer and Zionist polemicist Perez Smolenskin (1842–1885), who claimed that Mendelssohn had "doubly ensnared our people by weakening its sense of national unity and insisting on the continued total obligation of the religious laws."[5] From Smolenskin's Zionist point of view, Mendelssohn's reduction of Judaism to a rational religion that did not threaten Christianity or the emerging Prussian state could only have been in the service of an attempt at assimilation to the German nation. As Allan Arkush has argued, Smolenskin's charge against Mendelssohn is both odd and unfair since a careful reading of *Jerusalem* shows that Mendelssohn does acknowledge Jewish peoplehood and is not merely apologetic but also quite subversive in criticizing Christianity as a religion of irrational dogma.[6] Nevertheless, Smolenskin's critique of Mendelssohn does express a common view of him and of German Jewish philosophy more generally: that Mendelssohn marks the beginning of the apologetic and delusional character of German Jewish confidence in a bright future for Jews and Judaism in Germany and in the European diaspora more broadly.

However, it is not only Mendelssohn's critics who fault him for constricting Judaism and for apologetics. The great neo-Kantian philosopher

---

5. Perez Smolenskin, cited in Isaac Barzilay, "Smolenskin's Polemic against Mendelssohn in Historical Perspective," *Proceedings of the American Academy for Jewish Research* 53 (1986): 12.

6. Allan Arkush, "Moses Mendelssohn Street," *Jewish Review of Books* 2 (Summer 2010): 49–50.

Hermann Cohen (1842–1918), Mendelssohn's heir and ultimate defender, charges him with the following:

> Although Mendelssohn unambiguously elucidates the relation of rea-son to religion in general, out of the spirit of the latter's philosophy, he obscures the concept of Judaism by limiting it to a religion of law.... It would appear to be an inner contradiction that Mendelssohn could bring about a new modification of the cultural life of Jewry and of Judaism as well on the basis of the isolation of Judaism under the law... Was Mendelssohn a hypocrite then, who obeyed all these laws with meticulous strictness all his life long and then wanted to burden the Jews with them? Or was he perhaps so ignorant of the world and so politically shortsighted, or even blind, that he did not see how this yoke was becoming lighter from year to year? Or was he perhaps so doctrinaire that he wanted above all to secure the religion of reason, even though Judaism might be slighted by a narrow definition? Or, biased by an enlightened indifference with regard to Judaism, did he believe that he had done enough in bringing out the differences between Judaism and Christianity and in thus bringing Judaism safely under cover?...[7]

Cohen goes on to attempt to vindicate Mendelssohn, by suggesting that once reinterpreted in light of Cohen's own *Religion of Reason*, we can see that Mendelssohn was right or almost right on a number of points, including his basic characterization of Judaism as a religion of reason and his critique of Christianity as a religion of irrational dogma.

In the German context, Jewish philosophical criticisms of Men-delssohn culminated in Franz Rosenzweig's (1886–1929) argument that Mendelssohn epitomized the compartmentalized and divided life that modernity, and especially the modern state, had created for Jews. As Paul Mendes-Flohr explains:

> Rosenzweig was aware that Mendelssohn merely sought to argue that intellectually and spiritually the Jew is preeminently a 'human being' (*Mensch*) and that he can therefore participate qua human being in

---

7. Hermann Cohen, *Religion of Reason out of the Sources of Judaism*, trans. Simon Kaplan (Atlanta, GA: Scholars Press, 1995), 357–58.

enlightened culture unencumbered by any doctrinal or cognitive demands peculiar to Judaism. But here is the rub. According to his own admission, Mendelssohn himself was not 'a unified human being,' as Rosenzweig put it. The Jew and the human being resided in him not as an integrated whole but next to one another (*nebeneinander*) as discrete entities. He was both Jew and a human being, or rather a human being who had attained enlightened culture. It was not surprising that Mendelssohn's contemporaries found him 'incomprehensible.' As Rosenzweig rhetorically asked, How were 'they to grasp that there stood before them not one person but two.'[8]

In rejecting what he regarded as Mendelssohn's bifurcated self, Rosenzweig sought to replace what he claimed was Mendelssohn's "or" with an "and." Again, as Mendes-Flohr describes it: "Since Moses Mendelssohn most Jews have not, in fact, faced an 'and' but an insidious 'or,' observed Rosenzweig – the exciting new world of imagination and the spirit opened by Deutschtum 'or' the seemingly anachronistic and increasingly inaccessible world of Judaism. This insidious 'or' must be replaced by an 'and.'"[9]

Rosenzweig, Cohen, and Smolenskin all argue that Mendelssohn's attempt to balance the truth of Jewish particularity with modern political arrangements ultimately fails because it apologizes for Jews and Judaism by trying to make them conform to external cultural standards and conceptions of truth. As Rosenzweig summed it up: "From Mendelssohn on, our entire people has subjected itself to the torture of this embarrassing questioning; the Jewishness of every individual has squirmed on the needle point of a 'why.'"[10] For the Zionist Smolenskin, the liberal Cohen, and the neo-Orthodox Rosenzweig, it is Mendelssohn's project that must be overcome.

Yet despite the characterizations of Mendelssohn just discussed, the irony may be that Mendelssohn's philosophy of Judaism foreshadowed

---

8. Paul Mendes-Flohr, *German Jews: A Dual Identity* (New Haven, CT: Yale University Press, 1999), 76.

9. Mendes-Flohr, *German Jews*, 86.

10. Franz Rosenzweig, *On Jewish Learning*, ed. Nahum N. Glatzer (New York, NY: Schocken Books, 2002), 78.

and to some extent gave rise to three different and, in many ways, dif-
ficult-to-reconcile paths taken by subsequent modern Jewish philosophers. Indeed, it may not be an exaggeration to suggest that, with the
admittedly significant exceptions of expressly Zionist or Haredi thought,
these three paths represent the dominant approaches and strands of
modern and contemporary Jewish thought. As will be discussed in
greater detail below, I will call these three paths "the rationalist model,"
"the historicist model," and "the political model." Each of these paths, I
will suggest, takes its bearing from Mendelssohn.

To begin to appreciate these three paths of modern Jewish thought
emerging from Mendelssohn, we need to turn in greater detail to the
broad contours of Mendelssohn's *Jerusalem: Or on Religious Power and
Judaism*. The relation between the title and subtitle of Mendelssohn's
book captures its argument. In the first section of the book Mendelssohn
alleges that, by definition, the state concerns power and coercion, while
religion, properly understood, does not. This means that Judaism, or
"Jerusalem," the book's title, is not concerned with power and therefore
does not conflict with the possibility of Jewish integration into the
modern nation-state. Thus, the book's subtitle, "On Religious Power
and Judaism," indicates that Judaism is not to be equated with religious
power. In the second section of the book Mendelssohn asserts that
the Jewish religion is not a matter of belief but rather of behavior. As
Mendelssohn puts it, "Judaism knows of no revealed religion in the sense
in which Christians understand this term. The Israelites possess a divine
legislation – laws, commandments, ordinances, rules of life, instruction
in the will of God as to how they should conduct themselves in order to
attain temporal and eternal felicity."[11] Hence, Mendelssohn concludes,
because Judaism does not demand belief *of any sort*, it by definition does
not conflict with enlightened reason and in fact only complements it.

Within this broad framework, Mendelssohn makes a more specific
claim vis-à-vis Judaism's particularity. Mendelssohn begins with the
assumption that there are timeless philosophical truths, which he calls
eternal truths. He then argues that Judaism doesn't contradict the eternal
truths of reason because Judaism's truth is historical and temporal:

---

11. Moses Mendelssohn, *Jerusalem*, 90.

Judaism boasts no exclusive revelation of eternal truths.... The voice which let itself be heard on Sinai on that great day did not proclaim, "I am the Eternal, your God, the necessary, independent being, omnipotent and omniscient, that recompenses men in a future life according to their deeds." This is the universal religion of mankind, not Judaism... A historical truth, on which this people's legislation was to be founded, as well as laws, was to be revealed here – commandments and ordinances, not eternal religious truths. "I am the Eternal, your God, who made a covenant with your fathers, Abraham, Isaac, and Jacob, and swore to make of their seed a nation of my own."[12]

Philosophically, Mendelssohn's claim that Jewish law demands contemplation and action is in tension with his claim that Jewish law is in essence irrelevant to the pursuit of universal truth and morality. This tension further bears itself out in the subsequent fate of Mendelssohn's philosophy. On the one hand, Mendelssohn provides a very traditional conception of the Jewish obligation to obey Jewish law. As he puts it: "He who is not born into the law need not bind himself to the law; but he who is born into the law must live according to the law; and die according to the law."[13] Yet on the other hand, Mendelssohn provides no philosophical or theological justification for obedience to the law and in fact, by virtue of his own definitions, he *cannot* provide any philosophical or theological justification for Jews to follow the law because he has argued that Jewish law is a temporal, historical truth whose legitimacy neither rests upon philosophical truth nor upon theological belief. Two different paths for thinking about what Jewish philosophy could mean emerge from Mendelssohn's predicament: the first is a reworking of the rationalist path that Mendelssohn seems to have set out to take and the second is the historicist path, which rejects the premises of the rationalist path but also has its roots in Mendelssohn's philosophy.

Let us turn to the rationalist path first, which, despite his criticisms of Mendelssohn, is perhaps represented most fully by Hermann Cohen. The rationalist model is an attempt to consider Judaism within

---

12. Mendelssohn, *Jerusalem*, 97.
13. Mendelssohn, *Jerusalem*, 134.

a strictly philosophical framework. Like Mendelssohn, Cohen sought to defend Judaism's confluence with enlightened reason and politics while also maintaining the necessity of Judaism's continued separation from contemporary political life. Also like Mendelssohn, Cohen made his arguments on the basis of a claim about Judaism's non-political yet legal nature. However, Cohen intensifies two of Mendelssohn's claims. First, whereas Mendelssohn was content to show that Judaism did not contradict reason, Cohen goes further and maintains that Judaism and reason are in an important sense synonymous. As Cohen puts it in *Religion of Reason out of the Sources of Judaism*, "If the unique God were not the creator, being and becoming would be the same; nature itself would be God. This, however, would mean: God is not. For nature is the becoming that needs being as its foundation."[14] For Cohen, not only is there no contradiction between Judaism and universal truth, Judaism and universal truth are one and the same.

Second, whereas Mendelssohn maintains that Judaism and Christianity are complementary, Cohen goes further in contending that Judaism, and only Judaism, preserves pure monotheism for all peoples. Cohen makes an argument for the preservation of Judaism, what he calls "Jewish isolation," in the context of his argument about the significance of Jewish law. Cohen writes:

> the law makes possible that isolation which seems indispensable to the care for, and continuation of, what is, at once, one's own and eternal.
>
> Isolation in the world of culture!... Monotheism is at stake;... With monotheism, the world of culture is at stake... Therefore, isolation is indispensable to Judaism, for its concept as well as for its cultural work.[15]

Reiterating Mendelssohn's argument, Cohen continues that even in its isolation the law is not negative but "a positive force that stimulates, inspires, fortifies, and deepens religious ideas and beliefs."[16] Much of

---

14. Cohen, *Religion of Reason*, 67.
15. Cohen, *Religion of Reason*, 366–67.
16. Cohen, *Religion of Reason*, 367.

German-Jewish philosophy followed Cohen in attempting to correlate the universal truths of Judaism with the universal truths of philosophy. We need but mention Julius Guttmann's seminal 1933 book *Philosophy of Judaism*, which sought to understand Judaism in modern, scientific terms.[17]

A second model of Jewish philosophy, which I will call the historicist model, rejects the rationalist model as a distortion of both Judaism and philosophy. Here I would like to expand two points made by Paul Mendes-Flohr and Alexander Altmann in order to describe and suggest that Rosenzweig, despite his criticisms of Mendelssohn, ought to be understood in terms of what I am calling the historicist model.[18] First, as Mendes-Flohr notes, in the context of Rosenzweig's rejection of an academic career, Rosenzweig's is not a "rejection of history per se: rather he is passionately rejecting the then-prevailing historical scholarship."[19] Second, as Altmann puts it, for Rosenzweig, "Through the eruption of revelation, history receives a clear and definite articulation.... revelation orients our historical perspective by offering an absolute standard of what is truly meaningful in history."[20] To take both of these points a bit further, I would suggest that Rosenzweig's criticism of historical progress and his arguments about revelation are attempts not to deny true meaning to history but rather to define history's true meaning. The true meaning of history begins, for Rosenzweig, with an appreciation of the truth of our historicity, which means not only that truth develops within history but, more deeply, that history itself produces truth. For Rosenzweig, the quest for truth begins and ends not with abstract philosophical reasoning divorced from our particular historical circumstances but rather with an understanding of how history has shaped and continues to shape us.

---

17. Julius Guttmann, *Die Philosophie des Judentums* (München: E. Reinhardt, 1933).

18. Paul Mendes-Flohr, "Rosenzweig and the Crisis of Historicism," and Alexander Altmann, "Franz Rosenzweig on History," in *The Philosophy of Franz Rosenzweig*, ed. Paul Mendes-Flohr (Hanover and London: University of New England Press, 1988).

19. Paul Mendes-Flohr, "Rosenzweig and the Crisis of Historicism," 157.

20. Alexander Altmann, "Franz Rosenzweig on History," 135.

Rosenzweig's historicist model for thinking about Jewish philosophy or philosophy rejects the notion that universal, timeless Platonic truths define either Judaism or philosophy. Against what he maintained was the overly apologetic stance of German Jewish rationalism, Rosenzweig argued that Jewish philosophy must acknowledge both its strengths and its inherent limitations. Rosenzweig writes:

> No one became a Jewish thinker within the private domain of Judaism. Thinking was not thinking about Judaism (which was simply taken for granted, and was more of an existence than an 'ism'); it was thinking within Judaism, learning – ultimately ornamental, rather than fundamental, thinking. Anyone who was to think about Judaism, somehow had to be drawn to the border of Judaism, if not psychologically then intellectually. His thinking was thus determined by the power that had brought him to the border and the horizon of his gaze was defined by the degree to which he had been carried to, near, or across it.
>
> Apologetics is the legitimate strength of this thinking, but also an inherent danger.[21]

For Rosenzweig, the equation of thinking about and thinking within Judaism is a troubling category error with grave practical consequences. Although Rosenzweig was deeply indebted to Cohen's thought, he maintains nonetheless that Cohen's conflation of Judaism and philosophy was the culmination of an overly rationalized approach to Judaism that ultimately deprived Judaism and Jewish life of vitality. Rosenzweig contends that the crisis of modernity for Judaism is the loss of a particularly Jewish language or, in other words, the replacement of thinking within Judaism by thinking about it. Rosenzweig's efforts at adult education by way of his famous Frankfurt *Lehrhaus*, from 1920 until his death in 1929, were motivated by the desire to establish an institution in which a particularly Jewish language for modern Jews could develop.

---

21. "Apologetisches Denken," originally published in *Der Jude*, Jahrgang VII (1923): 457–64. Translated as "Apologetic Thinking" in *The Jew: Essays from Buber's Journal Der Jude*, ed. Arthur A. Cohen, trans. Joachim Neugroschel (Tuscaloosa: The University of Alabama Press, 1980), 262–72; cited at 267.

While he departs from Mendelssohn in a number of respects, and while, as we saw above, Rosenzweig clearly sees Mendelssohn's project as that which must be overcome, the seeds for his historicist position are also found in Mendelssohn. Once again, in *Jerusalem* Mendelssohn claims that Judaism concerns itself not with eternal truths but with historical, temporal ones. Nevertheless, for Mendelssohn, history is itself an important source of truth. Mendelssohn's account of miracles is particularly significant for appreciating this: "for miracles can only verify testimonies, support authorities, and confirm the credibility of witnesses and those who transmit tradition."[22] For Mendelssohn, the importance of a miracle such as, for instance, the parting of the Red Sea in the Book of Exodus has less to do with the reconcilability or irreconcilability of the Bible and modern science and more to do with the trust that those living in the present ascribe to their participation in the Jewish tradition by the retelling and reinterpretation of the story of this miracle. Rosenzweig picks up on this aspect of Mendelssohn's argument and presents it at the pivotal moment in his *Star of Redemption*. Rosenzweig seeks not to argue for the truth of miracles, but rather for the *possibility* of the truth of miracles. This possibility, for Rosenzweig, rests upon the historical testimony of miracles. In Rosenzweig's words: "the most cogent proof of the miracle is the appeal to the martyrs, in the first instance of those martyrs who had to corroborate the testimony of their eyes with their martyrdom, but beyond this also to the later martyrs. With their blood, these validated the steadfastness of their belief in the credibility of those who had transmitted the miracle to them, that is, in the last analysis, of the eyewitness... The belief in miracles, and not just the belief in decorative miracles, but that in the central miracle of revelation, is to this extent a completely historical belief."[23] Like Mendelssohn, Rosenzweig shifts away from thinking about truth in terms of the scientific plausibility of miracles to thinking about how the stories we tell about ourselves constitute us in the present by connecting us to the past. Rosenzweig goes further than Mendelssohn in arguing that recognizing the significance of historical truth requires us to rethink

---

22. Mendelssohn, *Jerusalem*, 99.
23. Franz Rosenzweig, *The Star of Redemption*, trans. William W. Hallo (New York, NY: University of Notre Dame Press, 1985), 97.

our conceptions of truth altogether: "From those most unimportant truths, of the type two times two is four, on which people readily agree, without any other cost than a little brain grease . . . the path leads over the truths which have cost man something, on towards those which he can verify not otherwise than with the sacrifice of life, and finally to those whose truth can be verified only upon generations of risked lives."[24]

A third path of Jewish philosophy emerges from the historicist model: the political model. The impetus for thinking about the meaning of Jewish philosophy from the perspective of political philosophy emerges from the historical insight that liberal modernity breaks with the pre-modern Jewish past. Jewish modernity represents the advent of the modern nation-state and the subsequent shifting of the locus of political power from the corporate Jewish community to the individual Jew. The political model suggests that the terms "Judaism" and "philosophy" are only meaningful within particular political contexts. Leo Strauss (1899–1973) represents this third model when he argues that: "Liberal democracy had originally defined itself in the theologico-political treatises as the opposite, less of the more or less enlightened despotism of the seventeenth and eighteenth centuries, than of 'the kingdom of darkness,' i.e., of medieval society. According to liberal democracy, the bond of society is universal human morality, whereas religion (positive religion) is a private affair."[25] From Strauss's perspective, the impetus for articulating something called "Jewish philosophy" stems from the apologetic attempt to define Judaism in particularly Protestant terms, that is, as a confession of belief and/or truth. But the political model moves beyond, or at least attempts to move beyond, the historicist model by reconsidering the meanings of both Judaism and philosophy apart from their modern instantiations. For Strauss in particular, the political model allows us to rethink what are in fact permanent, and not just historical, human problems pertaining to definitions of the good life, justice, and wisdom. This means studying pre-modern Jewish philosophers, such

---

24. "Das neue Denken" in *Zweistromland. Kleinere Schriften zu Glauben und Denken*, in *Franz Rosenzweig: Der Mensch und sein Werk: Gesammelte Schriften*, vol. 3 (Boston and The Hague: Martinus Nijhoff, 1974–1984), 159.
25. Leo Strauss, *Spinoza's Critique of Religion* (Chicago, IL: University of Chicago Press, 1965), 3.

as Maimonides and Judah Halevi, not in order to return to the past but rather to help us in the present rethink our often-unstated assumptions about both "Judaism" and "philosophy."

Notably, in 1925, Strauss began his post-graduate job in Berlin working for the Academy of the Science of Judaism editing the jubilee edition of Mendelssohn's work. While Strauss, like Cohen and Rosenzweig, did not see Mendelssohn as a worthy predecessor, we can nonetheless understand Strauss's turn to political philosophy on the basis of Mendelssohn's own arguments. Rather than reflecting an incomplete philosophical program, or even an incomplete appreciation of the meaning of our historicity, the arguments of Mendelssohn's *Jerusalem* may be best understood as reflecting the tension between the modern splitting of theology from politics and the theological-political context that defined pre-modern Judaism. Mendelssohn's strained attempt to defend the necessity and centrality of Jewish law for the Jewish people while simultaneously denying that this law has any political or philosophical implications embodies precisely this tension and tells us as much about the demands of liberal modernity as about "Judaism" and "philosophy." The tensions in Mendelssohn's arguments in *Jerusalem* may well reflect the fact that, in Strauss's words, "Finite, relative problems can be solved; infinite, absolute problems cannot be solved. In other words, human beings will never create a society which is free from contradictions."[26] Whether Mendelssohn was aware of these tensions and, if so, what to make of this, likely long will remain persistent questions in the study of Mendelssohn. Still, what we see here is that Strauss's worry about, yet ultimate commitment to, liberal democracy in the face of any other alternative may be understood as continuous with Mendelssohn's own, albeit more hopeful, project.

As we have seen, there are multiple ways in which truth is conceived within the bounds of Jewish philosophy. Frank's important historical claim that "Jewish philosophy came into being as an attempt to delineate, along standard academic lines, a certain body of literature" is true for the nineteenth-century emergence of an academic field whose goal was to establish "Jewish philosophy" as a wholly independent field of study.

---

26. Strauss, *Spinoza's Critique of Religion*, 6.

But we have also seen that, today, understanding the thinkers who may fall into this category requires the crossing of disciplinary boundaries – between Judaism and philosophy, philosophy and history, and history and politics. These crossings do not lead to one conception of truth but to several, through which Jewish philosophers grapple with the many dimensions of modern Jewish life.

Section 5

Eilu ve'eilu:
Pluralism and Truth

In Our Time: Jesuits, Jews, and "Nones" in *Hevruta*

MARK S. DIAMOND

1 In the days to come,
The mountain of the house of Adonai shall stand
Firm above the mountains;
And it shall tower above the hills.
The peoples shall gaze on it with joy,

2 And many nations shall go and say:
"Come, let us go up to the mountain of Adonai,
To the House of Jacob's God;
That God may instruct us in divine ways,
And that we may walk in divine paths."
For instruction shall come forth from Zion,
The word of Adonai from Jerusalem.

3 Thus God will judge among the many peoples,
And arbitrate for the multitude of nations, however distant;
And they shall beat their swords into plowshares
And their spears into pruning hooks.
Nation shall not lift up sword against nation;
They shall never again know war;

4 But everyone shall sit under their own grapevines or fig trees
With no one to disturb them.
For it was Adonai of the heavenly hosts who spoke.

5 Though all the peoples walk, each in the names of its gods,
We will walk in the name of Adonai our God
Forever and ever. (Micah 4:1–5)[1]

In this oft-cited text, the prophet dreams of a world of peoples and nations living in peace, happiness, and harmony. Micah envisions pilgrims from across the globe joyfully flocking to God's Temple on the Mount to learn Torah and to receive divine justice. The end of the passage, however, with its exclusivist[2] vision of Judah and Jerusalem, seems to undermine this universalistic picture.[3] Though modern readers may be tempted to view Micah as a "proto-religious inclusivist,"[4] Prof. Daniel Smith Christopher cautions against reading too much universalism into this intriguing text:

Does this [Micah 4:5] presume some kind of affirmation of peoples walking in the name of their gods? If so, this would be unprecedented (contra Deut 18:20, 22), and it seems unlikely. More likely, it is an identification of the current state of the world and a further

---

1. Author's translation of Micah 4:1–5, based on *Tanakh: The Holy Scriptures: The New JPS Translation According to the Traditional Hebrew Text* (Philadelphia, PA: The Jewish Publication Society, 1988), 1046–47.
2. "The term exclusivism is generally used to denote a denial of the salvific function of other religions, or of their efficacy in attaining the highest religious goal...Exclusivism may be regarded as the default religious position, insofar as most religions present themselves as the ultimate truth or as the sole repository of truth, thus ruling out the presence of relevant truth in other religions." Catherine Cornille, *Meaning and Method in Comparative Theology* (Chichester, West Sussex: Wiley Blackwell, 2020), 45.
3. See, for example, Juan I. Alfaro, *Justice and Loyalty: A Commentary on the Book of Micah* (Grand Rapids, MI: Wm. B. Eerdmans Publishing Co., 1989), 48: "The contents of this verse are difficult to reconcile with 4:2, except when seen as a response of Micah's adversaries who reject his universal outlook and insist on their own exclusivist vision of Judah. They do not think of a conversion of pagans or an integration of nations in the Lord; they affirm their experience of the present and make it final and definitive. They effectively deny Micah's hope for the future."
4. "The inclusivist approach to the question of religious truth recognizes the possible presence of truth in other religions insofar as it may be reconciled with the truth of one's own religion...This is a fairly common and coherent religious position." Cornille, *Meaning and Method*, 54.

reassurance of God's presence as something that leads to the peace spoken of in the passage as a whole. On the other hand, Micah 4:3 speaks of negotiations between nations and says nothing of a mass "conversion" to the ways of God. That these other nations continue to walk in their own ways but not threaten Israel is a hopeful image.[5]

Micah's hopeful image comes to mind when I reflect upon my teaching at Loyola Marymount University (LMU), a leading Catholic university in Los Angeles. Throughout my career, I have found the Catholic community to be especially receptive to my needs and concerns as a rabbi, from the empathetic spiritual care offered to Jewish patients and families at Catholic hospitals to the high standards of theological and pastoral education for Catholic clergy which parallel modern educational standards for Jewish clergy. When I began teaching at LMU, however, I was faced with a new set of personal and professional questions. I wondered if and how the universalistic portion of Micah's vision would be operative for a Jew who espouses one time-honored view of religious truth in the company of Catholic educators and students with a different age-old view of religious truth, learning together at a Jesuit institution, which is guided by its own distinct concept of religious truth.

In my faculty orientation at LMU, I was reassured when I read the university's pluralistic[6] mission statement, which calls for "the encouragement of learning, the education of the whole person, and the service of faith and the promotion of justice."[7] LMU's undergraduate, graduate, and professional programs reflect the universal outlook and religious pluralism that are hallmarks of a Jesuit higher education. The university's commitment to the service of faith

> …honors the reality of religious pluralism on our campus and embraces inter-faith dialogue in formal and informal contexts. The

---

5. Daniel L. Smith-Christopher, *Micah: A Commentary* (Louisville, KY: Westminster John Knox Press, 2015), 138.

6. "The pluralist approach to questions of religious epistemology is based on the premise of the equivalence of all religions in matters of truth … The attitude of religious pluralism has evolved largely as a result of developments in religious studies and in the understanding of other religions." Cornille, *Meaning and Method*, 61.

7. *Our Mission*, LMU|LA, Loyola Marymount University, 2015, 1.

desired outcome of such encounters moves us beyond tolerance to mutual respect and understanding, deepens appreciation of one's own faith, and creates opportunities for engaging others who share a longing for meaningful lives.[8]

I have served as a lecturer and senior lecturer in Jewish Studies at LMU since 2016. My invitation to join the faculty came with a directive to develop and teach *Interreligious Experience and Engagement*, an upper-level core curriculum course for undergraduate students. The course syllabus reflects both my longstanding commitment to interfaith dialogue and LMU's requirements for a curriculum that integrates faith and reason and carries a "flag" for engaged learning. With a pedagogic focus on the Abrahamic faith traditions, students study the key beliefs and practices of Judaism, Christianity, and Islam, the formative texts of interfaith relations, and models of interfaith dialogue. Class visits to a synagogue, church, and mosque deepen students' exploration of the Abrahamic faith traditions while guest presenters share insights concerning interfaith dialogues on theological understanding and social justice. Assignments include research papers on interfaith milestones and controversies, reflections on interfaith relations in the media, and original interfaith engagement projects designed and presented by students themselves.

Greater Los Angeles offers students an ideal living laboratory of interfaith and intergroup relations. Los Angeles is one of the most diverse global cities in the world, a colorful tapestry of communities of faith, ethnicity, language, and national origin. Fifty-nine percent of Angelenos reside in homes in which a language other than English is spoken; 36.9 percent of the population is foreign-born.[9] In 1999, Los Angeles was already described as the most religiously diverse city in the world: "[m]ore than 600 separate faith communities have established religious centers in Los Angeles neighborhoods."[10] While thirty-two

---

8. *Our Mission*, LMU|LA, Loyola Marymount University, 4.

9. U.S. Census Bureau, 2017 American Community Survey (ACS) 1-year census, Censusreporter.org, accessed April 30, 2019, https://censusreporter.org/profiles/16000US0644000–los-angeles-ca/.

10. John Orr, "Religion and Multiethnicity in Los Angeles," Center for Religion and Civic Culture (Los Angeles: University of Southern California, 1999).

percent of the region's adults are Roman Catholic, greater L.A. has large populations of evangelical Protestants, mainline Protestants, historically Black Protestants, Jews, Muslims, Buddhists, as well as adherents of other faith traditions.[11] For their Interfaith Field Experience assignment, students select a religious site to visit outside class and write an essay detailing their encounter with an unfamiliar Western or Eastern religious tradition. The Interfaith Field Experience deepens students' appreciation of the multi-layered religious diversity of the community beyond their campus.

The Loyola Marymount University students who enroll in my interreligious classes come from diverse religious, cultural, and ethnic backgrounds. Their academic majors span the full range of educational disciplines – liberal studies, English, journalism, psychology, economics, urban studies, political science, international relations, marketing, communications studies, biology, health sciences, art history, recording arts, studio arts, music, dance, mechanical and civil engineering, computer science, finance, business, entrepreneurship, animation, screenwriting, and film and television production. My U.S. students come not only from California but from all across the country, and my international students hail from the four corners of the globe, including Mexico, China, Japan, Myanmar, Indonesia, Kuwait, Saudi Arabia, Poland, Ukraine, Croatia, and Israel.

When I ask my students what faith tradition, if any, they were raised in, their responses include Catholic, Protestant, Orthodox Christian, Jewish, Muslim, Buddhist, Shinto, and Hindu. When I inquire about their current religious identity, their answers place many of them into the functional category known as religious "nones," individuals without a particular faith affiliation. I remind students that I am a rabbi who teaches at a Catholic university and that I view the world through a religious lens. I explain to them that when I was their age, "nun" was a three-letter word for a Catholic woman who wore a habit and devoted her life to Jesus Christ. Today "none" is a four-letter word that encompasses the broad range of respondents who describe themselves as atheists or agnostics,

11. Pew Research Center, "Religious Landscape Study: Religious Composition of Adults in the Los Angeles metro area." https://www.pewforum.org/religious -landscape-study/metro-area/los-angeles-metro-area/.

or those who select "nothing in particular" when asked about their religious affiliation in demographic surveys. Michael Lipka of the Pew Research Center explains this growing phenomenon in the context of Pew's 2014 *Religious Landscape Study*:

> Religiously unaffiliated people have been growing as a share of all Americans for some time.... Religious "nones"... now make up roughly 23% of the U.S. adult population. This is a stark increase from 2007, the last time a similar Pew Research study was conducted, when 16% of Americans were "nones"... Overall, religiously unaffiliated people are more concentrated among young adults than other age groups – 35% of Millennials (those born 1981–1996) are "nones." In addition, the unaffiliated as a whole are getting even younger. The median age of unaffiliated adults is now 36, down from 38 in 2007 and significantly younger than the overall median age of U.S. adults in 2014. (46)[12]

My classes at LMU are filled with Catholic nones, Protestant nones, and Jewish nones – young men and women who were raised in a Christian or Jewish faith tradition but no longer identify with that religious affiliation or any other religion. We do ourselves a disservice, however, when we dismiss millennial and Generation Z nones as uninterested in religion and unworthy of our time and resources. Many of my student nones are searching for a spiritual identity, and a course in interfaith relations presents a fine opportunity to further their quest. It also presents the instructor with a welcome opportunity to explore with students one of the central questions of the course. Mindful of Abraham Joshua Heschel's admonition that "the first and most important prerequisite of interfaith is faith,"[13] we discuss and debate what seat, if any, religious nones have at the table of interfaith dialogue. What will interfaith relations look like in a world of religious nones? What ultimate purpose will be served by interreligious dialogue if participants are ill-equipped to

---

12. Michael Lipka, "A Closer Look at America's Rapidly Growing Religious 'Nones,'" Pew Research Center, May 13, 2015. https://www.pewresearch.org/fact-tank/2015/05/13/a-closer-look-at-americas-rapidly-growing-religious-nones/.
13. Abraham Joshua Heschel, "No Religion Is an Island," *Union Seminary Quarterly Review* 21, no. 2 (Jan. 1966): 123.

share their respective religious truths? Traditional models of interfaith dialogue and cooperation may need an upgrade or even an overhaul in the wake of demographic trends in religious identity.

The interfaith relations courses I teach at LMU meet once a week for three hours per session,[14] a format that affords students the opportunity to engage in class visits to houses of worship within the time constraints created by LMU class schedules and the infamous Los Angeles traffic. However, this presents the considerable challenge of preparing a lengthy lesson plan that is pedagogically sound and retains students' interest. One methodology that seems to work well is the time-honored *hevruta* method of textual analysis. In many classes, students break into cohorts of three for intensive study of primary sources, including the Hebrew Bible, the New Testament, the Qur'an, rabbinic literature, and documents of interfaith relations. Few of my students are familiar with *hevruta* learning, and I appreciate the opportunity to help them wrestle with difficult texts as they learn with and from one another.

The notion of a rabbi teaching at a Catholic university would be inconceivable were it not for *Nostra Aetate* ("In Our Time"), the seminal declaration on interfaith relations issued by Pope Paul VI at the Second Vatican Council in 1965. *Nostra Aetate* marked a radical departure from traditional Catholic supersessionist doctrines and constructs of religious truth. In a Copernican revolution in interfaith dialogue, *Nostra Aetate* proclaims:

> The Church...urges its sons and daughters to enter with prudence and charity into discussion and collaboration with members of other religions. Let Christians, while witnessing to their own faith and way of life, acknowledge, preserve and encourage the spiritual and moral truths found among non-Christians, together with their social life and culture...Since Christians and Jews have such a common spiritual heritage, this sacred council wishes to encourage

---

14. Beginning in 2021, the course meets twice a week for ninety minutes per session. This was one of the changes I made in response to the COVID pandemic and the consequent shift from in-person to virtual and hybrid learning. In 2022, I look forward to returning to in-person site visits rather than virtual tours of sacred spaces.

and further mutual understanding and appreciation. This can be achieved, especially, by way of biblical and theological enquiry and through friendly discussions.[15]

Nostra Aetate not only opened the door to Catholic-Jewish interfaith dialogue; it laid the groundwork for nearly all subsequent interfaith engagement between the scholars, clergy, and laity of the world's principal religious communities.[16] The declaration boldly transformed Catholic theology from a position of religious exclusivism to one of religious inclusivism, acknowledging that there is truth in faith traditions other than Christianity. *Nostra Aetate*, "In Our Time," presaged joint Catholic-Jewish theological enquiry and led to the introduction of Jewish Studies programs and interfaith dialogues on Catholic university campuses.[17]

In one assignment, my students learn the story of my Orthodox Jewish grandfather who admonished my parents to prevent me from joining a high school trip to Mexico, lest I be surreptitiously baptized with holy water in a Mexican church or cathedral and become a "goy."

---

15. Austin Flannery, ed., "Nostra Aetate: Declaration on the Relation of the Church to Non-Christian Religions," *Vatican Council II – The Basic Sixteen Documents, Constitutions, Decrees, Declarations – A Completely Revised Translation in Inclusive Language* (Collegeville, MN: Liturgical Press, 2014), 2, 3.

16. See Appendix.

17. It is critically important to understand and appreciate both the milestones and controversies that have marked the path of interfaith relations since 1965. The historic rapprochement in Catholic-Jewish relations since Nostra Aetate has seen serious obstacles along the way – the establishment of a Carmelite convent on the grounds of Auschwitz in 1984 and the lengthy delay until its dismantling by the authority of Pope John Paul II in 1993; the 1998 canonization of Edith Stein/ Teresa Benedicta of the Cross, born into an observant Jewish family and murdered at Auschwitz; the long-proposed canonization of Pope Pius XII despite his controversial role in the Holocaust; the release of Mel Gibson's contentious film *The Passion of the Christ* in 2004; Pope Benedict XVI's reinstatement of Holocaust-denier Bishop Richard Williamson in 2009; among others. The post-Nostra Aetate history of Catholic-Jewish relations demonstrates that sustained progress in interfaith dialogue is an uneven road marked by bumps and barriers, as befits all complex, evolving relationships. The challenge is how to build and nurture interreligious partnerships that enable participants to overcome setbacks and controversies with wisdom and *sekhel* (common sense).

Ironically, my trip to Mexico – and two subsequent visits – played a key role in my later decision to become a rabbi. Those student trips at a young age also fueled my personal and professional interest in inter-faith relations. In his time, my *zeida* (grandfather) left Kiev to escape persecution at the hands of Christians who were taught that Jews were Christ-killers. In his time, my grandfather felt the sting of antisemitism in his new home in Chicago and warned his children not to venture too close to Catholic churches and parochial schools lest they be assaulted by their Christian peers. In our time, his grandson works closely with Catholic judicatory leaders and clergy to plan interfaith services and projects, including a multi-faith visit to the Vatican and Israel. In our time, his grandson enjoys collegial relations with administrators and faculty members of a Jesuit university where he is warmly welcomed and where courses in Jewish Studies are valued and appreciated.

One of the highlights of the LMU Jewish Studies program is *Literature and Faith in the Holy Land*, an accredited student seminar in Israel. In May 2016, and again in May–June 2019, I joined Jewish Studies chair Professor Holli Levitsky and the Right Reverend Alexei Smith[18] as course instructors for a diverse group of LMU undergraduate and gradu-ate students. The curriculum includes classes on Israeli prose and poetry, visits to Christian, Jewish and Muslim historic sites, and presentations by educators, faith leaders, journalists, and artists, among others. We float in the Dead Sea, kayak down the Jordan River, and ride camels in the Negev Desert. Students are amused when I share a camel ride with my friend Fr. Alexei, leading to good-natured jokes that open with the line, "A rabbi, a priest and a camel walk into a bar together."

The central theme of the seminar is encountering the other, and the students soon learn that the other isn't always eager to encounter us. One morning during the 2016 trip, we toured Jerusalem's Temple Mount, where heavily armed security, video surveillance cameras, and eavesdropping guards are a stark contrast to Micah's serene vision of every person sitting peacefully under grapevines and fig trees. A guard

---

18. Fr. Alexei is the pastor of St. Andrew Russian Greek Catholic Church in El Segundo, CA, and serves as Ecumenical and Interreligious Officer of the Arch-diocese of Los Angeles.

from the Palestinian Waqf disturbed our peaceful and respectful tour by berating the Israeli guide for referring to the area as the Temple Mount. This is Al-Aqsa, he said, and you have offended us by saying there was a temple here. There never was a Jewish presence on this site, he admonished us.

At that moment, I thought of Micah in his universalistic mode and imagined him weeping in solidarity alongside us. After we descended the mount, the guide and course instructors corrected this mistruth. Shortly thereafter, I imagined the prophet crying again when two LMU Jewish students reported an encounter with an Orthodox Jewish shopkeeper in the Jewish quarter of Jerusalem's Old City. When they explained to her that they were part of a multi-faith, multi-cultural cohort from a Catholic university, she berated them for traveling with such a diverse group. They should only visit Israel with their fellow Jews, she said, and not waste their time learning about other religious faiths. Why were they not married already and lighting Shabbos candles for their husbands and children, she inquired.

Distressing as these episodes were for seminar participants, they were valuable teaching moments. LMU students witness firsthand the diverse and often conflicting narratives held by Israel's Christians, Jews, Muslims, Bahá'ís, and Druze, to name only some of the religious communities in the land. By the end of the trip, they understand and appreciate the mantra we recite from day one in response to almost every question: "It's complicated."

It's complicated teaching and experiencing interfaith relations on a student seminar in Israel. So too on a Jesuit university campus in Los Angeles. Several incidents highlight both the lighter and the more serious aspects of my work at LMU. Each semester, I allocate time during the first class of *Interreligious Experience and Engagement* to advise students what the course is and what it is not. The course is not a Sunday school class designed to reinforce their religious faith, I tell them, nor is it my intention to convert them to the Jewish faith. Nevertheless, to date, I have had two young Catholic women come to my office the very next week asking for advice on how to convert to Judaism. Notwithstanding the fact that they paid scant attention to my earlier admonition, I referred them to off-campus rabbinic colleagues who might be able to assist them in their quest. One can only hope and pray that the Jesuit brothers and

Marymount sisters do not censure this rabbi for leading students astray in matters of faith.

Professors and students of theology at Catholic universities are quite familiar with the writings of Abraham Joshua Heschel. I lecture about Heschel's life and work in the context of his role as a champion of interfaith dialogues of social justice and as an early proponent of Catholic-Jewish dialogue. One of Heschel's citations is a query to Catholic theologian Gustave Weigel, "Would it really be *ad majorem Dei gloriam* to have a world without Jews?"[19] I ask my students if they have seen the Latin words *ad majorem Dei gloriam* ("for the greater glory of God") before. Most have not, which is troubling on a Catholic university campus whose Jesuit motto is precisely this Latin phrase that can be found on the diplomas of LMU graduates.[20] I encourage students to call home to inform their parents that a rabbi taught them the four words of Latin that are the foundation of their Jesuit higher education!

In recent years I have witnessed – both on and off campus – an intense curiosity about Jews and Judaism that is at once charming and somewhat disarming. Wearing a kippah at a Catholic university engenders curious comments and questions. On several occasions, total strangers have approached me on campus and proudly shared the results of their DNA tests. "I'm sixteen percent Jewish," a young man exclaimed during a chance encounter in the elevator. For a brief moment, I considered answering, "sixteen percent mazal tov," but instead responded how nice it was for him to discover that he had Jewish ancestry. Upon serious reflection, these and similar affirmations of philo-Semitism are a welcome counterpoint to the prevalent antisemitism of the past, now current once again in many academic and communal settings.

My LMU teaching experience convinces me that educators play a vital role in responding to the rising tide of antisemitism, Islamophobia, and other noxious manifestations of hatred and intolerance in our midst. Teachers at all levels have a special stake in the struggle to build bridges

---

19. Heschel, "No Religion," 129.

20. In 2019, Loyola Marymount University developed a new visual identity for the university that replaced the traditional LMU logo. The new university seal, shorn of its Latin motto, now appears on student diplomas. The author laments this change.

of compassion and understanding for "the other." Eboo Patel writes that "the theology of the bridge, the practice of the bridge, the faith formation of the bridge is going to be key not only to civic life in the twenty-first century but to maintaining faith identity."[21]

Patel's message has special import on the campus of Loyola Marymount University. The diverse student body of LMU includes many Dreamers, young people who came to this country as undocumented children brought by their parents across the U.S./Mexico border. They listen with special concern when politicians pledge to erect higher walls and implement more restrictive policies designed to ostracize and exclude others. They witness with growing alarm and special sensitivity the extreme polarization of American society, marked by fearmongering, name-calling, and xenophobic rhetoric.

One of the ongoing assignments for students in my LMU courses is to research and write about interfaith relations in the media. With the rising tide of religious extremism across the globe, and the divisive political rhetoric in this country and elsewhere, there is no dearth of stories about interfaith relations. Indeed, as I tell students, "God, Allah, Jesus, Moses, and Mohammed are having a banner season." Sadly, the majority of prominent media reports are negative ones – ISIS terrorists killing Christians, Yazidis, and Hindus; politicians stoking firestorms of homophobia and Islamophobia; purveyors of hate fomenting virulent antisemitism throughout Europe and the United States; yeshiva students in Jerusalem spitting on Christian priests; the list goes on and on.

During a two-week period in the spring 2019 semester, my students and I studied and reflected upon horrific acts of violence against houses of worship of each of the Abrahamic faith traditions – mosques in Christchurch, New Zealand; churches in Colombo, Sri Lanka; the Chabad synagogue center in Poway, California. In his book *Not in God's Name*, Rabbi Lord Jonathan Sacks surveys the ongoing tragedy of religious violence in the world today and writes:

> When religion turns men into murderers, God weeps... It is not our task to conquer or convert the world or enforce uniformity of belief.

---

21. Eboo Patel, "Acts of Faith: Interfaith Leadership in a Time of Religious Crisis," *Virginia Seminary Journal* (Fall, 2009): 40.

It is our task to be a blessing to the world. The use of religion for political ends is not righteousness but idolatry... To invoke God to justify violence against the innocent is not an act of sanctity but of sacrilege. It is a kind of blasphemy. It is to take God's name in vain.[22]

The relationship of religion and violence is a compelling and timely theme in my LMU classes. It raises fundamental questions of how competing doctrines of religious inclusivism and exclusivism shape beliefs and practices in diverse faith communities. Proponents of interfaith dialogue ought to acknowledge that pluralism remains a minority viewpoint of faithful believers in many regions across the globe. Drew Christiansen of Georgetown University offered this analysis of the state of religious pluralism in a reflection on the Second Vatican Council and Nostra Aetate:

> The closing day of the four-day conference at Georgetown University celebrating the close of the Second Vatican Council was devoted to the council's opening to other faiths, especially Judaism and Islam. It was also a day for tough questions and cautionary observations from interfaith interlocutors. Abdulaziz Sachedina, professor of Islamic Studies at George Mason University and a veteran of the Muslim-Catholic dialogue, declared that "Vatican II deserves to be emulated by other exclusionary faith communities." Still, he observed that "religious communities have not come to terms with the demand that their own traditions should be regarded as one among many..." He added, "I can still hear clear and loud anti-pluralist sentiments coming from almost all monotheistic traditions in the (Middle East) region..."[23]

If someone holds dearly to a particular religious faith and affirms its truth in answering ultimate questions, why should he or she engage in interfaith dialogue? Why should that individual not seek to convert others to his or her own beliefs and practices?

---

22. Jonathan Sacks, *Not in God's Name* (New York, NY: Schocken Books, 2015), 3, 5.

23. Drew Christiansen, S.J., "Tough Questions for the Future of Interfaith Dialogue," *America: The Jesuit Review* (May 25, 2015). https://www.americamagazine.org/content/all-things/tough-questions-future-interfaith-dialogue.

I encourage my students to wrestle with these key questions of faith and truth. I teach them that interreligious engagement is most efficacious when participants come to the dialogue with open minds and hearts. This quest is not well suited to those who wear "religious blinders" and are unwilling to be self-critical about their own faith traditions. Nor is it a good fit for individuals who harbor deep suspicion of and antipathy toward "the other" and cannot comprehend or tolerate another religious faith whose beliefs and practices are built on a different set of truth propositions.

How, then, should we respond to religious exclusivists who believe that interfaith dialogue is antithetical to their faith? Rabbi Heschel answered this query more than five decades ago:

> Does not the all-inclusiveness of God contradict the exclusiveness of any particular religion? The prospect of all men embracing one form of religion remains an eschatological hope. What about here and now? Is it not blasphemous to say: I alone have all the truth and the grace, and all those who differ live in darkness, and are abandoned by the grace of God?[24]

It is understandable that individuals who affirm exclusivist views of religious truth often feel compelled to share their faith with friends, neighbors, and even total strangers who "live in darkness and are abandoned by the grace of God." They may well believe that interreligious dialogue presents an enticing opportunity to convert their interlocutors. Rabbi Heschel was prescient in decrying interfaith dialogue as a subterfuge for proselytizing:

> Dialogue must not degenerate into a dispute, into an effort on the part of each to get the upper hand … Thus any conversation between Christian and Jew in which abandonment of the other partner's faith is a silent hope must be regarded as offensive to one's religious and human dignity.[25]

Proselytizing has no sanction in programs of interreligious dialogue. My own interfaith work in the past two decades includes multi-year

---

24. Heschel, "No Religion," 126.
25. Heschel, "No Religion," 126.

dialogue projects with evangelical Christians and Latter-day Saints, two faith communities that invest significant resources to train and dispatch missionaries around the world. From the outset, interreligious dialogue participants recognize and appreciate the sensitivity of this issue for their Jewish dialogue partners. At no time have I witnessed any attempts to proselytize others in these programs, nor am I aware of anyone who has abandoned his or her faith as a consequence of participation in these interreligious encounters. Rather, I find that immersion in interfaith dialogue strengthens my Jewish identity, and many others, similarly, also discover that interfaith experiences deepen their own religious commitments.

A choice fruit of interreligious dialogue is the quest to uncover new truths about one's own faith and dispel misconceptions about the faith of others. While some of my students have grown up in religiously diverse population centers and are familiar with their friends and neighbors' faith traditions, many have never been inside a synagogue, and very few have ever visited an Eastern Catholic church or a mosque. These tours of sacred spaces, coupled with in-class studies of the three Abrahamic faiths, shatter common fallacies about the tenets and rituals of Islam, Judaism, and Christianity, and their respective denominations.

Interreligious engagement is an invaluable tool of inquiry in a milieu of growing religious diversity. It helps us appreciate how much our circles of faith have to glean from other religious practitioners. As a co-founder of the *Jewish–Latter-day Saint Academic Dialogue*, I have come to admire several aspects of Latter-day Saint communal practice, including the religious imperative of volunteerism and the mandate to tithe one's income in support of the church. I have also learned that church elders examined traditional norms of Jewish Shabbat observance as part of their campaign to enhance Sunday Sabbath practices among Latter-day Saints. This dual "holy envy"[26] underscores the inclusivist view that no single religion is the sole repository of truth in theology or praxis.

There is little an instructor treasures more than the opportunity to witness a student's "aha moment" of discovery and inspiration inside or

---

26. The term "holy envy" is credited to Krister Stendahl, who served as dean of the Divinity School at Harvard University and later as Presiding Bishop of the Lutheran Church in Sweden.

outside the classroom. Andrea, a student in the *Interreligious Experience and Engagement* course, shared this insight about truth after our class visit to a local mosque:

> The trip our class took (to the mosque) exceeded my expectations. I learned more than I thought I would about a religion strong in culture and rituals. Being able to tour a mosque, attend a service, and ask questions from a very knowledgeable source is the most beneficial way to learn more about Islam. In my notes, I wrote a line that I heard that sticks out to me most: "Truth is a primary value to achieve peace." I found this line very intriguing and spent some time thinking about its significance and importance to our everyday lives. I interpreted this to mean that it is through being truthful to others and to yourself that you will find peace both within yourself and with others.[27]

As I explore questions of faith and truth, I am cognizant of my privileges and responsibilities teaching interfaith relations to undergraduate students at a diverse Catholic university. I hope my students embrace the principle that diversity is an integral feature of the divine blueprint of creation. Our sacred mandate is to promote pluralism in a diverse world – to learn to live with one another and learn from one another in the pursuit of truth and peace. We are all created in the divine image. We are all in this together. Now, more than ever, we are called to live by the timeless message of the prophet Micah:

You have been told, O mortal, what is good and what Adonai requires of you:

> To act justly;
> To love mercy;
> And to walk humbly with your God.[28]

---

27. LMU student reflection paper, "Interreligious Experience and Engagement," fall semester 2019.
28. Micah 6:8. Author's translation.

Appendix

Religious leaders and scholars have issued numerous interfaith declarations since 1965. Catholic church bodies, including the Commission for Religious Relations with the Jews (part of the Pontifical Council for Promoting Christian Unity), and the United States Conference of Catholic Bishops, continue to issue guidance and elaboration of the core principles of *Nostra Aetate*. Their statements, guidelines, and interfaith declarations may be found at: https://www.ccjr.us/dialogika-resources /documents-and–statements/roman-catholic and https://www.ccjr.us /dialogika-resources/documents-and–statements/roman-catholic/us -conference-of-catholic-bishops.

Jewish responses to *Nostra Aetate* include "Dabru Emet" ("Speak the Truth"), a Jewish statement on Christians and Christianity that was written by four Jewish scholars, printed in a full-page advertisement in *The New York Times* in September 2000, and later affirmed by more than 220 rabbis and Jewish academics (https://www.bc.edu/content/dam/files /research_sites/cjl/texts/cjrelations/resources/documents/jewish /dabru_emet.htm), and "To Do the Will of Our Father in Heaven: Toward a Partnership between Jews and Christians," a 2015 interfaith declaration of twenty-five Orthodox rabbis that was subsequently signed by fifty-five additional Orthodox rabbis (https://www.cjcuc.org/2015/12 /03/orthodox-rabbinic-statement-on-christianity/). David Fox Sandmel offers an excellent summary and analysis of Jewish interfaith declarations in "Who Do You Say That I Am? Jewish Responses to *Nostra Aetate* and Post-Holocaust Christianity, in *The Future of Interreligious Dialogue: A Multireligious Conversation on Nostra Aetate*, ed. Charles L. Cohen, Paul F. Knitter, and Ulrich Rosenhagen (Maryknoll, NY: Orbis Books, 2017).

Catholic theologians have been joined by their Protestant colleagues in reassessing traditional Christian views of Jews and Judaism. "A Sacred Obligation: Rethinking Christian Faith in Relation to Judaism and the Jewish People," is a 2002 declaration produced by Catholic and Protestant theologians in the Christian Scholars Group. The "Willowbank

Declaration on the Christian Gospel and the Jewish People" is a document published in 1989 by a cohort of evangelical Christian leaders that presents an exclusivist view of Christian-Jewish relations in contrast to the inclusivism of *Nostra Aetate, Dabru Emet,* and "A Sacred Obligation." Another formative interfaith declaration, "A Common Word Between Us and You," was issued in 2007 by a group of Muslim leaders in response to controversial comments by Pope Benedict xvi. "A Common Word" was subsequently endorsed by 138 Muslim scholars and clerics as a definitive statement of Muslim-Christian relations.

For further information on these and other landmark documents of interfaith relations, see https://www.ccjr.us/dialogika-resources /documents-and-statements, https://www.bc.edu/research/cjl /cjrelations/backgroundresources/articles.html#dialogue, http://www .vatican.va/roman_curia/pontifical_councils/chrstuni/sub-index /index_relations-jews.htm, and https://www.acommonword.com /introduction-to-a-common-word-between-us-and-you/.

Diagonal Pluralism: A Short Essay on Truth

MICHAEL MARMUR

TWO IMPOSSIBILITIES

Here are two impossibilities. One is that there is Truth, absolute and incontestable and pristine, and I know it. I know it thanks to my extraordinary cognitive ability, which far outstrips that of all who err. Or perhaps I know it due to a stroke of cosmic luck which allowed me to born in the right place and the right time, and to have been reared on Truth from an early age. I regard all those fed the pap of error either with disdain (those wicked infidels!) or pity (those poor misguided fools!).

I regard this is an impossible posture because it is arrogant, blinkered, and demonstrably wrong.

Here, though, is another impossibility. It suggests that there is no such thing as truth, no facts, no evidence. Let's say you step on my toe. I saw and felt you do it. I have no external evidence that you were the perpetrator, although the bruise on my toe indicates that something has taken place, and my distinct memory of you approaching me, pointing to my foot, and saying "I will now step on your toe" provides further proof, if proof were needed. I know you stepped on my toe, but not only do you deny it, you speculate as to why I would be inclined to level a baseless canard against you. That's the psychological defense. Or you assert forcefully that you saw me inflict the wound on my own toe in a fit of rage. That's the psychopathic defense. Or you claim that my error derives from the fact that as your foot came close to mine, an angel came down from heaven and punished me. Let's call that the metaphysical defense. You may even blame me for brutally assaulting the sole of your boot with my sharpened toe in an unprovoked attack. Lastly, you may call in the heavy artillery and question whether anyone can ever say what transpired in the space between my toe and the sole of your boot. It's not unprovable because of the lack of video footage, but rather because truth cannot be verified. The undermining of specific truths is connected to the dismantling of the very concept of Truth.

Our world is dominated to an increasing degree by these two impossibilities. It is tempting to portray the current state of geo-politics as an epic confrontation between Holders of the Truth and Deniers of the Truth. More unnervingly still, many find themselves on both sides of the battlefield. I may hold with a raft of opinions – populist and chauvinist, liberal and PC, traditional and pious, whatever – which I assume to be True. At the same time, I may find myself adopting the strategies of the truth deniers – deflection, distraction, undermining the certainties of my opponent. We are engaged in a battle for truth, and we may not even be sure which side we are on.

What are we to do with the "truth" of others when it contradicts our Truth? If my opponent is simply a scoundrel, then presumably all I need to do is expose their lies. But what if they express a truth contradictory to my own with integrity and conviction?

THE TRUTH DILEMMA[1]

Truth is often portrayed as a precious commodity. "Truth is such a *rare thing*," according to Emily Dickinson, that "it is delightful to tell it."[2]

A talmudic teaching (b. Shabbat 104a) points out that the word *emet* comprises the first, middle and last letters of the Hebrew alphabet; they could not be farther apart. This implies both the all-encompassing nature of Truth, but also that it is seldom found. In contrast, the word *sheker*, lie, is comprised of letters adjacent to each other. Based on these observations, the Talmud concludes that "a lie is common, while the truth is rare."

---

1. A version of this section can be found in my essay on the ninth commandment "Don't Be That Person," in *Inscribed: Encounters With the Ten Commandments*, ed. Oren J, Hayon (New York, NY: CCAR Press, 2020), 167–76.

2. Emily Dickinson's Letter 342 to Mr. Higginson [1894]: http://archive .emilydickinson.org/correspondence/higginson/jnl342.html.

Truth is also highly contested in our own age. Its meaning and very existence are debated within and between philosophical schools. Theories of truth abound – a recent authoritative work[3] lists five classic approaches, which range from correspondence through coherence, pragmatism, deflationism, and semantic theories. Absolutists, sceptics, and relativists propound fundamentally different hypotheses on this and most other questions, and often talk past each other. "The absolutist trumpets his plain vision; the relativist sees only someone who is unaware of his own spectacles."[4]

To live in the twenty-first century is to encounter problems with the meaning of truth to a degree perhaps unprecedented in history. This is not due solely to the preponderance of contradictory understandings of the term, but also to cultural and technological changes which make it harder than ever to know what can be considered true. On the one hand, there has never been as much access to "the light of truth," since data is accessible and millions can be, in a sense, present at events which in previous generations would have been attended by hundreds. On the other hand, however, it has never been so easy for interested parties to divert and manipulate this light in pursuit of their own commercial or political agendas.

Felipe Fernández-Armesto[5] offers distinctions between four kinds of truth. First, he lists "the truth you feel," then "the truth you are told." The third type he calls both "the truth of reason" and "the truth you think for yourself," and the list is completed by "the truth you perceive through your senses." Most of us experience a combination of these dimensions of truth – we intuit it, take it on trust, deduce it, and perceive it. That's even true of those of us who argue that there is no such thing as truth, since human beings are selective in their adoption of philosophical positions. A friend who teaches at a large university described to me

---

3. Simon Blackburn, *On Truth* (London: Oxford University Press, 2018). For another vigorous presentation of different understandings of truth, see Lenn E. Goodman, *In Defense of Truth: A Pluralistic Approach* (New York, NY: Prometheus Books, 2001).

4. Simon Blackburn, *Truth: A Guide for the Perplexed* (London: Penguin, 2006), xix.

5. Felipe Fernández-Armesto, *Truth: A History* (London: Black Swan, 1998.)

faculty members in a literature department who tend to deconstruct all texts, reading against the grain of literal truth. All texts, that is, except their monthly pay slips, which are interpreted in a highly traditional manner. The list of benefits and rights is not to be understood as an allegory, and not to be reframed through the prism of indeterminacy. It means what it says, and any attempt to challenge this may result in legal proceedings.

Postmodern critics of old-fashioned truth discourse have challenged some of our most persistent assumptions about truth. Michel Foucault once made this point in an interview, in a characteristically provocative way: " ...I think that, instead of trying to find out what truth, as opposed to error, is, it might be more interesting to take up the problem posed by Nietzsche: how is it that, in our societies, 'the truth' has been given this value, thus placing us absolutely under its thrall?"[6] Foucault, whose emphasis tended to be on relations of power within social structures, was keen to decentralize this abstract notion of "truth," and to recognize that often the One Great Truth that we hold to be Out There is more an expression of an agenda than some metaphysical reality.

Richard Rorty offers a distinction between two schools, roughly equivalent to pre-moderns and modernists in one corner, and post-modernists in the opposite corner. He calls them metaphysicians and ironists. It is the former who insist "that what matters is not what language is being used but what is *true*."[7] The ironist, on the other hand, holds that sentences such as "is independent of the human mind' are simply platitudes used to inculcate...the common sense of the West." When an ironist reflects on this search for a better vocabulary, her description "is dominated by metaphors of making rather than finding, of diversification and novelty rather than convergence to the antecedently present."[8]

It would appear that the gulf separating these approaches is unbridgeable, that metaphysicians and ironists, absolutists and relativists, modernists and postmodernists, may not agree on anything regarding the truth, since the most fundamental questions of what that might mean

---

6. *The Truth about the Truth: De-confusing and Re-constructing the Postmodern World*, ed. Walter Truett Anderson (New York, NY: Putnam's, 1995),45.

7. Anderson, *The Truth*, 102.

8. Anderson, *The Truth*, 104.

are radically contested. When ironists invoke Friedrich Nietzsche and Michel Foucault saying that there are no facts, only interpretations, they see in these provocative words a strident and necessary corrective to a kind of naïve credulity. Others, however, see such views as dangerously close not only to a shapeless relativism, but also to a self-serving self-justification with alarming moral implications.

Karl Lueger was the mayor of Vienna until his death in 1910. A man of many contradictions, he seemed to espouse antisemitic views while maintaining close personal relations with a number of people of Jewish descent. Challenged to defend this apparent hypocrisy, Lueger is said to have responded: "*I* decide who is a Jew." His remark was to become one of the dark slogans of the twentieth century, emblematic of the risk and tragedy implicit in the loss of faith in a Great Truth Out There. In its absence the truth may be colonized by the strong, the unscrupulous, and the perverse. Contemporary history serves as a reminder of what is at stake in this debate about the nature of truth. The metaphysicians hold that once the notion of a truth external to my perception has gone, the potential for doublespeak and deception is increased. The ironists respond that hanging on to an indefensible concept of truth "out there" is itself an instrument of domination and manipulation. Many of us find ourselves prodded uncomfortably by the horns of this dilemma.

THREE IMAGES OF PLURALITY

The term pluralism is employed with regard to a wide range of topics, and, perhaps appropriately, it answers to no single authoritative definition. In the attempt to steer a path between the first impossibility I mentioned above and the second, between monism and relativism, between metaphysics and irony, the pluralist posits that truth has more than one currency, and more than one value. Some theorize a plurality of truth itself – not only does it fall from the sky in abstract moral absolutes, it also springs up from the earth (Psalm 85:12), nourished in different soils and set in varying climates. Others hold with the essential unity of truth, but emphasize the varied ways in which it is perceived and experienced.[9]

---

9. There is a voluminous and complex philosophical literature on these topics, but this is not the focus of our current essay. For excellent recent surveys of

I want to relate to three metaphors which have been used to conjure up the notion that truth is complex and multi-faceted, and that it may be perceived quite differently by persons of good faith. The images relate to language, vision, and topography respectively.

Languages of Truth

In the first of these metaphors, a controversial proposition is supposed. It is that the world looks different to people who speak different languages. Each language is a lens, and we see through the lenses in significantly different ways. The "language as lens" theory has not been without its critics. The noted linguist John McWhorter wrote a robust rebuttal of it in his 2014 work, *The Language Hoax: Why The World Looks the Same in Any Language.*[10] While he allows for some variations in the way languages express truths about the world, McWhorter wholeheartedly rejects the idea that one's worldview is formed by language. He states in a way which would be understood in any language that "the whole notion that how someone's language works determines, in any significant way, how they see the world is utterly incoherent, and even dangerous."[11]

A strong example of the counterclaim to this position is provided in the work of the Ghanaian philosopher Kwasi Wiredu. Wiredu is no relativist. He argues forcefully for the existence of universal truths, and is wary of the nihilistic implications of the alternative view.[12] Nonetheless, he points out that different languages offer different perspectives on

---

work on alethic pluralism and related fields, see *Pluralisms in Truth and Logic*, ed. Jeremy Wyatt, Nikolaj J.L.L. Pedersen, & Cory D. Wright (London: Palgrave /Macmillan, 2018); Nikolaj J.L.L. Pedersen, & Cory D. Wright, *Truth and Pluralism: Current Debates* (New York, NY: Oxford University Press, 2013); Jeremy Wyatt & Michael Lynch, "From One to Many: Recent Work on Truth," *American Philosophical Quarterly* 53. 4 (2016): 323–40. Critics such as Pascal Engel prefer a position which holds with "a pluralism about knowledge, but a monism about truth." See his 2013 unpublished paper "Against Truth Pluralism": https://www .academia.edu/10405063/Against_truth_pluralism_2013. See also Pascal Engel, "Truth Is One," *Philosophia Scientiæ*, 13.1 (2009): 1–12.

10. John H. McWhorter, *The Language Hoax: Why the World Looks the Same in Any Language* (New York, NY: Oxford University Press, 2014).

11. McWhorter, *The Language Hoax*, xviii.

12. See Kwasi Wiredu, *Cultural Universals and Particulars: An African Perspective* (Bloomington: Indiana University Press, 1996).

truth. Indeed, he demonstrates that the very term "truth" has different valences in the English and Akan languages, and that what has become known as the correspondence theory of truth in the Western philosophical tradition is rendered meaningless in another language tradition.[13] We can learn new insights by being alert to the differences between languages.

In 1960, Norwegian scholar Thorleif Boman presented an influential study titled *Hebrew Thought Compared With Greek*.[14] Decades after its publication, aspects of his argument might be derided as clumsy essentialism, but the essential thrust of the work deserves attention. He argues that Hebrew, auditory and dynamic, offers a different understanding of the world than does Greek, visual and static in its essence.

The multiplicity of languages represents a challenge to the idea that truth is universal and impervious to cultural or contextual influences. For our present purposes, it matters little if one regards linguistic variety as primarily a cause or a symptom of cultural diversity. In either case, it can be argued that the way in which truth is understood is significantly influenced by the linguistic filters through which it is expressed. The boiling point of water is, as a matter of fact, the same temperature, whether it is expressed in Celsius or Fahrenheit, in Serbo-Croat or in Swahili. However, the water itself appears to the speaker of English as a singular commodity, denoted by the singular noun "water." A Hebrew speaker knows of *mayim*, a plural word. Similarly, *life* is singular, *ḥayim* plural.

Language serves as more than a localized code for the purpose of imparting generalized truths. It is a primary conduit, some would argue the only and indispensable conduit, through which truths might be formulated and expressed. The fact that we use language differently and different languages to express these truths is more than an inconvenience. It bears on the truths we speak. The long-cherished dream to convert mathematics into that universal language so that all local mutations can be evened out has been realized in part with the advent of the computer

---

13. Kwasi Wiredu, "Truth and an African Language," in *African Philosophy: New and Traditional Perspectives*, ed. Lee M. Brown (Oxford: Oxford University Press, 2004), 35–49.

14. Thorleif Boman, *Hebrew Thought Compared with Greek* (Philadelphia, PA: Westminster Press, 1960).

age. But our understandings of truth continue to be mired in our cultural and linguistic assumptions.

In 1939, Ludwig Wittgenstein wrote:

No one *can* speak the truth; if he has still not mastered himself. He *cannot* speak it; – but not because he is not clever enough yet.

The truth can be spoken only by someone who is already *at home* in it; not by someone who still lives in falsehood and reaches out from falsehood towards truth just on occasion.[15]

Wittgenstein's observation is not to be read simply as a call for habits of ethical probity. Truth is presented here as a dialect: in order to be expressed, it requires fluency and familiarity. It is a language. Reading Wittgenstein's aphorism, an echo of an earlier word of wisdom, from the Book of Proverbs 12:19, comes to mind. It is perhaps illustrative of the general tenor of this section of the essay that the truth of the verse is difficult to capture in translation. Here are three attempts:

Truthful words will stand forever; lying speech but for a moment.

True words have the quality of permanence, untruths last only for a moment.

The lip of truth shall be established forever; but a lying tongue is but for a moment.

Truth is portrayed here as that which is conveyed through the medium of speech. The speech itself is the truth or the lie. Our first image of plurality with regard to truth is that of language. Even when capable persons of good faith are set the task of expressing truths, the vehicles of that expression, within one language system and certainly between language systems, are bound to create differences. The language of truth may stand forever, but we all speak it with different vocabularies, syntaxes, and pronunciations.

Many civilizations have held that the highest peaks of truth and beauty can be scaled only in their own language, and not in others. I interpret these statements not as defensible claims to exclusive truth.

---

15. Ludwig Wittgenstein, *Culture and Value* (Oxford: Basil Blackwell, 1980), 35e.

Rather, they should be understood as a call to resist the erosion of linguistic and cultural diversity. My world is enriched when I see water through the prism of "water" and also through the prism of the Hebrew word מים. And when a language and literature become extinct in the world, pathways to the truth are lost.

Optical Imagery

One of the strongest objections to dogmatic traditionalist claims, or for that matter to optimistic modernist claims that objective truth is clearly accessible and expressible, is the issue of perspective. To hold that one sees the "view from nowhere," that one can perceive reality *sub specie aeternitate*, from the perspective of eternity, is to make an overreaching claim. From the time of Friedrich Nietzsche (1844–1900) to our day, philosophers and historians have encouraged us to be more honest and more aware about our own role as observers. The truth I see is necessarily influenced by where I stand, and by the eyes through which I see. Along with this consciousness there is the danger is that once I acknowledge that my truth is no more than one perspective, I lay myself open to the claim by any unscrupulous actor that their lie is as much of a truth as my truth.

Nietzsche argued that such a risk is preferable to the "nonsensical absurdity" of the doctrine of "contemplation without interest." It is imperative to face up to the ways in which we employ perspectives as part of the constant act of knowing – "we can use the *difference* in perspectives and affective interpretations for knowledge."[16]

In rabbinic and later Jewish literature. we find the term *aspaklaria* (sometimes translated as speculum), usually referring to a way of seeing, an aspect of vision, or an obstruction to true sight.[17] A remarkable reflection on the ways in which divine truth is perceived appears in a number of forms in classical rabbinic literature and thereafter.[18] The version appearing in Leviticus Rabbah is worth quoting here:

---

16. Friedrich Nietzsche, *On the Genealogy of Morality* [1887] (Cambridge: Cambridge University Press, 1994), III.12, 87.

17. I have discussed the *aspaklaria* in Michael Marmur, *Abraham Joshua Heschel and the Sources of Wonder* (University of Toronto Press, 2016), 149f.

18. These traditions and their implications are discussed in Elliot R. Wolfson,

How is Moses to be distinguished from the other prophets? There is a response to this question in the name of R. Judah son of R. Ilai, and one in the name of our Rabbis. Rabbi Judah says: the prophets saw through nine *aspaklarias*, as it is written: "The vision I saw was like the vision I had seen..." (Ezekiel 43:3)[19], while Moses saw through only one *aspaklaria*, as it is written: "...clearly and not in riddles" (Numbers 12:8). Our Rabbis teach: all the other prophets saw through a dirty *aspaklaria*, which is as it is written: "I spoke to the prophets, gave them many visions, and told parables through them" (Hosea 9:10),[20] Moses saw through a polished *aspaklaria*, and this is as it is written: "...he sees the form of the Lord." (Numbers 12:8)[21]

Rabbi Judah does not assert that Moses's vision was better than that of the other biblical prophets. In some cases, possession of more lenses can enhance rather than corrupt vision. Moses certainly has the advantage of purity of untrammeled vision, but not necessarily clarity or accuracy.[22] In the alternative reading, a clear hierarchy is enunciated. The other prophets were hampered by the motes and speckles which are wont to plague ancient lenses. Moses alone is graced to see through a polished (or in some versions, an illuminated) lens.

The term *aspaklaria* is employed in a variety of ways through classical Jewish texts and in more contemporary contexts – it can refer to a mirror, a prism, a perspective, or a screen. In all of these cases, the term refers to ways of seeing, ways of perceiving. Sight in a sense beyond the merely physical is at stake here – indeed, some medieval commentators suggest that the real difference between the great prophets of old and Moses was that the former believed they had actually seen something when gazing

---

Through a Speculum That Shines: Vision and Imagination in Medieval Jewish Mysticism (Princeton, NJ: Princeton University Press, 1994).

19. The verb root implying vision can be counted nine times in this verse.

20. The reading here implies blurriness of vision.

21. Leviticus Rabbah 1.14. The translation is mine. The midrash and its parallels are a response to a number of theological questions raised in Numbers 12:6–8.

22. See b. Yevamot 49b, where the distinction is between an *aspaklaria* that does not shine and one that does.

at divine glory, while Moses's lucid speculum enabled him to realize that there was nothing physical to be seen.[23]

This tradition offers a way of thinking about multiple perceptions of a singular truth. Nietzsche's idea that multiplicity of perspective may help us achieve clarity of vision comes to mind in this regard. For Moses, perhaps, one lens would suffice to face up to ultimate truth. For the rest of us, multiple lenses may be required.

Some have also merged the symbolic fields of language and of vision, the first and second metaphors employed in this essay. Guy Deutscher published a work entitled *Through the Language Glass: Why the World Looks Different in Other Languages*.[24] Here, language itself is seen as an *aspaklaria* through which the raw material of the universe is processed. To cite a work on color: "Physiology determines what we see; culture determines how we name, describe and understand it. The *sensation* of color is physical; the *perception* of color is cultural."[25] I see the color through my eyes and express it through my language and the rest of my cultural equipment. Even as I accept that the color I see has a certain chemical composition, and that it is presenting a certain frequency of light waves to me, I acknowledge that there are particular ways in which I experience and relate to this. Herein lies the possibility of plurality in the face of truth without the need to posit falsehood or ill intent.

Vertical and Horizontal Pluralism

Following figurations taken from the domain of language and the visual realm respectively, let us now turn to the dimension of space. Among theorists of pluralism, a distinction between horizontal and vertical pluralism is sometimes employed. In the words of David Ludwig,"[h]orizontal pluralism is the claim that there can be different but equally fundamental

---

23. See Abraham Joshua Heschel, *God In Search of Man* (New York, NY: Farrar, Straus & Giroux, 1955), 277n23.

24. Guy Deutscher, *Through the Language Glass: Why the World Looks Different in Other Languages* (London: Arrow Books, 2011). John Mc Whorter's *The Language Hoax*, mentioned in a footnote above, was written in direct opposition to the key claims of this work.

25. David Scott Kastan (with Stephen Farthing), *On Color* (New Haven, CT & London: Yale University Press, 2018), 9.

descriptions in one domain, while vertical pluralism assumes different but equally fundamental descriptions across domains."[26]

The distinction is not watertight, but it is nonetheless helpful in thinking about differing concepts and degrees of plurality that may be allowed within discourse concerning truth. Here is a somewhat convoluted thought experiment which may help to illustrate the point. Let us suppose that two individuals are both charged with the task of describing the same rare and inaccessible waterfall on the same day, in a way which would capture its most significant and memorable aspects. One is a geologist reporting back to a scientific team researching climate change and water management. The other is a poet who has been asked to evoke the waterfall for an audience of readers who have never seen it. This would count as an example of vertical pluralism, because a category distinction separates the two tasks. It is reasonable to expect that the "truth" concerning the waterfall will look different in the two reports. To tolerate or celebrate that plurality is to engage in a form of vertical pluralism.

Now imagine that ten individuals have been invited to capture the truth concerning our waterfall. All are geologists or hydrologists, all charged with the same task. The reports they provide are not identical. Unlike the tradition concerning the ancient Jewish translation of the Hebrew Bible into Greek, according to which the seventy translators independently produced identical translations, in our experiment as in life, plural perceptions of the truth may be allowed. If you hold that only one of the ten experts actually spoke the truth (or perhaps none of them did), then your position is not pluralist in essence. Say, however, two hydrologists offer two differing accounts of the waterfall using the methodology of that discipline. They categorize it in different ways; explain the circumstances by which the waterfall came to be in different ways; predict its future development in different ways. You are so struck

---

26. David Ludwig, *A Pluralist Theory of the Mind* (Amsterdam: Springer, 2015), 104. I became acquainted with this distinction through the work of Michael Lynch. See Michael P. Lynch, *Truth in Context: An Essay on Pluralism and Objectivity* (Cambridge, MA: MIT Press, 2001), especially 6–8. Lynch refers his readers to an earlier article by Huw Price. See H. Price, "Metaphysical Pluralism," *Journal of Philosophy* 89.8 (1992): 387–409.

by the persuasiveness and creativity of those differing accounts that you hold both to be valid, both to contain aspects of truth. You are pleased that both reports were generated because this has added to your understanding of the waterfall in a way that one single report could not have done. All this qualifies you as a horizontal pluralist.

This distinction between the vertical and the horizontal comes to expression in discussions within and between religious traditions. In some cases, it is easier to grant validity to a truth claim expressed in a religion other than my own – it is possible to apply a version of vertical pluralism. But that someone should appear on my horizon, within my domain, and make a truth claim at odds with my own – that may prove harder to bear.

THE DIAGONAL PRINCIPLE

Throughout this essay I have suggested that imagery taken from a variety of fields can help express the notion that truth has more than one face. First, language diversity raises the possibility that individuals of good faith express the truth they see in different ways. To borrow from the third category, we might add that the difference in claims about Truth in English and in Akan are vertical differences – cultural and linguistic walls divide the two worlds of discourse. Arguments such as those that rage among philosophers using the same language are in this sense horizontal. An extreme monist might argue that one person among the thousands of thinkers who have formulated their understanding of Truth is correct, and the others simply wrong. Another view would hold that no one theory of Truth contains all the truth, but that the Truth is out there, perhaps preserved in fragmentary form in the thinking of many who have devoted their attention to this issue. According to a more explicitly pluralist position, truth has qualities of indeterminacy and fluidity. Thinking of it as a solid commodity, concealed by a playful deity in a cosmic game of Hide and Seek, is inadequate to truth's elusive quality. So I turn to the multiplicity of voices and perspectives, and in that messy search some glimpses of truth may be visible. Without the cacophony, no harmony is possible.

Modernity has been characterized in the West by a quest for objectivity, and no less by its rejection.[27] This tension is at the source of the fissure driving modernism and postmodernity apart. Faced with the impossibility of a truth fully monopolized, and a truth rejected wholesale, the search is on for a way of holding on to truth while admitting the possibility (and even the necessity) of diversity.

I want to say something in favour of a *diagonal* pluralism. While I acknowledge that reality is expressed differently in different languages, I celebrate a common humanity which unites people more than all the linguistic diversity in the world can divide them. While I appreciate that we see through different lenses, and mirrors, and perspectives, and veils, we are all endeavoring to peer at reality as best we can. This may be as through a glass darkly, through a speckled and impure *aspaklaria*, but the notion that there is no connection between our various ways of seeing seems too bleak, and also quite dangerous.

I recently had a conversation with a student who argued that religion involves a faith commitment which is simply in a separate category to that of reason. A vertical wall divides them, and one should not be expected to conform in any way to the dictates of the other. Indeed, a strict vertical pluralism implies that one can hold views which contradict each other so long as one confines them to different domains. According to this argument, not only is it possible to hold such contradictory opinions, there is no point attempting to harmonize one's positions across the domains.

I find this position to be logically defensible, yet unacceptable. It may be that my religious commitments cannot be fully explained and justified in terms of my general political or scientific outlook. The attempt to explain religious commitments often turns into an exercise in reducing them to domesticated categories borrowed from other aspects of life. So

---

27. Isaiah Berlin captures this ambivalence brilliantly in his 1960 essay, "The Romantic Revolution: A Crisis in the History of Modern Thought," in Isaiah Berlin, *The Sense of Reality: Studies in Ideas and Their History* (New York, NY: Farrar, Straus & Giroux, 1997), 168–93. See also Michael Morgan's "The Problem of Objectivity Before and After Auschwitz," in Michael L. Morgan, *Interim Judaism: Jewish Thought in a Century of Crisis* (Bloomington: Indiana University Press, 2001), 1–45.

it is that prayer is re-packaged as therapy, community as a social safety net, and study as mental exercise with health benefits.

While I resist the tendency to domesticate religious commitment in this way, I cannot countenance the idea at the opposite extreme: namely, that once a practice has been categorized as religious or traditional, no critique is justifiable. Like countless Jews before me, the God in whom I believe is called to be congruous with the world of concepts and ideas I inhabit. If I am to continue to recite the words of the liturgy, "who has chosen us from among all peoples," I am required to find an interpretation of these words which is not at odds with my beliefs concerning the humanity of all individuals. If I am to ask for God's help in healing a sick friend, I am required to interpret that prayer in a way that takes my understanding of causality and health into account.

My diagonal approach recognizes that the various domains in which my search for meaning and truth take place are not hermetically sealed off from one another. The vertical and horizontal each exercise a pull on the other – hence the diagonal motion.

I am unconvinced by attempts to do away with the multivocal and the multifocal. Arguing that there is only one prism through which the world can be genuinely understood – be it halakhah, or science, or politics, or whichever candidate is chosen – and that all other domains must bow before the one true perspective, is not a satisfactory position. Our world is perceived through the multiple prisms of the prophets, not the single lens of Moses. What I am terming diagonal pluralism occurs when the various perspectives impact on each other. As I look at the waterfall, the reports about it I have received from multiple disciplines combine in my mind. My field of vision is enriched.

Each strong truth commitment leaves a trace – exercises a pull – on every other strong truth commitment. That is why I am engaged in the increasingly beleaguered approach known as liberal religion. I hold my religious commitments in some way accountable to my philosophical, social, feminist, and other commitments, and I want them to bend toward the light provided by these other insights. My liberal Jewish forebears were wrong (to my mind) in their wholesale rejection of the esoteric tradition, of Hasidism, and more. I look to those areas, learn those languages, seek out those perspectives. But I do so irrevocably committed to values I can't leave at the door when I enter into these other worlds of discourse.

Here, then, is my suggestion, offered in the face of all the possibilities and impossibilities we confront: a pluralism rooted in humility and curiosity, stubbornly resistant to nihilism and atrophy, unable to accept a one-size-fits-all Truth for all people and all times. A multi-lingual, multi-perspectival, multi-level pluralism, moving forward in diagonal increments, like a bishop or a knight on a chessboard. If, like bishops and knights, the rest of us applied more of this diagonal approach in life, the search for truth might be better served.

In an era in which the Holders of the Truth square off against the Deniers of the Truth, another kind of discourse comes to be of great significance. Switching between codes and languages, shifting perspectives and domains, a diagonal pluralism is called for. It celebrates diversity of approach, respects difference, and feels the pull exercised by each iteration of the search for truth. It is realized whenever the profound truth of one language, one perspective, reaches out to another. Perhaps its watchword can be found in the Book of Psalms[28]:

תְּהוֹם אֶל תְּהוֹם קוֹרֵא לְקוֹל צִנּוֹרֶיךָ

One of the various published translations of this verse reads:

Deep calls to deep in the roar of your waterfalls

Deep calls to deep: a profound search for truth in one tradition, in one field of discourse, calls out to and impacts the depth inherent in another. The truth is not to be found in the victory of an exclusive understanding. The plural water as it cascades can best be perceived through the multiple *aspaklaria* afforded to the attentive observer when deep calls to deep. And, I believe, the depth of one truth has a bearing on the depth of another.

I don't pretend that this multi-layered approach will always be effective against those who seek to monopolize the truth and those who seek to explode it. If your interlocutor stubbornly denies stepping on your toe, invoking diagonal pluralism is unlikely to get you the apology you

---

28. Psalms 42:8.

were hoping for, and the pain of the bruise will persist. But even when deception and artifice are in the ascendant, the diagonal pluralist may be comforted by the belief that in time, despite the allure of competing impossibilities, searching for truth within a variety of domains and being attentive to the impact of each domain upon the other offers the prospect of meaning and resonance. Deep calls to deep.

Section 6

Lo Ye'uman ki Yesuppar:
Truth, Fiction, and Satire

Truth and Satire in the Bible, Yesterday and Today: Reflections on *Hayehudim Ba'im* (*The Jews Are Coming*)

WENDY ZIERLER, WITH CONTRIBUTIONS
FROM ASAF BEISER AND NATALIE MARCUS

Satirical parody of sacred figures and traditional Jewish texts hardly constitutes a new genre in Hebrew literature and culture. While few people readily associate the Bible with humor or satire – the term satire itself derives from Latin, and the corresponding genre from Roman literature rather than from Hebraic tradition – the Bible includes several texts that comically skewer important figures and institutions in the name of moral truth. It is this kind of humorous, satirical approach to the revelation of truth that Bible scholar Charles David Isbell detects in the narrative framing of Aaron the High Priest's speech to Moses in response to the debacle of the Golden Calf:

> "The people gave [miscellaneous pieces of gold] to me, I threw them into the fire, and out came this calf!" (Exodus 32:24). I am not arguing that the point of the golden calf is to serve as a backdrop for a standup comedy routine, nor do I overlook the implications of the text regarding the relative significance of Aaron vis-à-vis Moses. The fact that Aaron refused to accept personal responsibility for his actions also remains clear and the narrators could have made their point forcibly with arid prose. But they did not. They used a comical description of Aaron to great advantage.[1]

---

1. Charles David Isbell, "Humor in the Bible" in *Jews and Humor*, ed. Leonard J.

According to Isbell, humor helps highlight Aaron's moral and religious evasion. Along similar lines, Isbell and other scholars such as David Marcus point to the satirical unveiling of the truth in the story of the prophet Balaam and his miraculous, speaking she-ass from Numbers 22.[2] Marcus points to the elements of absurdity, fantasy, irony, ridicule, and parody inherent in this story about a she-ass who sees and speaks more prophetically than her would-be visionary master, all of which identify the story as satirizing the false pretenses of this non-Israelite prophet and which reveal, by contrast, the nature of divine Truth.[3] Marcus reads the Book of Jonah and other prophetic texts as having a similar, anti-prophetic, satirical bent. Remarkably, he notes, the Bible allows the subversive, truth-telling voices of satire to dwell comfortably and honestly in its prophetic midst, sharply targeting "behaviors considered unbecoming for prophets in Israel":

> Elisha is satirized for his cruel curse; the man of God for disobeying God; the old prophet for lying, and being concerned about his own remains; Jonah for disobedience, hypocrisy, and for being concerned with his own physical comfort. Because these stories criticize the imperfections of certain prophets, even though they are only prophetic types, they enable us to see how the writers and their audiences really feel about the standard bearers of prophecy. For satires, by their very nature, reflect a certain conservatism and a desire to uphold the traditions. The satirist uses his art "to shore up the foundations of the established order." Thus when our satires criticize the behavior of the prophets, there lies the unspoken wish of what the proper behavior should be.[4]

This essay attempts to pick up where the biblical stories leave off, highlighting the ways in which one contemporary work of Hebrew satire – the

---

Greenspoon (West Lafayette, IN: Purdue University Press, 2011), 3. For an extended satirical take on this biblical episode see the following skit from the second *Hayehudim Ba'im* Season 2, Episode 12, https://www.youtube.com/watch?v=1cuVhCel_mY.

2. Isbell, "Humor," 6.

3. David Marcus, *From Balaam to Jonah: Anti-Prophetic Satire in the Hebrew Bible* (Atlanta, GA: Scholars Press, 1995), 9.

4. Marcus, *From Balaam to Jonah*, 170.

Israeli Academy Award-winning *Hayehudim Ba'im* – has aimed, over the course of over four masterful seasons, to reveal tough truths about Jewish history and contemporary Jewish/Israeli society through the medium of biblically-based or Jewish-text-based Hebrew satire.

As scholar Derek Penslar notes in *Israel in History: The Jewish State in Comparative Perspective*, parody and humor about Jewish holy books were an integral part of Haskalah literature in the nineteenth century as well as of Jewish culture in the Zionist Yishuv from its earliest days. From newspaper columns to cabaret acts, pre-State Jews laughed at themselves and at rival groups via satire and parody of such Jewish books as the Bible, the Talmud, and the Passover Haggadah.

According to Penslar, however, after 1948 Israeli satire became less religious and more secular, focusing more on political issues of the day or on ethnic divisions in Israeli culture. Increasingly, Israeli humor became removed from Jewish content and the Jewish past. "How many secular Israelis today would identify themselves, as did Yishuv parodists during the 1920s and 1930s, with Israel in Egypt, and how many would conceive of the manifold crises confronting contemporary Israel in terms of the Passover narrative?" Penslar asks woefully. "This is not solely a question of lacking textual knowledge; rather, it is a sense of distance, even alienation from the Jewish past and its creation."[5]

A decade and a half later, however, the picture seems to have considerably changed with *Hayehudim Ba'im* (*The Jews are Coming*), a satirical skit show, which completed its first broadcast season in January 2015, and is now filming its fifth season. Here is a contemporary Israeli television program, broadcast on Israel's historic Channel 1 – for many years the only TV channel in the country – devoted to producing sketches that draw from the entire history of the Jewish people, from biblical times to the present. Here the laughs and the truth-telling depend not on an intimate knowledge of all the ins and outs, scandals and skirmishes of Israeli politicians and their parties, but on central moments in Jewish history and culture throughout the ages. The title of the series itself marks a shift in focus, announcing, as it were, the coming home of Jews and Jewishness to Israeli comedy and satire.

---

5. Derek Penslar, *Israel in History: The Jewish State in Comparative Perspective* (London and New York: Routledge, 2007), 185.

The cast of Hayehudim Ba'im *with Creators Asaf Beiser and Natalie Marcus and Director Kobi Havia*

To be sure, *Hayehudim Haba'im* is not the first Israeli show to feature satirical skits on the Holy Book. *Niqui Rosh*, a famous post-1973 sketch program, featured an unforgettable sketch in which Moses flees the site of the burning bush after God tells him to take off his shoes, because it was simply too hot to stand barefoot in the hot desert sand.[6] The skit reveals the absurdity of a God, and by extension a religion, that would ask a prophet to stand barefoot in a Middle Eastern desert. *Haḥamishiyah haqamerit*, which ran on Channel 1 from 1993–1997, featured a celebrated spoof of the story of the sacrificial ethos that undergirds the story of the Binding of Isaac, replete with a candid camera host and a bikini clad "angel" as Abraham's prize.[7] Likewise, in 2010, the cast of the satirical news show *Eretz Nehederet* released the film *Zohi Sedom*, an extended lampoon of the biblical story of the destruction of Sodom (Genesis 19).

But whereas material based on biblical and other Jewish historical and textual materials was the exception rather than the rule of these other satirical comedy shows, in *Hayehudim Ba'im*, offering a satirical perspective on hallowed stories, personalities, and events is the show's

6. See *Nikui Rosh*, https://www.youtube.com/watch?v=QIzm-ZoyDW.
7. https://www.youtube.com/watch?v=KyJ2mwG2VKc.

comic bread and butter, and also facilitates its broader social criticism and truth-telling. No sacred cow is too holy to escape the razor-sharp blade of its wit – as represented by the opening of every episode, which features a circumcision knife. The truth often hurts, as is evident from the very first skit of the very first episode of the show: a send-up the various inconsistencies and hypocrisies of the Ten Commandments. A stuttering insecure Moses gives the commandments, only to be besieged by questions from the Israelites about each and every one, most trenchantly the prohibition against murder, given the biblical mandate to wipe out the Amalekites and other indigenous groups.[8]

While the irreverence of *Hayehudim Ba'im* might be viewed by some as virulently anti-religious, the show clearly demonstrates a positive investment in the Jewish religious past that is unprecedented in Israeli pop culture. The secular-religious divide in Israel used to be an established fact. But the rise, over the past decade of secular *batei-midrash* (Houses of Study) and related organizations such as Bina, Elul, and Oranim, committed to the idea of secular Jewish study and spiritual activity, has narrowed and complicated the schism between secular and religious life in Israel, pointing to new ways to be an engaged and learned Israeli Jew. The mission statement of one such new organization, "*Harabbanut hahilonit beYisrael*" (The Secular Israeli Rabbinate) insists that to be a secular Jew means being part of a dynamic, ever-renewing, forward-looking community, with deep roots in a three-thousand-year-old historical tradition, a stance that considerably complicates establishment Orthodox religious truth.[9]

Steeped in this history, as well as in the best traditions of Jewish humor,[10] *Hayehudim Ba'im* is yet another expression of this new secular interest in Jewish text study, albeit in popular comedic form. To be expected, the show has garnered no small measure of criticism from the religious and political right. Skits like the mock advertisement in Season 1 Episode 5 promoting "the *Agudah lemilhamah be'Elohim*," (The

---

8. See https://www.youtube.com/watch?v=KmX9LAgv_z4.

9. http://www.harabanut.co.il/אודותינו/.

10. For more on Jewish comedy see Jeremy Dauber, *Jewish Humor: A Serious History* (New York, NY: W.W. Norton & Co., 2017) and Ruth Wisse, *No Joke: Making Jewish Humor* (Princeton, NJ: Princeton University Press, 2013.)

Society for War Against God) are not calculated to curry favor with the conventionally Orthodox.[11]

The brilliance of this mock-advertisement, however, is that all sides come under satirical attack. Simplistic traditional theologies may not satisfy those modern Jews looking for honest explanations as to how a supposedly benevolent God can allow great natural disasters to overtake innocent people all over the world. But the would-be truth-seeking, empirical, scientists featured at the end of this sketch, who hubristically proclaim their intent to wage war against the canard, which is God, similarly underestimate the enduring spiritual needs even of secular Jews. Here come the new TV Jews to bring comic relief to their spiritual woes. As critic Ariana Melammed writes about those who initially decried the series for its potential to stir-up controversy and dissent:

> האמת, צדקו. יש פוטנציאל להסתבכות, אבל בכל סאטירה טובה המשודרת
> בארץ לא כל כך נהדרת, פוטנציאל ההסתבכות גדול, וצריך שעל כסאות
> ההנהלה יישבו אנשים שלא פוחדים מהצל של עצמם ומוכנים לשחרר
> לעולם גם מוצרים טלוויזיוניים נשכנים ובועטים, לא רק נעימים ומלקקים.

> It's true. They were right. There is real potential for snags here, but in every good satire that is broadcast in this not-so-wonderful[12] land, there is great potential for snags, and thus it behooves those who occupy the seats of management not to be afraid of their shadows, rather to be willing to let loose onto the world television productions that have the capacity to bite and kick, and not just to make nice and kiss-up. [13]

According to Melammed, the creators of influential media need to have to have the temerity to wield the sharp instruments of their art. Asaf Beiser and Natalie Marcus, the co-creators of *Hayehudim Ba'im*, could not agree more, as evident from their attendance at Symposium 11 and their contribution to our discussion of pluralistic Jewish truths in our age of "truthiness."

As if building on the scholarly discussion of biblical satire presented

---

11. https://www.youtube.com/watch?v=jS-5Nmm_rp8.
12. A play on the satirical show *Eretz Nehederet* (Wonderful Land).
13. Ariana Melammed, "Hayehudim ba'im: ḥakhamah, matshiqah uvoʿetet, *ynet.* 8.11.14 https://www.ynet.co.il/articles/0,7340,L-4588826,00.html.

above, Beiser and Marcus begin their presentation on truth-telling in *Hayehudim Ba'im* by screening a famous skit from the first season of the show, based on the biblical Book of Esther. If scholars view the biblical book as taking satirical aim at the excesses of the Persian monarchy, *Hayehudim Ba'im* bravely dares to target the Jewish hero of the story for his questionable willingness to prostitute his niece for personal and national gain. In this way, Beiser and Marcus point to the ways in which the show performs the crucial social function of self-examination:

MORDECAI: That's it! Esther, Esther!

ESTHER: You summoned me, Uncle?

MORDECAI: I have a solution to our problem! Correct that Ahashverosh wants to kills us? And Ahashverosh hasn't been so thrilled with Vashti lately?

ESTHER: Nu...

MORDECAI: So here's my plan. You go to the palace, flirt with Ahashverosh, fool around with him, do some hanky panky. And voilà! Ahashverosh doesn't want to kill us anymore.

ESTHER: Okay, great idea, but you don't think that it's a bit problematic to send me to Ahashverosh? It sort of turns me into...

MORDECAI: What?

ESTHER: A whore?

MORDECAI: Why a whore?

ESTHER: Don't get me wrong, it's a great idea, but it sort of makes me look like, you know... a whore.

MORDECAI: How a whore?

ESTHER: Wait, let me get this straight. You want me to go to the palace, to flirt with Ahashverosh and fool around with him...

MORDECAI: To save the people!

ESTHER: That's like a whore.

MORDECAI: It's not like a whore.

ESTHER: It's not *like a whore*, it's a whore

MORDECAI: It's not a whore.

ESTHER: It is a whore

MORDECAI: How does it make you a whore?

ESTHER: How does it *not* make me a whore? You're sending me to be with a strange man?

MORDECAI: Yes.

ESTHER: You'll getting something out of it.

MORDECAI: Of course. I'll save myself from death!

ESTHER: So, I'll be a whore

MORDECAI: Wait a minute, Esther.

ESTHER: Whore!

MORDECAI: Esther…

ESTHER: Whore!

MORDECAI: Esther…

ESTHER: You want me to be a whore?

MORDECAI: Not a whore!

ESTHER: Whore!

MORDECAI: Can I get a word in?

ESTHER: Is that word, "Whore?"

MORDECAI: No.

ESTHER: So, no.

MORDECAI: Esther, try to understand, if our plan succeeds, our people will shower you with gratitude, they'll write songs about you and put you in the Bible…

ESTHER: Great: David the King, Jeremiah the Prophet, and Esther the Whore.

MORDECAI: Not a whore, a queen!

ESTHER: Queen of whores!

MORDECAI: Not a whore, heaven forbid, not a whore! You'll be the savior of our people. Your story will live forever. They'll name a holiday after you. A joyous holiday. And little girls will wait all year for this holiday, so they can dress up as Esther.

ESTHER: So they're going to get dressed up as whores?

MORDECAI: Only in high school.[14]

"The best satire," writes historian of satire Terry Lyndvall, "reveals the truth of self-recognition. If one does not first satirize oneself, one will either be a blasphemer or a bully. The best satirist writes out of his or

---

14. Translation by Wendy Zierler.

Esther making her case to Mordecai

her follies and vices."[15] In its willingness to target Mordecai, the Esther skit from *Hayehudim ba'im* follows in this tradition of satire as the truth of self-recognition," calling out the traditional reading of the book and reclaiming the text for secular Israeli Jews and for their liberal, modern, comic ends. If the biblical Mordecai is convinced of the rightness of this plan to send Esther into Aḥashverosh's harem despite his responsibility to care for her as his ward, the skit dares to unseat Mordecai from his purported righteousness. As co-creator Natalie Marcus notes, instead of hewing to Mordecai's perspective, the skit assumes Esther's point of view, thereby offering a feminist reading: "In the text there is this short passage where Esther says, וכאשר אבדתי אבדתי – 'If I perish, I perish.'[16] We zoomed in on those words and thought, Esther might not be so happy with Mordecai's plan. She's presented as a heroine, but she's also a victim. She sacrifices herself and her body. So what is the truth in this story? This is part of what we dealt with in the text: that there are other

---

15. Terry Lyndvall, *God Mocks: A History of Religious Satire from the Hebrew Prophets to Stephen Colbert* (New York, NY: NYU Press, 2015), 281.

16. Esther 4:16.

points of view and interpretations that we have not been previously identified and need to be told."

Part of what Esther and Mordecai are arguing about in this skit is the actual meaning of words and actions. The Esther of this skit insists on literal truth. She adduces a set of actions, matches them up with the dictionary definition of the word "whore," insists that the thing be called by its proper name, and not be spun to mean something else just because it redounds to someone else's advantage.

The feminist reading afforded by the Esther skit exposes a truth that the traditional or conventional reading had somehow blurred, as well as an insight about contemporary Israeli culture: the joke at the end of the skit about girls getting dressed up as whores "only in high school" dares to point out the way in which secular Israeli culture has accepted fashion norms that wittingly or unwittingly sexualize teenage girls.

To drive home the point that the show targets conservatives and liberals alike, Marcus and Beiser adduce another clip that derives not from the Bible but from the Nazi era in Germany. In the skit, two German men are sitting in an outdoor café, when one of them, a man named Hans, spies Hitler and says, "Is that him, that Nazi?" whereupon his friend chastises him, telling him that it's impolite call someone Nazi.[17]

"But it's him, what's his name? Hitler!"

"Don't call him that!"

"But he's the head of that party! He's a Nazi."

"Really, Hans. You can't just go around calling everyone with views you disagree with, Nazi. It lowers the level of the discourse!"

Beiser and Marcus explain how the skit, set in the Nazi era, serves as a critique of the contemporary Liberal Left, with its policing of language and reluctance to call things by their proper name. "What we're talking about here," says Beiser, "is truth. Whenever you narrow language, you narrow the truth. If there are fewer words that you can use, there is less truth in the culture. Political correctness limits what is true. The other side of the coin is that if you call people Nazis, no one will listen to you even if you are using the terms truly and correctly, against the likes of a

---

17. See https://www.youtube.com/watch?v=CCp4eg5w8ZI.

Hitler. There is a kind of language that makes the truth impossible for people to hear and accept."

Basic to this skit as well as to many of the biblically-based sketches in the show is a strategy of indirection: a truth about our own times is captured via material from the past. An excellent example of this comes from a skit from Season 3, in which Miriam complains to Moses about the lack of a prohibition in the Ten Commandments against rape.

> "But wasn't there something about rape? Something like "Thou shall not rape your mother and your father"? or "Thou shall not rape a calf in its mother milk?"
>
> "Nope."
>
> "So *you* add one in. You have good handwriting."
>
> "No. You need get them all together and tell them: "Thou shall not rape."
>
> "It can't wait?"
>
> "No, it can't wait." (The camera then pans down and you see a man trying to get under Miriam's skirt.)

Miriam and Moses

So Moses gathers everyone together, and tells them plain and simple that they may not rape but is immediately challenged by the crowd: What if she's dressed sexily and her cleavage is showing? What if she's unconscious? If she's dead? What if she says no, and you don't know if she really means it?

In an attempt to help out Moses, Aaron insists that specific circumstances don't matter: it's forbidden in all cases to rape. That is...unless you're an officer in the army! The very effort to abstract, simplify, and clarify the prohibition leads to even more obfuscations and exceptions. In the end Moses capitulates to the confusion of the crowd, insisting to a very unhappy Miriam that it's just too complicated to issue a prohibition against rape, an allusion to the persistent difficulty exposing and prosecuting cases of sexual assault that continues to this very day.

Asked about the context that led to the creation of this skit, Beiser explains that they weren't thinking first and foremost about the Ten Commandments, rather about a contemporary case about a wealthy man in Israel: "It was a few months before the #MeToo movement started to emerge. There was a story in Tel Aviv about a tycoon who was big in Tel Aviv night life; some twenty complaints of sexual misconduct came out about him. The writers on the show, we got together in the morning, and we were talking about current events, and this grey area that emerges when it comes to rape and sexual assault, which got all of us very angry. Our major complaint in the skit was not with the Ten Commandments for not including a prohibition against rape – those were different times – but with the failures of the present moment."

Marcus and Beiser talk about the way in which the shows' writers arrive at their readings of the Bible – about the "beit midrash" that is the writer's room of the show. "We sit together. We have a library, a lot of books, and of course, the internet. We do satire through history not through current events. That is to say, we address current trends or values or the lack of them, and then we use the Bible or history to get at them. Or we find a character in the Bible that we want to write about in a new way. Or both at the same time."

A great example of "both at the same time" comes in the form of yet another skit based on the biblical Book of Esther, one that deals indirectly with the repression of critique of the Israeli army, particularly that of *Shovrim Shetiqah* (Breaking the Silence), a movement founded by former Israeli soldiers for the purpose of telling the truth about their military experiences. This organization is extremely controversial in Israel; a law entitled *Ḥok shovrei shetiqah* (The Break the Silence Law) was passed to limit its activities and ban soldiers affiliated with this organization from going into schools and speaking about their experiences. The skit in question alludes to this controversy using Esther 9 to depict the failed efforts of a Jewish warrior in Shushan to tell the traumatic truth about the carnage described at the end of the biblical book.[18] At the beginning of the skit Mordecai invites a would-be warrior hero to talk about his experiences. The soldier leads off with a description of what went on in Shushan as simply terrible, a massacre: "Every time I close my eyes I see the corpses, I hear the screams. The horror of killing all of Haman's children. We killed 75,000 people for no reason, because of Haman?" With the mention of Haman, the audience begins spinning their *graggers* to drown out the name of Haman, following the traditional practice of drowning out Haman's name during the ritual recitation of the *Megillah* on Purim. But in the context of the skit, using noisemakers becomes a strategy to evade the darker truth of the text and by extension, of Israeli military service. Like the members of Breaking of the Silence who are deprived of their platform, the soldier is summarily whisked off stage on account of "all of his lies." Then Esther starts singing off-key, and comically, they drown her out too.

As Beiser explains, "These days the truth is in danger of being silenced. All Breaking the Silence wanted to do was to tell the story from the soldier's side. Once they are labeled as traitors, you have a silencing. If you use a noisemaker every time you hear your enemy's name you can never see the world from his side."

"As secular Jews," Marcus adds, "we know the texts very generally from reading them in high school or lower school. When we started reading Esther, we didn't remember that 75,000 were killed. We suddenly realized: our side killed a lot of people. That surprised us. We took that revelation about what we had missed in our younger reading of the story and merged it together with this very relevant contemporary issue."

---

18. See https://www.youtube.com/watch?v=S1lqwupIBhI.

The soldier in the skit specifically refers to Haman's son, Vayzata, pulling this one name from the list of the ten executed sons, which traditionally are recited very quickly together, all in one breath. As Beiser notes, "We know that these ten children are killed, but we never stop to ask ourselves who they are as individuals, and why they are killed." This too is a silence that the skit attempts to undo.

Special critique is reserved on the show for the corruption of religious institutions, such as in one skit that uses the story of the priests in the Temple who discover the Book of Deuteronomy[19] to obliquely target the self-serving actions of the Israeli rabbinate.

"We got to thinking," recounts Beiser, "about the Temple as a 24-hour steak house. Meat was brought in all the time; rivers of blood flowed from the altars. And then there was the other layer: that of power, politics, and the centralization of religious authority."

"Against the backdrop of all of this is the book of *Devarim* that is found by King Josiah,"[20] Marcus adds. "To us that seemed a bit too convenient. Here are these court figures named rabbit, weasel, mouse, who suddenly find a holy book. To us, all of this sounded like an invented story rather than a real one. How could it be possible that this holy book suddenly appears that brings the power and meat back to priests and recentralizes their control?"

Hayehudim Ba'im renders this skepticism in the face of the received tradition a sacred, moral stance, a position made clear in perhaps the most blatantly theological skit in the entire series, a rap music video entitled "Zeh Lo Hashem" (That's not my Name),[21] in which God, an old white haired man dressed in white, accompanied by a troupe of angelic, white-clad backup singers, recites all the various names and epithets that have been assigned to him throughout the generations in place of His proper name.

Marcus explains the origin of the skit as a secular effort to reclaim the voice of God: "There are a lot of people and streams in Israel who claim God for themselves, who say that they are the only ones who can speak

---

19. See https://www.youtube.com/watch?v=H04ZERVmfto
20. See 2 Kings 22.
21. Based on "That's Not My Name," by the Ting Tings. See https://www.youtube.com/watch?v=v1c2OfAzDTI.

in God's name and voice. We thought that as part of our movement and the way we look at things, we ought to attempt ourselves to speak directly to God. We started looking at all the names assigned to the divine; we found out that you can't say the letter *heh* anymore in naming God and have to say *daled* instead. We noticed that the connection with God was becoming more and more removed. We decided, as a result, to do a sketch from God's point of view, in God's proper name, one that said that if you need Me and you want to connect with Me, you can just say My name. And we chose as our God the actor Moni Moshonov, who is a kind of pop-culture god-figure in Israel."

At the end of the skit, God attempts to pronounce God's own four-lettered name but disappears mid-pronouncement. "Should anyone say Jehovah?" the skit implicitly asks, alluding to Monty Python's treatment of the same question in *The Life of Brian*. More than that: can God be God if God cannot survive humor? As Monty Python troupe-member Michael Palin asserts: "If anything can survive the role of humor it is clearly of value, and conversely all groups who claim immunity from laughter are claiming special privileges which should not be granted. The role of satire in works like *The Life of Brian* is to reveal what is true and good, not just mock it."[22] The same might be said about "Zeh Lo Hashem," which comes not to mock the name of God but to save it from chronic human misuse and obfuscation, and in that sense, to uphold a form of religious virtue. As John Morreall notes about the role of comedy and humor in religion, "the flexible thinking in comedy matches the complexity, diversity and movement of life itself."[23] Humor, Morreall argues "not only fosters virtues, but is best seen as itself a virtue, and like wisdom, it is an intellectual and moral excellence of a high order. And any religion purporting to show people how to live needs to take it seriously."[24]

---

22. Quoted in Lyndvall, *God Mocks*, 257.
23. John Morreall, *Comedy, Tragedy and Religion* (Albany, NY: SUNY Press, 1999), 22.
24. Morreall, 154.

Conclusion

God's Honest Truth: Some Final Literary Thoughts on Truth, Death, and Eternity

WENDY ZIERLER

A truth: some things get worse with time. The backdrop to the HUC Symposium that served as the basis for this book was, by all accounts, a fear-laden time for seekers of truth. "Truth decay," the term used by the Rand Corporation to describe what they saw as the "the growing disregard for facts, data, and analysis in political and civil discourse in the United States,"[1] had become a stark new reality, joining, as Michiko Kakutani ruefully observes in her book, *The Death of Truth*, "such now familiar phrases as "fake news" and "alternative facts.""[2]

Not to say that these were entirely unprecedented phenomena or fears. Some ten years earlier, British writer Simon Blackburn had already given voice to a sense of truth crisis. "It is easy to feel frightened," he wrote,

> at the beginning of the twenty-first century. And among the most frightening things are the minds of other people. The beliefs and faiths that move people to behave as they do are opaque to others;

---

1. Jennifer Kavanagh and Michael D. Rich, *Truth Decay: An Initial Exploration into the Diminishing Role of Facts and Analysis in American Public Life* (Santa Monica, CA: Rand Corporation, 2018), iii.
2. Michiko Kakutani, *The Death of Truth* (New York, NY: Tim Duggan Books, 2018), 12.

as we read or watch the news, lunacy together with mutual suspicion and contempt seem to be the order of the day.[3]

By all accounts, however, the backdrop for the writing of this conclusion – the fevers and coughs and stay-at-home lockdowns in the wake of the COVID-19 pandemic – is even more terrifying and dire. If one of the concerns voiced in the aftermath of the 2016 election, and the 2020 election, too, was the increasing impossibility of dialogue across the political divide, with people isolated and hunkered down in their partisan news siloes with their mutually exclusive truths, the literal isolation of people in their own homes for weeks and months on end and the mounting fear of outsiders and contagion makes the possibility of dialogue for the sake of common truths and compromise, seem ever more remote.[4]

But is that actually true? Is it not possible that the COVID crisis – the irrefutable, worldwide ultimacy of it, with 2.5 million dead at the time of this writing, and a global economy repeatedly crippled if not entirely ground to a halt – will finally make it possible for people to come together and acknowledge certain incontrovertible truths? Is death itself not an undeniable, human verity? Is that not the reason why the rabbinic blessing recited upon the death of a loved one is "*Barukh dayan ha'emet*" – Blessed is the Judge of Truth? More than mere wordplay, I daresay, the inclusion of the word "*met*" (dead) in the word *emet* (truth), would seem to register a fundamental fact.

My expertise as a scholar of Jewish literature certainly does not qualify me to prognosticate about the post-pandemic future of politics and human relations. It does equip me, however, to offer a few concluding observations about the intertwinement of truth and death in a selection of Jewish literary texts, as a means of framing the scope and findings of this collection of essays. Lest my subject appear too dreadful for the

---

3. Simon Blackburn, *Truth: A Guide* (Great Britain: Penguin, 2005), ix.

4. On the polarized response to the Coronavirus depending on which news outlet you watch, see Sarah Lyall, "A Household Divide: Which New Channel to Tune Into Each Day," *The New York Times* (Sunday April 19, 2020), A26. Published online as "The Cable TV Quarantine Fight," https://www.nytimes.com /2020/04/17/us/politics/fox-news-msnbc-coronavirus.html.

conclusion of a book, I will note that hand in hand with the Jewish literary and liturgical confrontation with death, and the evanescence of people and cultures, comes a reaching for some concomitant notion of eternity – of truth everlasting. Consider, for example, "The Gifts" (1883), a poem by American Jewish poet Emma Lazarus (1849–1887):

"GIFTS"

'O World-God, give me Wealth!' the Egyptian cried.
His prayer was granted. High as heaven, behold
Palace and Pyramid; the brimming tide
Of lavish Nile washed all his land with gold.
Armies of slaves toiled ant-wise at his feet,
World-circling traffic roared through mart and street,
His priests were gods, his spice-balmed kings enshrined,
Set death at naught in rock-ribbed charnels deep.
Seek Pharaoh's race to-day and ye shall find
Rust and the moth, silence and dusty sleep.

'O World-God, give me Beauty!' cried the Greek.
His prayer was granted. All the earth became
Plastic and vocal to his sense; each peak,
Each grove, each stream, quick with Promethean flame,
Peopled the world with imaged grace and light.
The lyre was his, and his the breathing might
Of the immortal marble, his the play
Of diamond-pointed thought and golden tongue.
Go seek the sun-shine race, ye find to-day
A broken column and a lute unstrung.

'O World-God, give me Power!' the Roman cried.
His prayer was granted. The vast world was chained
A captive to the chariot of his pride.
The blood of myriad provinces was drained
To feed that fierce, insatiable red heart.
Invulnerably bulwarked every part
With serried legions and with close-meshed Code,
Within, the burrowing worm had gnawed its home,

A roofless ruin stands where once abode
The imperial race of everlasting Rome.

'O Godhead, give me Truth!' the Hebrew cried.
His prayer was granted; he became the slave
Of the Idea, a pilgrim far and wide,
Cursed, hated, spurned, and scourged with none to save.
The Pharaohs knew him, and when Greece beheld,
His wisdom wore the hoary crown of Eld.
Beauty he hath forsworn, and wealth and power.
Seek him to-day, and find in every land.
No fire consumes him, neither floods devour;
Immortal through the lamp within his hand. [emphasis
   added][5]

Those who are familiar with Lazarus through "The New Colossus,"
the sonnet that furnished the lines emblazoned on the Statue of Liberty,
will recognize the illuminating lamp image at the end of this poem
from the last line of that better known 1883 work: "I lift my lamp beside
the golden door!"[6] But whereas "The New Colossus" fixes the lamp
in a particular place – in the hand of the statue that looms in the New
York harbor, a metonymic representative of the promise of America to
immigrants seeking a better life – The Gifts" uses the lamp to represent
an idea of Truth that transcends time and place.

Comprised of four ten-lined stanzas, "The Gifts" offers four individual national/cultural portraits, with the best saved for last – four different
decalogues, one might say, or encapsulations of core principles. In the
aggregate, the paradigmatic[7] forty lines of the poem project a Jewish
exceptionalist worldview. Recalling the midrashic interpretation of
Jacob's dream of the ladder in Genesis 28, according to which the angels

---

5. Emma Lazarus, "Gifts," https://www.poemhunter.com/poem/gifts-15/.
6. Emma Lazarus, "The New Colossus," https://www.poetryfoundation.org
/poems/46550/the-new-colossus.
7. Forty is a paradigmatic number in the Bible: the rain falls for forty days and
nights in the episode of Noah's flood; Moses ascends to Sinai for forty days; the
Israelites wander for 40 years in the desert; and the period of time for purifica-
tion after the birth of a boy is 7 plus 33 days = 40. For more on this see Aaron
Pinker, "The Number 40 in the Bible," *Jewish Bible Quarterly* 22:3 (1994): 163–72.

that first ascend and then descend the ladder represent the rise and subsequent fall of the ancient world powers,[8] Lazarus's poem depicts a series of empires that come and go. The Egyptian Pharaohs pray to the World-God for the gift of wealth so as to assert godlike majesty and to vanquish death, but death ultimately turns their gift to dust. The ancient Greeks importune the same World-God for the gift of beauty, but little of that ancient imperial gift remains intact. The Romans plead and kill for the gift of power, but alas, the worm of death burrows and gnaws at Rome from within, bringing down its imperial roof.

Against these fallen empires, Lazarus adduces the Hebrew, who prays to an (infinite) Godhead rather than an ephemeral World-God, and relinquishes wealth, beauty, and power in favor of the eternal gift of Truth. A connection between Truth and Torah is suggested in the three concluding images of the poem, all of which derive from the Hebrew Bible. The image of the truth that remains unconsumed by the fires of persecution calls to mind the burning bush that is not consumed from Exodus 3:2. "Neither floods devour" evokes the saving of Noah from the deluge in Genesis 6–9, while the figure of the everlasting lamp conjures up the *ner tamid* from Exodus 27:20–21. Other cultures may spurn this hoary, aged Hebrew and his Torah-itic truth, condemning him to a nomadic, exilic fate, but this wandering ensures his worldwide influence. Jewish and American exceptionalism merge here, as Lazarus simultaneously rejects the outworn values of the Old World and raises up the everlasting contribution of the Hebrew Bible, its Puritan American and Jewish avatars alike.

In 1883, in the aftermath of the Russian pogroms in 1881–1882, Lazarus had a polemical point to make. If Jews were being beaten, raped, pillaged, and killed in Russia, then it was up to America to recognize the truth of their contribution to civilization and to welcome them into the fold.

That said, her confident assertion of the immortality of the Hebrew and his Truth cannot help but come across to any post-nineteenth-century reader as more than a little quaint and naïve, especially given the

---

8. See Genesis Rabbah 68, and Exodus Rabbah 32:7. For a detailed discussion of the various interpretations of Jacob's dream see James L. Kugel, *The Ladder of Jacob: Ancient Interpretations of the Biblical Story of Jacob and His Children.* (Princeton, NJ: Princeton University Press, 2009).

millions of Jewish deaths that ensued in the first half of the twentieth century. Comedian John Stewart's brutally truthful, satirical "Timeline of Democracy," with its acerbic reference to the would-be protective power of Israelite chosenness upon receiving the Ten Commandments, immediately comes to mind: "God gives Ten Commandments to Israelites, making them His Chosen People and granting them eternal protection under divine Law. Nothing bad ever happens to Jews again." [9]

To believe after the Holocaust in the protective power of Jewish, Torah-based Truth, Stewart's satire suggests, constitutes the height of laughable gullibility. Stewart, of course, was hardly the first to target Jewish credulousness. Isaac Bashevis Singer's iconic story "Gimpel Tam" (Simple Gimpel) raised the very same idea when it was published in 1945, in the aftermath of the Holocaust. The protagonist of Singer's story is the butt of everyone's jokes in his town for his willingness to believe anything and everything he is told. One lie after another is practiced on Gimpel, many of which expose the town's own theological/liturgical doubts. Early in the story a Yeshiva *bachur* says to Gimpel, "You, Gimpel, while you stand here scraping with your baker's shovel the Messiah has come. The dead have arisen [*es iz tkhies-hameisim*]." [10]

Gimpel claims that he knew all along, "*az es iz nisht geshtoygen nisht gefloygen*," – that the purported resurrection didn't "climb up, didn't fly." Saul Bellow's English translation demetaphorizes the Yiddish expression and adds an assertion of truth: "To tell the truth, I knew very well that nothing of the sort had happened," but the Yiddish original deliberately keeps the word truth away from this story of sham messianism – a nod, perhaps, to Singer's earlier novelistic representation of false messianism, *Der Sotn in Goray* (1935).

The first appearance of the word truth in "Gimpel Tam" actually comes when the town proposes to marry off Gimpel to Elka, the town

---

9. See John Stewart, "Timeline of Democracy," in *America: A Citizen's Guide to Democracy Inaction* (New York, NY: Warner Books, 2004), 4.

10. Isaac Bashevis Singer, *Collected Stories* (New York, NY: Farrar Strauss and Giroux), 1983), 4. Yitshak Bashevis Zinger, *Der Shpiegel under andere dertseylungen* (Jerusalem: Hebrew University and Techerikover Motsi'im la'or, 1975), 34. All further citations from these texts will be noted in parentheses in the body of this essay.

whore – an evocation of the folk practice of plague weddings, wherein orphans or other marginal figures would be married off in a cemetery as a means of expiation for the town's sins and of petitioning for the intercession of pious ancestors in order to stave off the contagion.[11] (Reading of a crowded Plague Wedding in this contemporary time of plague and social distancing itself constitutes a veritable assault on scientific truth.) Gimpel, as it turns out, does not even register concern for physical contagion. Rather, in a faint show of individual rights, he declares that his status as an orphan entitles him to the truth regarding his marriage: *"Zog mir dem emes"* – "Tell me the truth," he pleads, "are you really a virgin and is that mischievous Yechiel actually your little brother? Don't be deceitful with me, for I'm an orphan." (Yiddish, p. 35/English, p. 5). But Elka keeps lying, as do her fellow townsfolk. The wedding itself is a veritable parody of folk piety. The cemetery backdrop of the wedding, with its lingering specter of death, does nothing to coax out the truth from the townsfolk. Gimpel alone persists in being faithful to those around him. One night, Gimpel comes home and finds Elka in bed with another man, requiring him by decree of the town rabbi to leave her at once; but Gimpel later retracts his testimony about Elka's infidelity, making room for an alternative halakhic ruling that allows him to return to his wife.

Halakhic truth thus joins the list of arbitrary or incredible notions that are debunked in this story. "The Truth is out, like oil upon water, Maimonides says it's right, and therefore it is right" (English, p. 10/ Yiddish p. 42). Notably, the term used in the original Yiddish with respect to the ruling by Maimonides is not "right" but kosher – a ritual rather than ethical or epistemological term. The effect, of course, is similar, insofar as halakhic rulings are shown to be a species of magical thinking that perpetuates a larger theological mistruth. Having received the ruling enabling him to return to Elka after their temporary separation, Gimpel leaves his bakery at night and makes his way home. Outside, he hears his Christian neighbors' dogs barking – an intimation of the use of dogs in the Nazi roundup of the Jews and in the death camps. Says

---

11. For more on the Plague Wedding, see https://www.tabletmag.com/jewish -life-and-religion/300726/plague-weddings.

Gimpel: "Bark your teeth out. What are you but mere dogs? Whereas I am a man [*mensch*], the husband of a fine wife, the father of promising children." Every detail of this assertion, however, proves to be a lie. Elka hardly qualifies as a fine wife; immediately upon returning home, Gimpel discovers yet another infidelity on Elka's part, which he willfully disregards on the grounds that belief itself is beneficial. On her deathbed, Elka confesses that none of the children she bore were actually his; every debasing fact about his life with her and in this town renders him less than a mensch, not only in the eyes of his community but also in the context of the larger Gentile world. Alas, Gimpel is brought to a breaking point. In the wake of Elka's confession and under the influence of his hitherto absent *yetzer ha-ra'*, he sets out to exact excretory revenge on the townspeople by pissing into his baker's dough. No longer can baker Gimpel work to sustain the community with his bread, with his behavior and simple faith as fodder for jokes and amusement. Enough is finally enough.

If the story were to have ended here, its truth would be clear: religious belief is a fraud; and the promises of people are a lie, too. But this is where the story takes a crucial turn, reinstating and recuperating faith as something abidingly true. Just as Gimpel is about to wreak his vengeance, the dead Elka comes to Gimpel in a dream. Just because I was false, Elka says, does that mean that you should be too? In contrast to everyone else, she insists, "*du tam*"[12] (Yiddish, p. 45) – you are whole, blameless, innocent, not a jaded cynic. As Janet Hadda argues in an article cleverly titled "Gimpel The Full," Elka explains to Gimpel, despite her prior, cynical mistreatment of him,

> that there is neither need nor gain in seeing the world through the eyes of the average person, who perceives slights and proceeds to redress them, using methods as low and stupid as the perpetrator. She asks him to realize that his general perspective, which has set him apart from others, was in fact no less accurate than that of everyone

---

12. The English translates this as "You fool," as it does the word "*tam*" throughout the story, beginning with the title. This translation misrepresents the full meaning of this term as well as this particular moment in the story. Elka is not so much scolding Gimpel for foolishness as reminding him of his identity as a *tam*, an innocent rather than a clever trickster. See "Gimpel the Fool," 13.

else, even though he was alone in his view and they were united in theirs…Gimpel *tam* is complete in the way he loves, and for this readers love him.[13]

That said, from this point on in the story, the notion of truth is lodged even more resolutely alongside the fact and site of death. Gimpel's apprentice sees him burying the tainted dough in the ground, like a body, and in his incredulity, ער ווערט בלייך ווי א מת " – he looked as pale as a corpse (Yiddish, p. 45 / English, p. 3). The Yiddish words א מת (a corpse) and אמת (truth) are a mere orthographic space or step away from one another. In the aftermath of the burying of the dough, Gimpel leaves his bakery once and for all, not to return home but to go out into the world, the very image of the wandering Jew. Rather than renouncing his former credulity, however, Gimpel re-embraces it in the guise of storytelling! "Going from place to place, eating at strange tables, it often happens I spin yarns – improbable things that never could have happened" (English, p. 14). The Yiddish original recapitulates here the phrase *nisht geshtoygen nisht gefloygen* (Yiddish, p. 46), which had been used earlier in the story in the context of the Yeshiva *bachur's* effort to trick Gimpel into believing that the Messiah had come and the dead had been resurrected. Here, though, instead of standing for bogus faith, *nisht geshtoygen nisht gefloygen* represents the restorative powers of the imagination. As Adam Cohen notes in an article commemorating the 100th anniversary of Singer's birth,

> "Gimpel" is, in the end, a sly rebuke to rationalism, and is a story in which the author explains, and defends, his decision to become a writer. In his Nobel lecture, Singer argued that storytellers might have the best chance of anyone to "rescue civilization." Writing fiction might not seem like the most direct way to improve the human condition, but Singer suggested that in a world where politics often failed, or worse, succeeded disastrously, intelligent, logical interactions with the world – the kind Gimpel spent a lifetime avoiding – may well be overrated.[14]

---

13. Janet Hadda, "Gimpel the Full," *Prooftexts* 10:2 (May 1990): 293–94.
14. Adam Cohen, "On Singer's 100th Anniversary, the Debate Still Rages Over a Famous Fool," *The New York Times* (December 26, 2004), https://www.nytimes

By the end of the story, then, Gimpel has been transformed from laughable gull to writerly sage, a stand-in for immigrant Singer, himself, and an echo of Lazarus's wise hoary Hebrew in "The Gifts." According to this transformed Gimpel, nothing really is false, but not in the simple, credulous sense of his earlier self. "‏אודאי איז די וועלט אן עולם־השקר,‏ ‏אבער זי איז איין טריט פון דער אמתער וועלט‏ – "No doubt the world is an imaginary world [lit. a world of lies], but it is only once removed from the true world" (Yiddish, p. 46 / English, p. 14). As Nancy Tenfelde Clasby notes, "Gimpel's insight that 'there really are no lies'" is linked to a vision of an infinitely meaningful universe.[15] In that true world of death, only one step away, sage Gimpel avers, "all is real, without complication, without ridicule, without deception." The poignant ending of "Gimpel Tam" marries truth, fiction, and death, both literally and figuratively. The plot of the story begins with Gimpel's wedding to Elka in a cemetery and ends with Gimpel living in a cemetery, awaiting his reunion with Elka in death. Hovering in the background of the story – its dating, its barking dogs, and its notion of the unimaginable coming true – is the hitherto inconceivable death of millions of Eastern European Jews in the Nazi death camps. The fact of the Holocaust is the undeniable[16] truth undergirding Singer's tragicomic tale; in the face of that reality, even Gimpel, endless butt of jokes, cannot be deceived.

Still, the ultimate lesson of Gimpel is hardly simple or cynical. On one level, the story seems to indict those, like Gimpel, who continue to believe in God and humankind in the aftermath of the Shoah or who resign themselves to the perfidies of this world. On the other hand, the wise, contented, faithful tone of the ending suggests an affirmation of the enduring value of the stories we tell ourselves to endow our lives

---

.com/2004/12/26/opinion/on-singers-100th-anniversary-the-debate-still-rages
-over-a-famous.html.

15. Nancy Tenfelde Clasby, "Gimpel's Wisdom: I.B. Singer's Vision of the True World," *Studies in American Jewish Literature* 15 (1996): 96.

16. The ongoing phenomenon of Holocaust denial points to the fact that even the documentation of millions of death does not necessarily prevent mistruths. For more on this see https://www.splcenter.org/fighting-hate/extremist-files /ideology/holocaust-denial. See also Deborah Lipstadt, *Denying the Holocaust: The Growing Assault on Truth and Memory* (New York, NY: Free Press, 2012).

with virtue and meaning. This meaning is not refuted by the facts of mortality and human evil; rather, these realities lend storytelling even greater urgency.

So where does all of this leave us? I began this essay tentatively suggesting that the fact and finality of death might be a means of measuring or reclaiming truth. I showed, however, how truth and death go hand in hand in Singer's "Gimpel Tam" in ways that ultimately complicate rather than simplify its meaning. Is it possible that, so long as we live on this earth, this ambiguous notion of truth is the best we can muster? Is it possible that the immortality of truth, as Lazarus imagines it in the last stanza of "Gifts," actually depends on it meaning more than one thing? If so, is it truth after all?

Leah Goldberg's "The Moon Sings to the Stream" (1945),[17] another postwar Jewish text, underscores this dilemma with respect to truth. The third in a cycle of poems entitled "Mishirei Hanahal" (From Stream Songs), "The Moon Sings to the Stream" depicts the moon as a unitary figure, whose singular, celestial truth is duplicated and multiplied by the stream below.

iii. The Moon Sings to the Stream	הַיָּרֵחַ שָׁר לַנַּחַל
I'm the oneness on high	אֲנִי הַיָּחוּד בַּמָּרוֹם,
I'm the many in the depth.	אֲנִי הָרִבּוּי בַּמְּצוּלָה.
Look at the stream, there am I	תַּשְׁקִיף מִן הַנַּחַל אֵלַי
My likeness, my likeness, twice kept.	דְּמוּתִי, דְּמוּתִי הַכְּפוּלָה.
I'm truth up on high	אֲנִי הָאֱמֶת בַּמָּרוֹם,
I'm illusion below,	אֲנִי הַבְּדָיָה בַּמְּצוּלָה,
Look forth from the stream, there am I,	תַּשְׁקִיף מִן הַנַּחַל אֵלַי
My likeness in her treacherous tow.[18]	דְּמוּתִי בִּכְזַב גּוֹרָלָה.

---

17. Leah Goldberg, "Hayareah shar lanahal," from "Mishirei hanahal," *Shirim 2* (Tel Aviv: Sifriyat Hapo'alim, 1986), 11–15. My translation.

18. Literally, the lie or betrayal of her fate. In the translation I meant to evoke the image of being towed or pulled treacherously by the stream. Another translation option would be to consider "goral" as a throwing of lots or dice: "My likeness in her treacherous throw."

Above – clothed in quiet,	לְמַעְלָה – עוֹטֶה דוּמִיּוֹת,
Below – song and blare.	הוֹמֶה מְזַמֵּר בַּמְצוּלָה.
On high I am God yet,	אֲנִי בַּמָּרוֹם – הָאֵל,
In the stream, I am prayer.	בַּנַּחַל אֲנִי הַתְּפִילָה.

The word "yiḥud" in the first line of the poem calls to mind the "Shir hayiḥud," a liturgical *piyyut* that, while dedicated to the oneness and singularity of God, ironically offers a lengthy compilation of multiple images or descriptions of that Oneness. Goldberg's poem exploits and develops that paradox, offering a succession of contrasts between the moon as unitary truth on high, and the stream as a medium of reflection, representation, or interpretation on earth below. The stream's inability to accurately represent the godlike moon is presented as a form of illusion or betrayal, but also as as constitutive of the human act of prayer. As the river's reflection is to the moon, so too are our liturgical, theological, and literary musings to the idea of divine Truth: at best approximations, tenuous imaginings, gestures in the direction of something virtuous, real, enduring. Such is "*kezav goralah*," – the treacherous fate of truth.

The idea that there is a divine Truth up there that we human beings, floating down our ever-flowing, ever-changing streams, only partially capture or reflect might lead to a sense of relativism, nihilism, or despair. And yet the last stanza of the poem, offers a distinctly positive framing. God as moon in the heavens is clothed in silence. Our stream reflections add sound, voice, word, and shape to this dark silence and isolated Oneness. Not just that: as night's reflection of the moon in the stream, our prayers are no mere words or bluster. They cannot expect to completely capture the original, but they have a distinct and recognizable relation to it. Indeed, they contain more than a little truth. And as *tefilah*, the Hebrew word itself coming from the root פלל and the reflexive *hitpa'el* (*lehitpallel*) form, there is an added notion of self-reflection or self-judgment in the composition of our prayers. Represented this way, the stream of our prayer is an expression of the Highest within us and above us.

A word about the structure of the poem. Throughout the three stanzas, a pattern is established in which the moon first describes himself from a heavenly perspective and then as he appears on earth, repeating some of the same words but with a difference so as to underscore the differences between the moon on high and the stream's reflection below. The poem utilizes a call and response structure similar to that of many traditional Jewish prayers, most notably the Kedushah and Kaddish. God's name is magnified liturgically in the Kaddish and Kedushah through the liturgical choreography of multiple voices saying the same things in response to one another, sometimes cacophonously. Add to this the theme of both of these prayers, which looks forward to a future time when God's name will be more widely and definitively known. According to Jewish liturgical standards, one best magnifies God's name and recognizes God's Oneness not with one voice, but through a multiplicity of voices calling and responding to one another.

And so it is. Death and the threat thereof do not diminish the Jewish quest for truth but, rather, lend this quest its moral and historical necessity and urgency. And in almost every case, the quest for absolute Truth finds itself encountered by other virtues: pluralism, ethical considerations, and changing social norms. The goal: to sing with many voices, in good faith, with hopes for better times.

List of Contributors

Rachel Adler, the David Ellenson Professor of Modern Jewish Thought Emerita at Hebrew Union College – Los Angeles, was one of the first to integrate feminist perspectives into interpreting Jewish texts and law. Her book *Engendering Judaism* (1998) is the first by a female theologian to win a National Jewish Book Award for Jewish Thought. She has published over sixty articles on Jewish Thought, law, and gender, and on suffering and lament in Jewish tradition, as well as the whimsical *Tales of the Holy Mysticat*, a resource for adult Jewish education.

Leora Batnitzky is Ronald O. Perelman Professor of Jewish Studies and Professor of Religion at Princeton University. Her teaching and research interests include philosophy and religion, modern Jewish thought, hermeneutics, and contemporary legal and political theory. She is the author of *Idolatry and Representation: The Philosophy of Franz Rosenzweig Reconsidered* (Princeton, 2000), *Leo Strauss and Emmanuel Levinas: Philosophy and the Politics of Revelation* (Cambridge, 2006), and *How Judaism Became a Religion* (Princeton, 2011). She is also the co-editor of *The Book of Job: Aesthetics, Ethics and Hermeneutics* (De Gruyter, 2014), *Institutionalizing Rights and Religion* (Cambridge, 2017), the anthology *Jewish Legal Theories* (Brandeis Library of Modern Jewish Thought, 2018) and the journal *Jewish Studies Quarterly*.

Marc Zvi Brettler is the Bernice and Morton Lerner Distinguished Professor of Judaic Studies in the Department of Religious Studies at Duke University. His books include *The Creation of History in Ancient Israel; How to Read the Jewish Bible; The Jewish Study Bible* (edited with Adele Berlin); and *The Bible and the Believer* (with Peter Enns and Daniel Harrington). He co-edited *The Jewish Annotated New Testament*, and co-authored *The Bible With and Without Jesus: How Jews and Christians Read the Same Stories Differently,* both with Amy-Jill Levine. He is deeply committed to making the Jewish community more aware of the richness of Jewish literature from the past, including the New Testament, and to introducing academic biblical study to the broader community, as reflected in TheTorah.com, which he co-founded.

Mark S. Diamond is a Senior Lecturer in Jewish Studies at Loyola Marymount University, Los Angeles, where he teaches core curriculum courses on Jewish thought and interfaith relations. He also teaches graduate courses in practical rabbinics at the Academy for Jewish Religion CA. He is the former executive vice president of the Board of Rabbis of Southern California and a past president of the Los Angeles Council of Religious Leaders. Rabbi Diamond is co-editor of Understanding Covenants and Communities: Jews and Latter-day Saints in Dialogue, a joint publication of the Religious Studies Center of Brigham Young University and the Central Conference of American Rabbis.

David Ellenson is Chancellor Emeritus of Hebrew Union College-Jewish Institute of Religion and served as HUC-JIR President from 2001–2013 and again in 2018–2019. He is also Professor Emeritus of Near Eastern and Judaic Studies at Brandeis University where he was Director of the Schusterman Center for Israel Studies from 2015–2018. His most recent book, co-edited with Michael Marmur, is an anthology, *American Jewish Thought Since 1934: Writings on Engagement, Identity, and Belief,* published in 2020 by Brandeis University Press.

Joshua Garroway serves as the Sol and Arlene Bronstein Professor of Judaeo-Christian Studies at the Hebrew Union College – Jewish Institute of Religion in Los Angeles. He is the author of *Paul's Gentile-Jews: Neither Jew Nor Gentile, But Both* and *The Beginning of the Gospel: Paul, Philippi, and the Origins of Christianity.*

Christine Hayes is the Sterling Professor of Religious Studies in Classical Judaica at Yale University and a specialist in talmudic-midrashic studies. She has authored introductory volumes (*The Emergence of Judaism* and *Introduction to the Bible*) in addition to scholarly monographs. Her most recent book, *What's Divine about Divine Law? Early Perspectives,* won the 2015 National Jewish Book Award in Scholarship. She has served as president of the Association for Jewish Studies and is a Senior Research Fellow with the Shalom Hartman Institute of North America.

Lawrence A. Hoffman is Professor Emeritus of Liturgy, Worship and Ritual at HUC-JIR in NY. He has written or edited 48 books and 150 articles, both scholarly and popular. He is past president of the North American Academy of Liturgy, the academic address for Jewish and Christian liturgists, and the recipient of its annual Berakah award for lifetime achievement. He was also co-founder and co-director of Synagogue 2000/3000 (1995–2015) which pioneered the transformation of synagogues to become moral and spiritual centers for the 21st century, and visits synagogues around the globe as scholar-in-residence and consultant on synagogue change.

Michael Marmur is Associate Professor of Jewish Theology at HUC-JIR in Jerusalem. He is the author of *Abraham Joshua Heschel and the Sources of Wonder* (2016) and co-editor (with David Ellenson) of *American Jewish Thought Since 1934: Writings on Identity, and Belief* (2020). He previously served as Dean of the Jerusalem School and Provost of HUC-JIR.

Dalia Marx is the Rabbi Aaron Panken Professor of Liturgy and Midrash at HUC-JIR's Jerusalem campus. A tenth-generation Jerusalemite, she earned her doctorate at the Hebrew University and her rabbinic ordination at HUC-JIR. She is active in promoting liberal Judaism in Israel and writes for academic and popular journals. She has written and edited several books, and most recently served as chief editor of the Israeli Reform siddur, *Tfillat HaAdam* (2020). Her book, *From Time to Time: Journeys in the Jewish Calendar* (Hebrew 2018), is currently translated to German, Spanish and English.

Geoffrey A. Mitelman is the Founding Director of Sinai and Synapses, an organization that bridges the scientific and religious worlds, and is being incubated at Clal – The National Jewish Center for Learning and Leadership. His work has been supported by the John Templeton Foundation among others, and his writings about the intersection of religion and science have been published in the books *Seven Days, Many Voices* and *A Life of Meaning* (both published by the CCAR press). He is an internationally sought-out teacher, presenter, and scholar-in-residence, and lives in Westchester County with his wife, Heather Stoltz, a fiber artist, and their daughter and son.

Benjamin Sommer is Professor of Bible at the Jewish Theological Seminary and Senior Fellow at the Kogod Center for Contemporary Jewish Thought of the Shalom Hartman Institute. His book, *Revelation and Authority: Sinai in Jewish Scripture and Tradition*, received the Goldstein-Goren Prize in Jewish thought and was a finalist for a National Jewish Book Award. The Israeli newspaper *Ha'aretz* described Sommer as "a traditionalist but an iconoclast – he shatters idols and prejudices in order to nurture Jewish tradition and its applicability today."

Wendy Zierler (Co-Editor) is Sigmund Falk Professor of Modern Jewish Literature and Feminist Studies at HUC-JIR in New York. She received her Ph.D. from Princeton University, an MFA in Fiction Writing from Sarah Lawrence College, and rabbinic ordination from Yeshiva Maharat. She is the author and editor of several books and articles in the fields of Modern Jewish Literature and Thought and Jewish Gender Studies, most recently *Movies and Midrash: Popular Film and Jewish Religious Conversation* (Finalist for the National Jewish Book Award). In 2017, she was appointed Co-Editor of *Prooftexts: A Journal of Jewish Literary History*, a leading scholarly journal in the field of Jewish Literature.

Index to Bible and Rabbinic Works

General Index